Self, Religion, and Metaphysics

THE MACMILLAN COMPANY
NEW YORK • CHICAGO
DALLAS • ATLANTA • SAN FRANCISCO
LONDON • MANILA
IN CANADA
BRETT-MACMILLAN LTD.
GALT, ONTARIO

James Bissett Pratt

Self, Religion, and Metaphysics

ESSAYS IN MEMORY OF JAMES BISSETT PRATT

edited by
GERALD E. MYERS

New York   The Macmillan Company   1961

The editor gratefully acknowledges permission from the following publishers and copyright holders to quote from their publications: Chatto and Windus, Ltd., Curtis Brown, Ltd., and the Viking Press, *Thought and Action* (1959) by Stuart Hampshire; The Macmillan Company, *Personal Realism* by James Bissett Pratt, Copyright 1937 by The Macmillan Company; Harper & Brothers, *Dynamics of Faith* by Paul Tillich (Torchbook Edition), Copyright 1957 by Harper & Brothers; and The University of Chicago Press, *The Moral Life and the Ethical Life* by Eliseo Vivas, Copyright 1950 by the University of Chicago.

First Printing

Printed in the United States of America

The Macmillan Company, New York
Brett-Macmillan Ltd., Galt, Ontario

Library of Congress catalog card number: 61–7062

Preface

Among things inevitable I would include, if not this particular volume, one at least like it, for it was bound to occur to someone that a tribute to the career and person of James Bissett Pratt was appropriate, desirable, and overdue. As a member of the Williams College Department of Philosophy, I can vouch for the fact that Professor Pratt is vividly remembered (seventeen years after his death) by the Williams College community, where he lived and taught for thirty-eight years, as having been one of its most distinguished members. The decision to undertake a volume honoring her late husband developed out of conversations with Mrs. Pratt, a warm friend and neighbor; and her suggestions, while modestly offered only when requested, were indispensable to the completion of this book.

For a fuller account of his distinguished career as teacher and author, the reader is referred to the biographical sketch of Professor Pratt at the back of this book. It is sufficient to note here that, in addition to his years of teaching as the Mark Hopkins Professor of Intellectual and Moral Philosophy at Williams College, Pratt was at one time President of the American Philosophical Association, at another time President of the American Theological Society, an active member of the Critical Realist group, and a recipient of honorary degrees from Amherst and Wesleyan. His books on India, Buddhism, and religious experience are still widely consulted. His name, I discovered while attending the Third East-West Philosophers' Conference at Honolulu in the summer of 1959, was a familiar and respected one to almost all of the Eastern representatives. S. Radhakrishnan, philosopher and Vice President of India, very kindly wrote to me of his high regard for Pratt's writings, and, had the duties of his office permitted, he would have contributed an essay to the present work. Besides Radhakrishnan, there were others who wished to participate but for various reasons could not, and I thank all of them for their encouragement.

v

To those who were both willing and able to contribute so generously of their time and thought to this memorial volume are extended, of course, the deepest thanks. Contributors were asked to write on a topic or in an area of special interest to Professor Pratt, and they were free to refer or not to Pratt's own writings. Our intention was that these essays, while collected together for a memorial occasion, should constitute original contributions to philosophical literature, and thus be of interest to professional and nonprofessional philosophers as well as to associates of Williams College. Most participants, when their subject allowed, adopted the editor's suggestion of commenting on the nature and value of metaphysics. If there is any thread of unity running through these essays, it would be this interest in assessing the potential of metaphysical philosophy. But, in general, the reader should not seek a definite, underlying theme in all of the essays, for he would indeed be disappointed if he did so. He should rather consider each essay on its own, understanding that it is included here because of its relevance to issues and topics regarded as especially important by Professor Pratt.

Without the encouragement and financial assistance provided by President James P. Baxter, III, and the Trustees of Williams College, this book would not have been possible. In behalf of those who worked creatively on this project, I want to thank President Baxter and the Trustees for so effectively supporting the whole endeavor.

A special word of appreciation is due Professor Charles A. Moore, of the University of Hawaii, and the Steering Committee of the Third East-West Philosophers' Conference for the grant that permitted me to attend that Conference. The opportunity was thus afforded of meeting Dr. Datta, Dr. Suzuki, and Professor von Rintelen, and discussing with them the essays they were generous enough to compose for this occasion.

To my colleague Laszlo Versenyi I owe a particular debt for his willingness to undertake the not unformidable task of translating Professor von Rintelen's article. Also, I must thank Deborah Lee for research assistance of various kinds, but especially for her work in compiling a bibliography of Professor Pratt's publications. Her efforts were enormously facilitated by the expert and friendly assistance of Mr. Wyllis Wright, Librarian of the Williams College Library, and members of his staff.

GERALD E. MYERS

Contents

PREFACE   v

Some Glimpses of James Bissett Pratt   1
     William Ernest Hocking, Emeritus, Harvard University

PART I: THE CONCEPT OF SELF

The Self: Existence or Substance?   11
     M. Holmes Hartshorne, Colgate University

An Imputation Theory of Free Will   26
     Lawrence W. Beals, Williams College

Existence—Self—Transcendence   45
     Fritz-Joachim von Rintelen, University of Mainz, Germany

Self and Introspection   66
     Gerald E. Myers, Williams College

PART II: PHILOSOPHY AND RELIGION

Theology   83
     Walter Kaufmann, Princeton University

Religion as a Pursuit of Truth   110
     Dhirendra Mohan Datta, Santiniketan, India

Comprehending Zen Buddhism   122
     Daisetz T. Suzuki, Kamakura, Japan

What Metaphysics Is Good For   127
     C. J. Ducasse, Emeritus, Brown University

PART III: PHILOSOPHY AND METAPHYSICS

Metaphysics and Empiricism   145
     Sterling P. Lamprecht, Emeritus, Amherst College

CONTENTS

On the Nature of Things   156
   Virgil C. Aldrich, Kenyon College

American Realism: Perspective and Framework   174
   Roy Wood Sellars, Emeritus, University of Michigan

Three Bases of Objectivity   201
   Warner A. Wick, University of Chicago

James Bissett Pratt: A Biographical Sketch   219
   Gerald E. Myers

Notes   229

Bibliography of the Works of James Bissett Pratt   235
   Deborah Lee

Self, Religion, and Metaphysics

Some Glimpses of James Bissett Pratt

A man's contemporaries are his fortune—he can hardly be said to deserve them: like his habitat they are there, factors of destiny.

It has been my good fortune to count among my contemporaries James Pratt. And though I can barely suggest in a few words what he has meant to me, as one of my heroes, it is a privilege to recall some of our moments of tangency, touching the mental history of our times. I trust I may be pardoned the inevitable scraps of autobiography involved in the mutual picture.

It was a happy accident that I first encountered Pratt as a fellow foreigner in a German university—a fellow student at the University of Berlin in the winter of 1902–03. And it was a bit less accidental, though unplanned, that in the following year we turned up together in a course at Harvard offered by William James. It was, I believe, James's first academic attempt to formulate something called "pragmatism"—"a new name for some old ways of thinking." In any case, this our seminar of 1903–04 was a testing ground for those ideas which James afterward presented in Boston as Lowell Lectures, and then at Columbia; and which, as published in 1907, were destined to become a focus for much American thinking. On each of these occasions, we were both fortunate in our contemporaries, i. e., in those older contemporaries whose instruction we were enjoying.

In Berlin we were hearing Dilthey, Paulsen, Stumpf, Simmel, with lively rumors in the offing of Rickert, Windelband, Husserl—with whom I had been studying. Through these and a wider constellation of thinkers, including a Marburg School and a Kuno Fischer calling "Back to Kant," German philosophy was moving away from naturalism, feeling its way to a firm ground for truth, beyond the reach of a psychological relativity: the campaign

1

against "psychologism" under Husserl's flag was gaining momentum.

In Harvard, Royce, Münsterberg, and Palmer were in lively debate with James; Santayana cavalierly independent, with rumors of Charles Peirce and John Dewey in the offing. Without realizing it, we were at a turning point in American philosophy, *reversing the German trend.* The hitherto reigning outlook—an idealism in which the intellectualism of Leibniz and Hegel was strongly tinctured with the will element of Kant, Fichte, Schopenhauer, and especially Lotze (Royce's teacher)—this idealism was being put heavily on the defensive.

James stood for the new direction. He had come to philosophy almost experimentally, by way of anatomy and physiology in the Medical School, and then of laboratory psychology in the College. He was encouraging the spirit of empirical exploration in philosophy, rejecting the shelter of a priori certitudes in the interest of a malleable empirical truth. He was putting some strain on his long-time friendship with the German psychologist Carl Stumpf, who wrote him, "I cannot reconcile myself to pragmatism and humanism." [1] And while Royce, with his own strong element of volition in the determination of truth, was inclined to absorb something of the pragmatic into his own system, James continued pulling together with zest the grounds of his running dissent from Royce, wholly without strain upon their friendship. James could say to Royce, in the presence of a photographer, "Look out Royce! I say 'Damn the Absolute,'" without offense to Royce. How the Absolute felt about it remains a mystery. We profited immensely from this atmosphere of free difference and mutually admiring discussion, which I like to think of as characteristic of the American temper in philosophy, and perhaps especially of the Harvard of that "golden age."

As one illustration of this temper which involved Pratt, I recall vividly a moment in the course on pragmatism when James referred to Royce as having added to the three traditional proofs of the existence of God an entirely new proof, an outstanding achievement of speculative power. James then turned to the members of the seminar—there were perhaps thirty of us—asking whether any one could give an outline of Royce's proof. There was but one volunteer. James Pratt gave a clear summary of Royce's argument from the possibility of error! Not that he accepted the argument; but that, with characteristic integrity, he reached his own position by the hard road of thinking through the strongest statement of diverging positions.

After taking his doctorate at Harvard in 1905, Pratt began his long and distinguished career of teaching at Williams College. His first published books, *The Psychology of Religious Belief*, 1907, and *What Is Pragmatism?*, 1909, show in his relation to James a degree of continuity of theme with a strong independence of direction.

During these years there was a liberating wind blowing from another quarter. Royce's great work, *The World and the Individual*, had made a particularly devastating onslaught on "realism," considered as a doctrine that Nature's reality is independent of the thought that knows it: in holding that this independence is inconsistent with any likeness whatever, his demolition appeared to many a critic too thorough! Two contemporaries of our generation, Ralph Barton Perry and W. P. Montague, had sprung to realism's defense. The first trumpet of a new and militant realism had been sounded. It opened a way to do full justice to the empirical world picture of science and common sense, and to the Otherness of things that calls for the obediences of duty, law, and religion, without the special elasticities of pragmatism which, to many a thinker, suggested a marshy spinelessness. Pratt's inclinations were already leading him toward a realism of his own: he was to find his place in that movement and become one of its leading spirits.

But his immediate journey was to take him through a more direct and personal contact with religious experiences of widely different types—broader in scope than those considered in James's *Varieties*. After Pratt's marriage in 1911 to Caterina Mariotti of Rome, equally concerned with the thoughful inquiry into religious experience and the realities within it, and uniquely combining deep personal conviction with a noble breadth and magnanimity, the way was opened for a year's travel and study in India, 1913–14. The resulting book, *India and Its Faiths*, 1915, was the first of a notable series of contributions—not more to scholarly lore about system than to a sympathetic understanding of faiths and observances animating markedly different civilizations—the rarest and yet the most genuine achievement of scholarship.

Such understanding, essential prelude to an adequate philosophy of religion for our time, is a matter whose importance to an age in which disruptive pressures, chasms undreamed of, make an unprecedented demand for new apprehensions of the deepest moral bonds of mankind, only the prophetic intuition of a true philosopher could have discerned.

Almost at the moment of the completion of Pratt's first journey to the Orient in 1914, the shadow of war in Europe was spreading over this nation the anxious problem of our own involvement. This problem touched Pratt with a special sense of urgency. He had earlier been attracted to the law, had given a year to its study in Columbia University Law School. The issues of public order and world peace were never during this period absent from his interest. His work, *Democracy and Peace,* published in 1916, expresses the immediate concern of a citizen clear as to the special responsibilities of philosophy in a contest involving the principles of international relationship in their widest scope.

That concern led to another meeting between us. My limited military experience, beginning at Plattsburg in 1916, and continuing in Britain and France in 1917, was coining itself into views regarding the causes and issues of the struggle, its psychological and economic factors, the rights and wrongs of pacifism and pugnacity, the moral obligations of individuals and of nations not immediately involved, the psychology of the soldier and of the public, the problems of morale. Williams College asked me to present these views to its Training Corps between November 16 and January 4 of 1918. Pratt's sponsorship and unfailing aid during this effort made the task a joint undertaking, and went far to qualify it for a further year of work under our War Department.

During the years following the war, Pratt and I were frequently brought together by the work and meetings of the American Philosophical Association, though he was a far better citizen than I of that important fellowship group. He belonged to the central nucleus of that lively body, together with Lovejoy of Johns Hopkins, Montague of Barnard, Spaulding of Princeton, Sheldon of Yale, Ralph Perry of Harvard, and others of the chief bearers of its institutional burdens.

It was from such associates that *The Journal of Philosophy* was born early in the century. And it was in this journal that Pratt began publishing his comments, with mingled agreement and difference, on the "New Realism" which, in 1912, had made a corporate stand against the idealist theory of knowledge. It was in 1916 and 1917 that Pratt published "The Confession of an *Old* Realist" (my italics) and "A Defense of Dualistic Realism," foreshadowing two important departures: first, his sturdy participation in the *Essays in Critical Realism* of 1920, with Drake, Lovejoy, Rogers, Santayana, Sellars, Strong. Second, his growing discontent with a discussion of *how we know the world,* dissociated from a discussion of the world's nature—epistemology without metaphysics. To Pratt, metaphysics is the kernel of philosophy.

In any case, though I took no immediate part in this debate, adopting no party title as my own, I was quite rightly classed among the critics of "natural realism" in behalf of a "realism of social experience," close neighbor to an absolute idealism (*The Meaning of God*, page 290), therefore metaphysically on the defensive—trying in a way to bridge the gap between the contending parties.

But bridgers of gaps are allies of none of the fighters: their claims to unite the contending parties in the role of amicus curiae recommend them to none; they are destined to a certain loneliness of spirit. It was, therefore, with a peculiar sense of healing and readoption that I responded to an invitation to join Pratt, in June of 1923, at the shrine of Mark Hopkins, in a new tie of colleaguely fellowship, amid the beauties of the Berkshire Hills. He and his wife were habitués of the upland trails, and we of the seacoast prized the rare privilege of climbing with them.

At that moment, Pratt was planning his second journey to the Far East. On May 18th he had written me, "Preparations for our trip are going on in due order—vaccinations, inoculations, and all sorts of other vexations. I confess that *bugs* disturb me much more than *bandits*." During 1923–24, he was to trace "The Pilgrimage of Buddhism" to its East Asian shores in China, Siam, Japan, in preparation for the notable work of that name which appeared in 1928. After a third of a century this major opus retains its place for historical perspective and sensitive justice of judgment.

Though these studies of Oriental religion, as one basis for a philosophical view of all religion, were long-time common interests, neither of us could then have guessed that they would lead to a further meeting, some eight years later, in the heart of the Himalayas. It was on the high pass between India and Tibet, in December of 1931. Pratt, with his family, was on his way to a term of teaching at Rabindranath Tagore's school in Santiniketan. I, involved in a "Laymen's Inquiry," was just then studying at a Buddhist monastery in Darjeeling. We joined forces for a Christmas dinner in that town, where amid local year-end festivities we enjoyed an exchange of views about the character and mission of Gandhi (who had recently returned to India from the London Round-Table Conference), and the possible future of his *Satyagraha* in a world already stirred by mutterings of a coming storm. Pratt and I had been present in 1926 at the Sixth International Congress of Philosophy in Cambridge, at which our proceedings had been interrupted by an immensely cheering telegram: Germany had been admitted to the League of Nations. Hans Driesch of Leipzig had been reading a paper; as the telegram was read, a French delegate on the platform rose and took the German speaker's hand—a moment of intense feeling stilled the assembly. And now, five years later, with the collapse of the American economy, and the heavy repercussions in Europe—especially in the hard-hit Weimar Republic—the hopes of peace in Europe were fading. The severe words of Pundit Das Hupta opening a Buddhist temple at Sarnath seemed justified: "Christianity has failed: I welcome the new Hindu-Buddhist civilization of Asia; nowhere has the advance of Buddhism been achieved by force." Could Gandhi be the prophet of a new world era?

The following decade saw the ripening of Pratt's thought and influence. In 1935 he was president of the American Philosophical Association. His *Personal Realism* appeared in 1937, his *Naturalism* in 1939. And through this period of mature effectiveness ran the enlivening influence of a work finished in 1930 and published the following year, *Adventures in Philosophy and Religion,* written "in the spirit of good-humored fun," but with serious intent. To my mind this collection of dialogues has a most important message to all professional philosophy—the call to insert one's convictions into the current of daily life and conversation, partly on the ground that whatever is important for mankind must be capable of simple statement, in parable as well as in technical language; and partly on the ground that the relieving temper of humor is an essential aspect of truth, through the recovery of proportion. The technical road jams that block a just perception of the idea of survival after death have never been more effectively disposed of than in Pratt's brief dialogue "Adventures on This Side and on the Other."

The motives of his metaphysics came to firm expression. As his latest message, he felt it his most imperative word. The idealism he opposed ran the danger of abstraction, discounting not only the solid reality of the physical world but also its significance for the soul of man. The stuff of experience is our teacher. The absolutes that reach a final unity of Being by way of pure form, as in Bradley's logic of relationships, leave human history without significance.

On the other hand, a naturalism that makes the method of physical science the clue to metaphysical truth leads to a futile effort to reduce mind to a phenomenon of energy, measurable in c.g.s. or electrical-field units. The literal reality of the self, its genuine effectiveness in decision and action, must be the foundations of every future metaphysic. "Man characterizes nature as much as she characterizes him." There are objective reasons for holding that the cosmos is the scene of an immanent purpose.

With this realist and dualist view of Being, Pratt points out that Buddhism and Christianity have both borne witness to valid aspects of metaphysical truth.

But my most prized impression of Pratt comes later than this period of ripening power: it belongs to an ensuing period of suffering. I have spoken of the joy he and his family found in the hills about Williamstown. An accident that led to the necessity of amputating a leg came as an exceptionally severe deprivation. He met it not only with fortitude; he continued his teaching, meeting his students in his home.

He and I were approaching the scheduled age of retirement from active service: I, two years older, had reached it in 1939, but my frist was continued to 1943. As usual on retirement, my colleagues at Harvard set up a dinner party, and invitations were sent out to friends elsewhere. To my amazement, my old friend and colleague to whom travel was practically impossible was aided into the room— I could have wept.

At that moment, a number of us were retiring: Sheldon at Yale, Montague at Columbia; and Lovejoy had just retired from Johns

Hopkins. I had a speech to make. In it I proposed the founding of a new society based on a curiously contradictory association I had encountered in the Himalayas, a colony of sannyasins, a sannyasi being vowed to a life of solitude. We five were now to be *emeritus*: Why not, with a trifling change of spelling, *eremiti?* Why not a *Societas Eremitorum,* a group of intimates, devoted to the cause of philosophy; a society with no rules, no program, no dues, no duties—except to continue the hermit's function of meditation and to keep in touch with one another, perhaps with an occasional foregathering in summer, informal and free?

There was no objection to the formation of a society so evanescent in its demands, so essentially—shall I say?—spiritual. It existed nowhere but in our several fancies. There was an unwritten understanding that we might come together sometime soon at Pratt's home. Before that moment came, Pratt had left the scene of his work, his courage, his triumph.

We do not lose the continuing summons of a spirit of truly heroic mold.

WILLIAM ERNEST HOCKING
Emeritus, Harvard University

Part I

THE CONCEPT OF SELF

The Self: Existence or Substance?

The nature and existence of the self has been a persistent problem in modern philosophy. Forsaking the theocentric perspective generally characteristic of medieval thought, modern philosophers like Descartes began not with God but with man—with the self as the indisputable starting point for philosophical reflection. All thought must begin with the thinker. All philosophy must begin with the philosopher. This orientation of modern philosophy is epitomized in Descartes' argument: *Cogito ergo sum.*

Professor Pratt made the question of the self his continuing concern. It raised for him all the metaphysical issues that confronted Descartes' successors: the mind-body problem, the problem of knowledge, the nature of the real, etc. For Professor Pratt, any solutions proposed to these metaphysical problems had in large part to be judged by their implications for the understanding of the self. He was persuaded that both idealism and naturalism tend to lose the self. In the former, with its concern for the necessary, a priori conditions of an intelligible order, the concrete self evaporates. In the latter, the self is reduced to a material object, a mere phenomenon. Both positions, he contended, violate common sense. Too often philosophers devote themselves to a kind of detached and sterile thinking that leads them to ignore the indubitable testimony of self-consciousness; and psychologists, particularly the behaviorists, have joined them in this. There is a Kierkegaardian flavor about Professor Pratt's keen judgment: "We have trusted what we read in strangers' books about the secrets of our own hearts." [1]

Professor Pratt was, of course, no Pascalian or Kierkegaardian. He was in part tough-minded empiricist, strongly influenced by his beloved teacher William James. Like James, he combined with his empiricism a profound religious sensitivity, so that his empiricism was widely conceived to include the evidence of the heart. The catholic character of his philosophical study reflects the broad

11

humanism of the man. His experience of life was warm and rich. A philosophy which failed to see the self in both its earthy concreteness and its spiritual grandeur and outreach was for him folly.

Moreover, Descartes' argument convinced him: "The more this question is analyzed and clarified, the more certain does it seem to me that *since I think therefore I am.*" [2] The self, he argued, is a substance. No other explanation does justice to the evidence. Therefore metaphysics, which he regarded as a best guess as to the nature of things, ought to support this judgment. The personal realism which Professor Pratt espoused, with its dualistic solution to the mind-body problem, functioned in considerable measure as a metaphysical justification of his conviction as to the central importance of the self. "Dualism seems to me the only position that can safeguard man's spiritual interests. Nor do I know of any philosophy that can better satisfy the demands of the religious consciousness." [3] Our immediate spiritual awareness of ourselves is indubitable. *Ergo sum.*

Professor Pratt was quite aware that the Cartesian argument has been called into question, and radically so. "The *cogito ergo sum* of Descartes has been often attacked, and never more seriously than in our generation." [4] It was characteristic of him to welcome critical inquiry. In his view the task of the philosopher is never finished; philosophy has its life in continual open-minded questioning. He would have welcomed this book of essays, each of which seeks to take a fresh look at problems to which he devoted a lifetime of reflection. For my part in this endeavor to honor his memory, I want to begin with Descartes' argument for the existence of the self and to make another inquiry into the question of the self as this is posed by the argument.

1.

"I think, therefore I am." Having seen clearly that to think it is necessary to be, Descartes went on to draw the conclusion that I, a thinking substance, exist. But the argument of itself gives no warrant whatever for inferring the existence of the *res cogitans.* As Professor Pratt observes,[5] the argument appears to be an analytic statement. "I think" and "I am" do not assert two different things. The argument is asserting only that thinking is a mode of human being. The Latin has the merit of putting the subject where it belongs, in the verb form, thus avoiding the impression that the thrust of the argument is toward the establishment of the ego. An analysis of man's being (one should probably write this "be-ing" in order to underscore its verbal form) will disclose thinking as an aspect of it. If *cogito* then *sum*. Essentially the argument is only a modest and simple reflection upon the character of human existence. In order to think, I must *be;* the sheer givenness of my be-ing is the *sine qua non* of illustrating it through thinking. The inference that a thinking substance exists not only cannot be drawn from the argument; it entails also, as we shall see, a wholly different usage of the verb "to exist" (or "to be"). The proof, in short, is not a deduction from a given premise which enables us to assert a substantive; it is a statement of what is logically necessitated by the "I think."

Had Descartes followed more closely the Augustinian form of the argument, from which he appears to have borrowed his own, he might have paused to reflect upon the fact that Augustine drew no such conclusion as to the existence of a substantive self. Augustine's argument is simply this: Doubt cannot consume its own ground. My doubting presupposes my existing.

It is beyond question that I exist, and that I know and love that existence. In these truths there is nothing to fear from the argument of the Academics: what if you are mistaken? Since if I am mistaken, I am. One who does not exist cannot possibly be mistaken. Thus, if I am mistaken, this very fact proves that I am. Because, therefore, if I am mistaken, I am, how can I be mistaken as to my existence, for it is certain that I exist, if I am mistaken? Accordingly, since I must exist in order to be mistaken, even if I should be mistaken, it is beyond doubt that I am not mistaken in this, that I know myself as knowing. It follows, then, that I could not be mistaken as to the fact that I know myself as knowing. For, as I know myself to exist, so, also, I know this, that I know.[6]

What is being argued here is that I cannot doubt that I exist. The existence of the self is not the conclusion of the argument but its necessary condition. Yet as soon as we express the argument in terms of the self and its existence, we becloud the issue by giving the impression that the point of the argument is to establish some substantial entity rather than to analyze human existence. Actually the argument is a reflection upon the character of human existing, and it employs the word "exist" in a special sense. If the peculiar "proof" of man's existence is in terms of doubt and thought, then the word "exist" cannot be used of mountains and flowers and mice without a change in its usage. Heidegger makes this distinction clearly: "The being that exists is man. Man alone exists. Rocks are, but they do not exist. Trees are, but they do not exist. Horses are, but they do not exist. Angels are, but they do not exist. God is, but he does not exist." [7] To put this in analytic language, the propositions "I exist" and "The moon exists" do not have the same logical form. Whether the first word be *cogito* or *dubito,* the argument cannot lead to a conclusion of the form, "The moon exists." It cannot establish a substantive self, whether one thinks of that self as the objectively discoverable empirical ego or as the knowing subject. All assertions about the self as a substantial entity are of the form "The moon exists," not of the form "I exist." Descartes' error was to confuse this logical distinction. In Augustine's development of the argument this error is not made. The conclusion of the argument is but a clarification of what is affirmed at the outset: I exist "because" I doubt. The argument is concerned with a verb, not with a noun. It binds us to an analysis of "existing" as expressive of the peculiarly human mode of be-ing—as expressive of that which is a necessary condition of all questions and assertions whatever. Let us consider this verb.

2.

"To exist" is derived from the Latin *ex(s)istere—to step out, stand forth, emerge, appear;* hence also *to be visible, be manifest, be.* The word has thus an active and a passive sense: "to stand forth" is strongly active, "to be visible" is passive. This distinction in meaning is discoverable in the uses of "exist" in our philosophical tradition. The root meaning of the verb, "to stand forth," points to its logical usage in Augustine's form of the argument. "I exist" is not a proposition which predicates the property of existence of the substantive *I.* Critical philosophy from Kant to Russell has known that existence cannot be a predicate in this sense. But neither is "I exist" simply our ordinary linguistic form for asserting "I," the empirical ego. "I exist" expresses the possibility of this (and any other) empirically verifiable assertion, because it exhibits the a priori conditions of cognitive experience. To exist is to step out from—to step out from the world and so to behold it, to question it, to find oneself in it, to know it. In knowing I stand forth from the phenomenal me and from the world to which it belongs. In Kantian terms this standing forth is a transcendental movement which makes possible the oppositing of the self to the world. The being of things is given only to the being whose be-ing is given in thought. This is man. What is appears to us who exist because we stand forth. In other words, existing is characterized (in part) by the polarity of subject and object, knower and known, self and world. The recognition of this is the truth implicit in all dualism. Human existence is standing forth from the world.

"World" must not be confused with "environment." Everything that is has an environment. Man alone has a world. And he has a world precisely in questioning his environment, in standing forth from it, in discovering its problems, and in discovering it as his problematic. As Hume and Kant saw, the world cannot be discovered empirically or studied scientifically. World is a dimension of existence. "World" is a meta-word. The standing forth which characterizes human existing entails the subject-object dichotomy as a fundamental condition of human being. In doubt a man stands over against the world, questioning, probing, seeking. Only thus does the world manifest itself. Only thus does anything, including his empirical self, reveal itself. Therefore, if we say, "The empirical self exists," this proposition has the same logical form as "The moon exists," and here the passive meaning of *existere* is used ("to be visible," "to be"). But if we say, "The world exists," this has the same logical form as "I exist," and is entailed by it. This use of "exist" depends etymologically upon the primary or active meaning of the Latin *existere*.

Augustine concludes his argument with the phrases "I know myself as knowing" and "I know that I know." This formulation guards against the faulty conclusion "I know myself," i.e., I have knowledge of my empirical ego. Empirical self-knowledge is certainly possible, but it cannot be won from this kind of argument. A man finds out about himself as an empirical ego in the way in which he finds out about stones and squirrels—by observation. But precisely because he can discover and in some measure understand himself, he never finds himself: i.e., he is never identical with the self that he discovers, for he is the discoverer. He is both knower and known. But he is more. He is also the discovering. He is the transcendental unity of knower and known, a priori to their distinction. "Man is always more than he knows about himself." [8] This dictum of Jaspers does not refer to the limited character of our cognition and hence to the fact that self-knowledge, like all knowledge, is fragmentary, provisional, and problematic. Jaspers is pointing to the transcendental character of the "I exist" as logically prior to every question which I can ask about myself. A man's existence is the presupposition of his discovering anything; and in discovering anything he stands manifest.

Our ordinary language, whose form reflects the subject-object polarity, does not lend itself to the expression of what is logically antecedent to this polarity. In philosophy we are compelled to express in object language what is nonobjective. Thus we must say: In knowing himself (in existing) a man is not merely the knower and the known: he is the knowing. He cannot be identified with either himself as subject or as object, for his existing—his standing forth—is the unity of subjectivity and objectivity, logically prior to both, and this constitutes his being as a man. In discovering himself he discovers that he is the discovery. He knows himself as knowing. He knows that he knows. He knows that he exists.

3.

The Cartesian and Augustinian expressions of the ontological argument for the existence of the self can be differentiated, as we have seen, in terms of the logical usage in each of the proposition "I exist." The Cartesian argument has generally been employed to establish a substantial self. The Augustinian argument has been used as a reflection upon and analysis of existence. But these two expressions of the argument differ also in their point of departure, *cogito* in the one, *dubito* in the other. Because they differ in starting point, the thrust of the argument in each case is different.

Descartes' starting point served to direct him out upon the broad and secure domain of clear and distinct ideas. Although he doubted, his was a methodological skepticism, which confidently revealed certain truths to be indubitable—*non posse dubitanda*. For Descartes such ideas repulsed by their very clarity the attack of doubt. Certainty was thereby won, because self-evidence rendered doubt impotent. Understandably, then, the argument seemed to Descartes to point to the clear and distinct idea of a thinking substance. *Cogito ergo res cogitans sum.*

In the Augustinian form of the argument the skeptical element is decisive. Doubt is directed against its own ground. Doubt cannot, however, consume itself. Even the most radical doubt must presuppose what it calls into question, namely, doubting itself. Against the simple-minded dogmatism of the skeptics, who asserted as true the privileged proposition that no propositions can be established as true, Augustine let his doubt reach to its own roots: I doubt that I exist. The result, however, is not the discovery of indubitable ideas, such as the clear and distinct idea of a substantive self. Rather, my doubting illustrates, is the expression of, my existing. It presupposes what it appears to deny. Doubt is the expression of the very existence that it calls into question. Doubt cannot consume its own ground. But this ground is not a substance; it is our be-ing.

In each form of the argument both assertion and doubt are present—and necessarily so, for they are dialectical elements in all questioning. Thinking and doubting can be distinguished, but they cannot be separated. Their basic identity points to the fact that existence is questioning, asking. Indeed, another statement of the argument, alternative to both the Cartesian and Augustinian, would read, *rogo ergo sum.*

Thinking and doubting, asserting and questioning, belong together. An assertion necessarily implies a question, the question for its truth. The life or movement of an assertion is a movement from possibility to affirmation, from question to answer. But the answer can never avoid the thrust of the question: it is constantly under the criteria that determine its adequacy. Thus in science the problematic status of every hypothesis and theory must be maintained, else science is perverted into superstition. A statement adjudged tautological is nonetheless a statement made in time, subject to logical error and ignorance. The pervasive presence of the question is the critical element in every assertion. When thinking ceases to have the character of questioning, it becomes formalized, sterile, dogmatic, superstitious. Thinking is questioning; it is a mode of our existing.

Questions demand answers. Without answers questioning is frustrated and is thereby threatened with meaninglessness. But answers that foreclose our questions in that measure destroy our humanity, for they negate our existence as questioning. Our questions drive us to seek clear answers; but answers that are immune to doubt falsify the very existence that seeks them. This points to the demonic character of dogmatism in any form. It appears to fulfill our existence, because our quest for understanding seems to reach its goal in the moral and religious and intellectual certainties which are thereby authoritatively provided us. But precisely so our existence ceases to be what it is: questioning. In saving us from the peril of uncertainty and insecurity, in eliminating doubt, orthodoxy succeeds only in perverting our existence. For man's existence is questioning. It is the ceaseless probing of doubt. The unexamined life is not worth living just because it is not genuine. To exist is to ask, to examine, to wonder, to stand forth from every possibility and every actuality, and so to question it. Accordingly, he whose living is not essentially asking cannot exist authentically. His standing forth is perverted so that question yields assertion without criticism, dogma without doubt, self-affirmation without humility. Authentic existence combines assertion and criticism, answer and question, in such wise that a man remains what he is: questioning. The answers to our questions express the essential dynamic of existence only as they quicken it through constantly renewing the questions.

Thus man is the being who asks. This is not intended as an empirical statement, although it can be taken as such, and on purely empirical grounds might well be adjudged true. Men do in fact ask all manner of questions, and culture appears to be a consequence of this human propensity. But the statement "Man is the being who asks" is not here intended as an assertion predicating something of the empirically discoverable existent, man. The statement is analytic of human existence. To be (as a man) is to ask. In existing I stand forth from, and in this "movement" the Why is born. The Why which is man's being is threefold, according as man stands forth from the world, from existence, and from himself. In standing forth from the world, confronting the multiplicity of its events, I ask, Why this? Why that?—and there is science. In standing forth from existing, in "knowing myself as knowing," I ask, Why the why? Why is there being rather than nothing?—and this asking is metaphysics. In standing forth from myself in my irreplaceable and inexplicable uniqueness, in the awareness of the final and irrevocable responsibility which is mine for living my own living, I ask for the ultimate meaning of *my* existing—and then the question for God has been uttered. In each case I am this questioning. If in my asking I win no answers, my existence is threatened with meaninglessness; if I win answers, my existence is threatened with closure, with self-negation. For I am, only as I ask.

4.

The contemporary understanding of science has made clear the proper relationship of question and answer. Science per se is an expression of authentic human existence, because it regards every conclusion as a hypothesis for further study and every theory as open to continual empirical check and consequent revision. To obscure the problematic character of our knowledge of the world is to pervert our existence: it is to pretend that we can become as gods, knowing without questioning. To know is thus to ask. Our knowledge is fragmentary. Man advances in knowledge only through the continual illumination of his questions. Where questions and answers are final, not open to criticism and review, they presume to give man the status of a god. They blunt the critical edge of thought, stifle inquiry, darken the intellect. This is the perennially valid insight of pragmatism, which Professor Pratt understood so well. Orthodoxy in any form perverts existence. It does not, however, annihilate existence, for it involves the recognition of the power of the question (and hence of the thrust of existence itself) which it perversely seeks to eliminate by answers which do not themselves participate in the interrogatory character of existence. To pursue knowledge under the discipline of science is to embark upon a course of open and unending inquiry. To be is to ask.

5.

Only so is the life of the mind nurtured and sustained. What is true of science is true also of metaphysics. The significance of metaphysics lies in its questions, not in its answers, for genuine metaphysical thinking also participates in the interrogatory character of human existence.

In its most general form metaphysics is the question for the meaning of being. What does it mean that something *is*, that it can be named, that it stands forth, revealing itself as there? Why is there anything at all rather than nothing? This question is both a reflection upon and a reflection of existence. Man asks: thus he exists. In asking he stands out from what is and from himself and asks therefore about the sheer givenness of his own being and of being itself. His own being, his peculiar mode of being that we denominate "existence," is precisely this reflexive movement, that he knows himself as knowing. Man asks about being because he is aware of his own being. Not only does he ask about the variety of phenomena that appear to him in the world, seeking to explain their interrelationships, but he asks also about his own asking, he questions himself as questioning. And he does not ask this accidentally. This question is implied in his asking anything; that is, it is implied in existence as such. To be sure, only as philosopher does he ask the question "Why the why?" explicitly; but every question, judgment, action, conviction presupposes this question. There is a sense in which we cannot avoid asking this question, because every question about anything whatever drives back to the why of our existence—to the why of there being anything at all.

Thus our existence as questioning is the ground of every question, including the question for the meaning of being. Because he exists, man can ask about what appears to him; because he exists, he can ask about his own appearing as the one who asks. What is stands forth for us in our standing forth. Heidegger observes that the word *physis* in the Greek denotes "self-blossoming emergence (e.g., the blossoming of a rose), opening up, unfolding, that which manifests itself in such unfolding and perseveres and endures in it." [9] Things stand forth only for the questioner in the questioning. Their being is not a property which can be predicated of them; it is not anything at all. Things manifest themselves in existence—in standing forth in our standing forth. They are for us. It is man who gives to every creature its name.

The question for being, which expresses the fundamental concern of metaphysics, is asked only in radical awareness that there is anything at all—that anything is, that anyone exists. Such an awareness is identical with the awareness of one's own possible nonbeing. The recognition of the fact that things and persons in the world are contingent (e.g., that all men are mortal) does not of itself lead to the question of being and nonbeing. Asked objectively, with scientific detachment, any question about anything or anyone in the world leads only to an inquiry into their causal relationships. Nonetheless, consideration of the possible non-existence of anything can raise the metaphysical question *if* (and only if) the questioner becomes involved in the question—i.e., if he finds his existence thereby called into question. The metaphysical question is asked, therefore, only in the situation of dread (*Angst*), in which the ground of all questioning and answering is itself in question. A metaphysical question thus expresses the *existential* awareness of nonbeing—the awareness that nonbeing is part of one's own being, that existence is radically contingent, that our being (as Heidegger expresses it) is a being-toward-death. This understanding of metaphysics requires recognition of the distinction between "All men die" and "*I* must die"; "All men doubt" and "*I* doubt" (i.e., I find myself plunged anxiously into the sea of doubt).

Thus the metaphysical question "Why is there anything at all rather than nothing?" is not a question for information, which can be answered by an appeal to some first principle or final cause. Metaphysical answers of this sort always presuppose that the principle of sufficient reason is not itself called into question. The radical questioning which is the life of metaphysics exempts nothing from doubt, and so brings the questioner into a radical confrontation with the sheer givenness of his existing. That I exist is inexplicable, yet is the ground of all explanation. In radical amazement (to use Abraham Heschel's expressive phrase) before existence, we ask for the meaning of being.

The question for the meaning of being, then, is not a question about anything in particular. That kind of inquiry is the form of a scientific question; and when metaphysical questions take that form, questions and answers are alike nonsense. A metaphysical question is genuinely metaphysical only where no answer is expected save the insight won through the exploration of the depth of the question. The question is the rational expression of our existence as questioning, pointing to our finitude (our essential incompleteness) and to our transcendence (our stepping forth from). The point of a metaphysical question is not to elicit an answer. Metaphysics cannot establish a transcendent cause or supply a plausible hypothesis by which the totality of all things (itself a meaningless phrase) can be explained. Metaphysics asks ultimate questions, though not in the sense in which Professor Pratt used this phrase.[10] If one might legitimately offer "ultimate guesses" to ultimate questions, as he believed, both question and answer would be deprived of their ultimacy. An ultimate question is ultimate precisely because no answer can be offered to it, because as a question for information, as a question having an answer, it would be completely nonsensical. Metaphysics is a legitimate and crucial philosophical concern only when it is understood as giving expression to the the reflexive character of man's existence as doubting, thinking, questioning.

Thus the question "Why is there something rather than nothing?" does not have the same logical form as the question "Why is this precipitate blue rather than white?" The latter is a legitimate question about something in the world, and can be appropriately answered by recognized scientific (empirical) procedures. If the question "Why is there something rather than nothing?" is presumed to have the logical form of an inquiry into the contingent conditions under which some specific phenomenon can be observed, then it can only be answered by adducing some transcendent (and essentially unknowable) principle or substance as a sufficient reason. The outcome is nonsense. If, however, the metaphysical question is understood as a reflection upon the givenness of human existence (not as an empirical fact but as a priori to all facts), then the question expresses the character of existence as questioning, standing forth, doubting. What-is manifests itself as there only in the existential relationship, i.e., only as a man stands forth from it and sees himself in relation to it. What-is is for us. Our existence does not *explain* it: it is a logical presupposition of it. Were not human existing of this character, a standing forth in which doubt probes the given, we could assert nothing. Hence the question "Why is there something rather than nothing?" is both an exclamation upon the givenness of existence and a reflection of its fundamental interrogatory character. The task of metaphysics is the elaboration of the metaphysical question implied in existence and expressive of it. Metaphysics does not attempt to answer its questions save by delineating and clarifying the a priori conditions of metaphysical concern.

6.

The Why that issues in science and the Why that issues in metaphysics are both implied in existence as such. There is, as well, a third Why implied in our existence. We ask not only about the existents in the world, not only about being as such, but we ask also about the meaning of *our* being. What is the ultimate meaning of my existence? In this question the "my" is crucial. The question is not about being per se or about human being in general; it is about my being. Each man has to do his own existing, and this entails confronting the question as to what he must become in order to be himself. As Luther observed, every man must do his own believing just as he must do his own dying. A man must live his own living; he must decide for himself what *his* life shall be. He must himself carry the burden of his doubting and of his hoping and the anxieties that belong to them. No ideal pattern or image of human life can relieve him of this responsibility, for whether he accepts or rejects such a pattern, the decision will be solely his. Every man stands ultimately naked and alone in the midst, as it were, of the question as to what he shall do with his life. His existence contains this question, and so he cannot avoid putting to himself the query "What is required of me?"

Again we must recognize that although the question "What is the ultimate meaning of my existence?" has the same grammatical form as any question for information, its logical form is different. It is not a question that asks for the psychological, sociological, physiological, religious, cultural, or other determinate factors that explain one's existence. Such a question would be entirely legitimate. It would give an answer in relative terms as to one's relationships to these factors. But in this type of question, the word "existence" would mean "occurrence in the world." The question would have the same logical form as the question "What are the factors which account for the decline of the Roman empire?"

The question "What is the ultimate meaning of my existence?" on the contrary, is a question concerning *my existing*, not the conditions of my occurrence as an event in the world. It asks: "What must I be? What is required of me?" This is the religious question, the question for God. It is a question that can be answered by any god or by God. From the point of view of biblical faith, God can be distinguished from the gods precisely in this: that when God speaks in answer to a man's question, the reality of the question is not destroyed. When a god speaks, a man's existence is consumed by the answer. The intellectual expression of this latter state of affairs is dogmatism; the ethical expression, absolutism; the religious expression, idolatry. Any answer to the question that constitutes a man's existence is demonic if it eliminates doubt. The One who answers without answering is alone God. This is the meaning of the holiness of God in the biblical tradition. The God whose clear call summons Israel to his service and whose commands are transparently given in the Law of the Covenant is nonetheless the One of whom the prophet says:

> For my thoughts are not your thoughts,
>   neither are your ways my ways, says the LORD.
> For as the heavens are higher than the earth,
>   so are my ways higher than your ways
>   and my thoughts than your thoughts.
>   —Isaiah 55:8, 9

Thus man asks for God, and when he appears to possess God, he possesses in reality only an idol, which corrupts his existence. Authentic existence is possible only in the situation in which our idols are destroyed. God's presence is the death of our gods. Doubt purifies faith. "Thus it may be permissible to make the paradoxical statement that the real proof of God is the agonized attempt to deny God." [11] The same insight is expressed in Nietzsche's famous argument against gods: "*If* there were gods, how could I endure it to be no god! Therefore there are no gods." [12] Faith and atheism are not far removed: they lie in the continuing life of the question for the ultimate meaning of my existence. A proved God is no God at all. God manifests himself in the depth of the human question where that question is asked with ultimate concern (Tillich). Atheism represents the persistent insight that man is always tempted to answer for himself the religious question, thus falsifying his existence by creating his gods in his own image. A man cannot answer the question that constitutes his being; he cannot transcend the boundary situation which defines him as the being that asks. In Augustinian terms, he is the creature who asks for his Creator. In biblical terms his existence is defined by God's covenant with him. The answer must be given, and in such wise that man's life as questioning is not destroyed. God, like oneself, cannot be found. Neither has locus in the world. The self that one finds is only the empirical ego; the god one finds is only the projection of one's vanity. The boundary remains, because a man cannot ultimately escape from being what he is, a questioning. Each man must ask for God. This is his existential concern, this is *his existence.* "Thou hast created us for thyself, and our hearts are restless till they find their rest in thee." [13]

M. HOLMES HARTSHORNE
Colgate University

An Imputation Theory of Free Will

The unique nature of the self has been a persistent theme in the history of Western philosophy. To be sure, naturalists and mystics (strange affinity!) have essayed to reduce or appropriate the self to some other and more inclusive mode of being. But, from the protest of Socrates in Plato's *Phaedo* that Anaxagoras abandoned "Nous" as a principle of explanation and had "recourse to air, and ether, and other eccentricities," down to the sharp distinction drawn by Descartes between *res cogitans* and *res extensa*, dualistic philosophers have stubbornly resisted the reduction of the self to the not-self. Professor Pratt identified himself with this great tradition. One of his most powerful arguments for mind-body dualism was an attack upon the absurdity of the monistic proclivity for reduction or "nothing but" theories. "To say that consciousness *is* a form of matter or of motion is to use words without meaning. The identification of consciousness and motion indeed can never be refuted; but only because he who does not see the absurdity of such a statement can never be made to see anything. Argument against any position must regularly take the general form of the 'reductio ad absurdum.' He, therefore, who chooses at the beginning a position which is as absurd as any that can be imagined is in the happy situation of being armor proof against all argument. He can never be reduced to the absurd because he is already there. If he cannot see that, though consciousness may be *caused* by motion, it *is* not itself what we mean by motion any more than it is green cheese—if he cannot see this there is no arguing with him." (*Matter and Spirit*, page 12.)

In more recent times, the Existentialists have made their own contribution to upholding the uniqueness of the self. With Ortega y Gasset they have maintained that "In the case of other beings, the assumption is that somebody or something already existing acts." In the case of Man, however, "we are dealing with an entity that has

26

to act in order to be. . . . Man, willy-nilly, is self-made, auto-fabricated. Man is the entity that makes himself." Or, in the widely known assertion of Sartre that, as regards Man, his "existence precedes essence."

The present essay allies itself with all these pleas in behalf of the uniqueness of the self. It aims to show that the attribute of "freedom" —a traditional attribute of the self—can be established only by abandoning the way in which an attribute is ascertained to belong to an object. An object possesses its attributes independently of anything we impute to or affirm about the object. But, we maintain, this does not hold of the self: one cannot make a radical separation between what *is* true about a self from what is *held* to be true. In what follows, the application of this dictum will be limited to the problem of the self's freedom. My central contention will be that assertions concerning the freedom of the will cannot be tested for their truth or falsity by reference to an alleged state of affairs commonly designated as "the facts." Constructively, I shall urge that the presence or absence of freedom depends finally upon the act of imputing it or denying it. By "freedom" I mean that a person is responsible for what are called his "acts." I claim that no one *is* responsible until he is *held* responsible. What follows is elucidation and defense of this position.

The genesis in the life of the individual of the idea of personal responsibility discloses the primacy of being *held* responsible. A child first becomes aware of himself as a veritable agent when he is held accountable for doing something "naughty." He becomes conscious of possessing a will of his own when, on the occasion of a parental Thou shalt not, some limitation is placed upon his originally unchecked behavior. The transition to self-conscious agency and at the same time to moral accountability occurs when the child becomes able to check his own behavior. I recall an amusing occasion of once being the undetected witness of what must certainly have been almost the first appearance of moral consciousness in a two-year-old boy. Having had his hands sharply slapped by his parents for tumbling books off shelves onto the floor, he was seen on one occasion first to ascertain whether anyone was looking and then to extend his reaching fingers slowly toward the forbidden books. Just as his fingertips made contact, he quickly grabbed them with his other hand and at the same time scolded himself, "Naughty! Naughty!" The switch had taken place from "other-directedness" to self-direction.

It is no news that the conscience that doth make cowards of us all is first acquired from others. That it very quickly becomes our own and is uniquely individuated—not merely "the mores within"— is revealed by the fact that the most characteristic and unmistakable instances of conscience are "conscientious objections." Similarly— and this is only to repeat what has been said in different words— we are first held responsible. The responsibility is no less our own even though not originating in solitude. More to the point is the observation that the actuality of responsibility occurs only as it is *taken.* "I am responsible" is not the conclusion of an inference from any fact or state of affairs. It is inseparable from one's assertion of it. Whoever, therefore, comes to treat me as either accountable or not accountable for my behavior cannot reach his decision without taking into account what *I* affirm with regard to my *own* responsibility. This affirmation is not traceable to, based upon, or justified by any previous state of affairs that could be appealed to as constituting its factual ground. The price for saying "I did it" consists in renouncing every attempt to establish its truth on the basis of antecedent fact.

I can think of two major objections to the view I am putting forward, one practical and one philosophical. The practical objection is that the imputation view destroys the possibility of testing the correctness or propriety of specific imputations of responsibility. Aren't there occasions when a person may be *held* responsible for an act when a better knowledge would show that what he did was not under his own control? That there are well known and important procedures of establishing criminal liability in cases of alleged insanity appears to put the imputation view in an embarrassing position. A plea of insanity on the part of a defendant's legal counsel leads to calling in alienists to see whether the psychological facts about the defendant are capable of sustaining the plea. Don't these familiar procedures show that the decision to *hold* a person responsible must wait upon the discovery of whether or not as a fact he *is* responsible?

The philosophical objection can be stated briefly, but its full import will become more apparent after we have dealt with the practical objection just outlined. The objection is based on the assumption that all assertions other than those in pure logic and mathematics are either emotive or capable of empirical verification. Our imputation theory offends on the ground that it blatantly contravenes the central thesis of contemporary as well as traditional empiricism. This thesis is that the truth of what is said is always independent of the fact of saying. It is averred that there are no statements whose very occurrence embodies both necessary and sufficient reasons for the truth of our belief. Our contention with regard to moral responsibility is, of course, that until a person *says* he is responsible it cannot be known that he *is* responsible, and that unless he *says* he is responsible there is no way of identifying either its meaning or its presence. In this head-on disagreement, I am fully aware that I am not on the side of the prevailing view!

When it is urged in the name of practical common sense that the activities of alienists in connection with the administration of justice constitute evidence that factual inquiry forms the basis of asserting or denying criminal responsibility, my reply is twofold: first, that on the basis of facts alone, and leaving out what any person avers to be the case concerning his own responsibility, it turns out that *no one can be proved to be responsible. Evidence can always be found against it.* Secondly, that no psychologist invited to give testimony in a criminal case where a plea of insanity is involved has ever omitted reference to what the defendant affirms with regard to his own responsibility.

The observation is almost commonplace that the effect of recent depth psychology has greatly reduced an earlier confidence in the very possibility of ethical responsibility. Although the existence of our legal system is rooted in the assumption of free will and in-dividual responsibility, modern psychiatry suggests that to a disturb-ing degree very few people are wholly in charge of their acts. This deterministic tendency is interestingly illustrated in a recently attempted revision of the test applied to murder cases where insanity is plead as a defense.[1] For more than a century our courts have employed a legal definition of insanity known as M'Naghten's Rule, which stated that a person is not responsible when, because of a "disease of the mind," he is unaware of the "nature and quality" of his acts and is unable to distinguish the "morally wrong" from the right. Both jurists and psychologists have long been dissatified with this criterion: a person may be aware of the moral quality of his act and still be the helpless victim of a compulsion to perform it even when it constitutes a crime. A new principle, known as the Durham Rule, has recently been invoked as a defense in several state and federal courts. This says, "An accused is not criminally responsible if his unlawful act was the product of a mental disease or mental defect." The revised rule allows psychiatrists to present as evidence everything they can ascertain about the defendant's mental condition. Under it, whenever a plea of insanity is supported by psychiatric testimony, the prosecution must prove beyond a reasonable doubt that the defendant is sane or that his deranged mind was not the cause of his deed.

The new proposal makes a wide appeal as a definite advance along the road of a humane jurisprudence. Needless to say, however, its application permits a large increase not only in the number of acquittals when a plea of insanity has been made, but also tends to add greatly to the number of defendants who plead insanity. Perfectly reputable psychiatrists are often able to find that the mental state of a person just before he committed murder may be accurately described as an instance of mental "defect," and it is all but impossible to prove that the defect was *not* the cause of his crime. The door to an extreme leniency is thus swung wide open. Indeed, the assumption that appears to underlie the proposed revision in the test for insanity is that the very nature of a major crime is such that only a mind that is *not* responsible for originating its deed *could* commit a criminal act! It is, I suggest, a moot question whether the advance in humaneness deriving from deepened insight into human motivation is not offset by an increasing reluctance to hold men responsible for their evil acts.

For if there is not only an increasing tendency to withhold imputing responsibility from criminals who plead insanity on the basis of widening the meaning of insanity, there is also an increased hesitation to believe that people can be held responsible for many acts which, though not of a criminal sort, are morally reprehensible or even merely socially offensive. Must we not be tolerant of the weaknesses of human nature, and avoid rushing in with superior moral judgment to condemn, when what is called for is understanding and sympathy? Nor are there lacking those who will quietly point out that we, who sit in judgment and insist upon treating the average criminal as guilty and not just "sick," are ourselves as "sick" as those on whom we pass judgment. It is no longer regarded as improper to denigrate the righteous as well as the unrighteous—a person may be no more responsible for his stake in virtue than for his propensity for evil.

What makes the situation here described especially troublesome is our underlying conviction that there is a good deal of truth in the allegation that people should not be held responsible for much of what they do in the way of either good or evil. That we have been forced as it were almost against our wills to acknowledge that full moral responsibility is not so widespread as we once believed has been viewed as being as much an advance in the direction of a triumphant determinism as a step ahead in humaneness. As already suggested, one sees a kind of cancellation process in the fact that we are being held increasingly responsible for our mistake in holding others responsible who ought not to be held responsible!

Here I should like to propose a more hopeful reading both of the situation as described and of the inference just now drawn from it. It is fallacious to view the advance of psychiatry as undermining our legal system, but it is equally wrong to take undue pride in our moral superiority for treating as "sick" those whom our forefathers treated as "guilty." Both pessimist and optimist are mistaken: there has been neither retrogression nor advance. What there has been is simply a change in the manner in which we have in recent times been doing what men have always done as long as they have been men, viz., to maintain the conditions under which moral responsibility can be either imputed or withheld. If we ask what would happen were the psychiatrists to discover that no one could be held accountable, the answer would not be, as so many think, that we would have to treat everybody as "sick." We could do whatever it pleased us to do, since the condition would have been destroyed which could hold us morally responsible for dealing inhumanely with, say, the criminally insane. The only imperative to discover just who is and who is not to be held accountable is *a moral imperative based only on our holding ourselves responsible for adhering to this very distinction!* Or, turn it around the other way. If we ask what would happen were we to treat as morally responsible all those we would not now dream of treating as responsible, the answer again is that we would be destroying a condition of maintaining the distinction. This is most easily seen if we envisage the consequence of imputing full responsibility for our own or others' behavior in all cases of behavior. It would appear that unless we can somehow effect an operative and functional distinction between will and act, the very concept of moral responsibility seems inapplicable. The innocence of merely animal consciousness is largely the outcome of our being unable to make this distinction in connection with them. Animals do what they will, and will what they do. Thus only sentimentalists hold animals morally responsible for what they do! F. H. Bradley held that you could "correct" but not "punish" a dog, since there is no evidence that the animal is capable of ever entertaining the idea of an act for which he is *not* responsible. It is because at the level of human self-consciousness we make the separation between will and act via disclaiming responsibility in some instances as well as claiming it in others that the condition of the meaning of both is maintained.

We may now return to the consideration of the psychiatrist who is called in to report his findings as they bear upon establishing the truth or falsity of a plea of criminal insanity. Whatever he has found, of one thing we may be sure: he has had to address inquiries to the defendant and get most of his information about him from what the defendant himself has told him. Unless you can get a man to talk about his own state of mind, you have no ultimate source or test for statements concerning his mental state. Questions addressed to someone with a view to ascertaining his sanity eventually go beyond the attempt to get the examinee's report of his passive states of consciousness. They aim to get the person to say whether or not he intended to do the act at the time that he committed it. *Any evidence that supports the conclusion that a man was not responsible because of insanity must make some reference to what that person himself says or fails to say about his own responsibility.* The "facts" on the basis of which responsibility is imputed or withheld necessarily include an imputation that is *not* based on fact, viz., the pure act of holding oneself to be responsible.

The practical objection to the imputation view has now, I think, been met. It is possible to agree that mistakes may be made in imputing responsibility, while at the same time maintaining that the ground of making an intelligent decision cannot be described as a set of facts existing independently of imputation itself. The objection errs in supposing that only a factual situation can serve as a ground.

The position here taken is that what we are dealing with is a reflexive situation having to do with the self-maintenance of the very standpoint from which the problem gets launched. We agree with the objector's demand that something does and must control our detailed imputations of responsibility. But we urge that what controls imputations of responsibility in detail is nothing other than the maintenance of responsibility in principle.

The philosophical objection to the imputation theory is that it fails to separate the question of "what is so" from the question of "what is held to be so." Both determinists and indeterminists traditionally assume that arguments for or against human responsibility and freedom can be produced which make no reference to the fact that anybody *says* "I am responsible." Indeed, the appeal to any personal factor in establishing free will is almost universally dismissed as the height of philosophical naïveté. The fact that a person *feels* that he is free is usually regarded as a jejune and outmoded consideration in establishing the *fact* of his freedom. The truth about the self, like the truth about anything else, is not to be established by any reference to pronouncements made *by* the self. Since much of what a person happens to think or avers to be so is controlled by what he would like to be so, isn't it obvious that most people tend to hold the flattering view that they often really are responsible for what they do? Belief in free will is wishful thinking. The truth or falsity of the belief is quite independent of what we think or wish. Such is the prevailing view.

Since philosophers can sustain almost any criticism except that of being naïve, it seems strategic to defend the imputation theory against its philosophical critics by proposing that the naïveté may reside in the camp of the objectors. How *else*, do they think, can freedom of the will be established if *not* by imputation? One well-known effort has taken the form of finding freedom as an exception to a general rule. If only some objective indeterminacy could be found in Nature, it then seemed that free will had the peculiarly desirable sanction of physical science itself. If in principle it were impossible to predict both the velocity and position of certain subatomic particles, the conclusion seemed to follow that this somehow gave the green light to a scientifically reputable belief in human freedom. However, the case was never clearly made out, and in retrospect it seems strange that the indeterminists grasped such an insubstantial straw with such enthusiasm. At present, the prevailing tendency is to show that when the meaning of natural determinism is properly understood, there is nothing about determinism which is incompatible with holding human agents responsible for their acts. Though this is a much sounder approach to the problem, it has a twofold drawback: it forces us to conclude that the problem was wholly gratuitous and would never have occurred at all if philosophers hadn't been guilty of mental carelessness and confusion. And, secondly, it certainly doesn't establish free will as a fact merely to show that it is not incompatible with something else alleged to be a fact, viz., natural determinism.

But the folly of supposing that one has discovered an objective indeterminism is matched by the equal folly of supposing that the determinism, which no one is any longer disposed to question, is itself a kind of truth discovered about the objective order. Hence the question, "How establish determinism?" must be asked along with the question of how one would establish freedom. The answer here proposed is that the orderly and determined world of nature as a fact of our experience is a corollary of the wholly unconditioned resolve on the part of a human agent to maintain that he is responsible for what he does. Free will and determinism are opposite sides of the same coin! The imputation theory of freedom thus becomes not only the only way in which the reality of free will can be asserted but also the only way in which an objective determinism can be established.

To say that no one is responsible until he is *held* responsible will strike many as a very shaky foundation indeed for freedom. But it does so only because it is mistakenly thought that the foundations of determinism lie in another and more trustworthy area, viz., the region of what is *so* quite apart from what anybody "holds." But it is naïve to think this. It is to confess that one has not learned the lesson of David Hume, viz., that necessary connection gets no meaning as a fact about the world that we empirically observe. One can't just find it. Hume thought that since the idea of necessary connection could not be traced to any external sense it must be due to mental habit externally projected after numerous passive experiences of repeated succession. Agreeing with Hume that causality cannot be found as a fact about external Nature, Kant proposed that it was a category of the understanding presupposed in the very identification of anything as a natural fact. Hence necessary connection can be given no meaning as applied to an order of things abstracted from the knowing subject. The world appears as a causal order because such is the precondition of its appearing at all to a rational subject. The price that Kant was willing to pay for this conclusion was the confinement of knowledge to the phenomenal world and the subsequent proposal that access to the world of reality is to be had only through some nonintellectual function of the subject that transcends the limits of pure reason.

The claim here advanced not only acknowledges indebtedness to the Hume-Kant agreement that causal determinism is not a fact about an alleged independent objective order but goes along with the view that causality is, in some sense, introduced from the side of the subject. The further development of this theme will be the major preoccupation of what follows. Its purpose will be to show, as already stated, that "the orderly and determined world of nature as a fact of our experience is a corollary of the wholly unconditioned resolve on the part of a human agent to maintain that he is responsible for what he does."

That some sense of the reality of his own agency must have existed in the consciousness of primitive man seems scarcely open to doubt. The earliest arts and skills by means of which men were able to gain some control over their environment in the interests of survival and safety were characteristically admixtures of direct and indirect control. To the extent that no spiritual or psychic purposes other than their own were viewed as relevant, primitive men could view themselves as solely responsible for the outcome of what they did. Their control was direct. But what chiefly distinguishes primitive man is the fact that so little direct control was asserted or acknowledged by him. He saw most of his acts as falling within an environment abounding in the presence of multiple spiritual forces, of numerous specifiable loci of spontaneous agency with which he had somehow to reckon before he dared launch his own act. One had to deal with the gods before planting a field, taking a mate, or going into battle. To effect desired consequences, centers of purpose and force, agents other than human, had to be invoked, petitioned, perhaps placated before one's own agency could wisely be exerted. Hence the most important control over the outcome of desired events was indirect rather than direct.

The trouble with the spiritualistic world of early man is that it was a capricious world, so much so, indeed, that we may be mistaken if we think he even thought of his environment as part of a unitary "world." Who could really tell what the gods would do next? Those who thought they could occupied the highest places of respect and honor in primitive societies. But the lives of medicine men and tribal priests were highly precarious: perhaps not "poor, nasty, and brutish" but at times "solitary" and "short"! And even when favorable outcomes resulted from not acting until wise men had been consulted, who could really tell whether the desired result was due to one's own efforts or to nonhuman agencies? Where nonhuman spiritual forces are admitted at all, there necessarily remains the lurking possibility of doubting whether men themselves are solely responsible for their deeds. "Men of an extraordinary success, in their honest moments, have always sung, 'Not unto us, not unto us.' According to the faith of their times they have built altars to Fortune, or to Destiny, or to St. Julian." Thus wrote Emerson in *Spiritual Laws,* documenting his celebration of the Over-Soul as the original source of the deeds of great men. Thus, to intend an outcome and exert oneself to bring it about is insufficient ground for claiming responsibility for what has happened so long as the environment is viewed as a region of spiritualistic controls. One may cast a stone but have little assurance that hitting the target is one's own act if it is assumed that stones have purposes of their own. Such expressions as "it flew from his hand" and "headed straight for the target" suggest the persistence of animistic modes of viewing objects. The point to be noted is that when objects are viewed as harboring subjective intentions of their own, their behavior is unpredictable and human control essentially doubtful. The despiritualization of the world of objects had to occur before men could gain assurance of the efficacy of their own purposes and intentions. To say "*I* threw it" presupposes a stone devoid of interiority and uninfluenced by spirit controls in the environment. The claim to have *acted* does not and cannot occur until the environment is seen as a nonspiritual, impersonal, lawful region of pure objects. A responsible self demands a naturalistically construed environment. In such an environment, stones have observable properties that can be counted on to fulfill or frustrate human purposes: unlike dry leaves, they are useful for ballasting boats. Hume could see no reason why we should expect bread to nourish us tomorrow. Thus he supposed that expectations of being nourished were quite irrelevant to the identification of "bread." That meaning in general and identification in particular could be claimed for specific kinds of objects at the same time that one alleged that "anything might happen in the future" attests to Hume's consistency as a radical empiricist and throws light on his incapacity to do justice to the idea of Nature. The predictability of the behavior of objects once we attain to knowledge of their natures provides the simultaneous assurance of the presence of an environment that can be designated "Nature" and of the possibility of introducing local changes that can be unambiguously imputed to human agents. Thus freedom is not only compatible with determinism but presupposes it!

That the presupposition is mutual may appear as a claim not easy to grant. However, it must be insisted on. What I want to avoid is all suggestion that the world is first discovered to be a naturalistic rather than a spiritualistic region, and that in the second instance we learn that only a despiritualized Nature provides the conditions of freedom. For Nature does not furnish the occasion for act unless in some sense Nature is the outcome of act. Indeed, it is now an old story that so long as action in principle was seen as falling within an independently defined order of Nature, the only alternatives were either to assert action as a strange exception to the determined objective order, or to deny the possibility of action in order to maintain an intact and seamless Nature. The choice was never easy to make as between a dualism that affirmed free will at the expense of making an exception to a general principle, and a monism that maintained the universal sway of Nature but discredited the autonomy of the mind that could propose this very view. Both alternatives may be rejected when their common premise is seen to be inadmissible.

Both prevalent and persistent is the view that man's increasing knowledge of his environment is why he abandoned a primitive spiritualistic outlook and gradually adopted a naturalistic or "scientific" position. This view, I am convinced, is mistaken. It makes the naïve assumption that man's general outlook on the world can be altered solely by detailed investigations and discoveries. But the mode of understanding what takes place in the environment is neither dictated nor altered by empirically observable properties of detailed events. For example, it was not the observation of some new phenomenon in the heavens that led to the Copernican proposal of a heliocentric theory to supplant the geocentric view of Ptolemy. Even less likely is it that such an over-all shift in outlook as that from the belief in spirit control to the belief in control by natural causes could have been brought about by increased knowledge of an already assumed environment of objects. Hard as it is for us of today to realize, the original spiritualistic mode of viewing the world simply did not entertain the idea of the environment as "Nature," i.e., a universal common order of objects. For us to whom such an idea seems both obvious and inescapable, it is highly plausible to suppose that like ourselves the primitive mind was speculative and theoretical, but because it was also ignorant and superstitious it adopted the "mistaken hypothesis" that spirits rather than natural causes were responsible for environmental events. We then go on to argue that it must have been the increase of knowledge that eventually led men to see it was not the wrath of Zeus that accounts for thunderstorms but rather the rapid vertical ascent of a column of warm, moist air. That such an account of the shift from spiritualism to naturalism is essentially naïve will be attested by anyone who has ever tried to win a philosophical argument by an appeal to what he himself calls "the facts." One makes no impression on one's opponent for the reason that he not only sees other facts but that he calls into question the criteria in terms of which the adduced evidence is interpreted as having factual status! There is a story about a scientist whose hobby was mountain climbing and of the difficulty he had in getting a native Chilean guide to accompany him on the ascent of a rather formidable peak in the Andes. It seems that the reluctance of the natives derived from their belief that the spirits residing among the high crags resented all human intrusion into their domain. The scientist finally succeeded in getting an unenthusiastic native to accompany him. As they approached the final steep ascent to the summit, the unhappy Chilean offered as concrete evidence of their mountaintop unpopularity the fact that boiling water didn't get hot enough to cook with. It was thus that the spirits of the place disclosed their resentment. Producing a compact pressure cooker from his knapsack, the scientist carefully explained that the "real" reason for the low temperature of boiling water at high altitudes was the lower atmospheric pressure. When he had finished explaining, the native guide said he found this very interesting but extremely complicated, and that he saw no reason for abandoning his own theory. "But *I* know how to get boiling water hot enough to cook. Just you wait!" To this exasperated protest in favor of science over superstition, the Chilean calmly replied, "You sir, must enjoy the special favor of the spirits."

Although we may assume that for every fact that the scientific mind may invoke to explain an occurrence in the environment, a believer in spirits will be able to invoke some explanatory spiritualistic fact, nevertheless the latter mode of explanation leaves the believer as helpless as before, whereas the scientist *can* get his boiling water hot regardless of altitude. In the long run, the only fact that will unseat a belief in spirit controls is not a truth about the environment at all, but rather the fact that such a belief is inconsistent with what must be believed by one who proposes to say "I can." To the mind or self that does not propose to assert its own responsibility for what takes place, there is no compulsion whatever to adopt the scientific attitude and no argument under heaven for arriving at a naturalistic view of the world.

That the transition from the spiritualistic outlook of the primitive mind to the naturalistic interpretation of events is understandable only as a step—and perhaps the very earliest step—in the long career of man's determination to claim autonomy for his acts and mastery of his environment comports with what has long been familiar to students of ancient philosophy. The entire tonality of the *De Rerum Natura* of Lucretius is that of celebration of the mind's emancipation from the anxieties and fears which no longer victimize and debase our human lives once we have come to see the world as a vast impersonal order infinitely receptive to rational inquiry. Hegel observed that it was the Greeks who discovered Reason, and Ortega y Gasset has more recently pointed out that only with them did man first come to see himself as "cogniser" of his world. Concerning the world as spiritualistically interpreted, there can be no knowledge of natural happenings in their generic forms, but only prophecy of specific future occurrences uttered by those to whom the gods reveal their basically inscrutable purposes. Again, it is well known that the figure of Socrates stands for emancipation in the area of morals: freedom from unreflective convention, the thought-blocking ethical cliché, and the cringing conformism of the merely prudent egoist. It is, however, no accidental concomitance that the legacy of Greece is both the beginning of scientific naturalism and the beginning of a morality of inwardness. Socrates was not put to death by the followers of Democritus. It is true, of course, that Socrates expressed disappointment with Anaxagoras because the "Nous" of the latter seemed to have only a material and not an ideal purport. Socrates cannot be credited with having effected any conjunction between Nature and morals. When in the *Timaeus* Plato elaborated a cosmology in order to provide objective anchorage for his ideal Republic, his picture of Nature was scarcely such as to suggest that the form of the environment is rooted in the finite human demand to be responsible. What is here contended is not that the Greek world established connection between freedom and Nature, but that an identical impulse in the career of Reason gave articulation to both concepts.

Nature as the region in which thought finds grounds, reasons, or causes for whatever takes place cannot itself be viewed as an object, regarded as a whole, and referred to some ground, reason, or cause. The Kantian critique of the cosmological argument may be said to stand firm. Oddly, though, many who agree with Kant continue to think of Nature as a kind of superobject "out there," like a good non-Berkeleian tree. And thus it is held that if only the mind of primitive man had not been clouded with animistic superstitions deriving from ignorance-bred frustrations in the quest for certainty, he, like us, would have been able to see Nature as it "really is," viz., an impersonal and orderly region of causal determinism. Even when a more modest view is taken of contemporary enlightenment, and skeptical doubts are expressed concerning whether the scientific view of Nature corresponds to "the way things really are," the conception of Nature as a kind of absolute object remains an unquestioned assumption. From this point of view, it is necessarily urged that, no matter how anyone *thinks* Nature, it *is* what it is. This, it should be noted, is the exact counterpart of the claim that the will is either free or not free *as a fact* quite apart from any act of imputing responsibility. Just as we found it necessary to reject this latter claim, so now must we reject the former. An imputation theory of determinism is the only tenable counterpart of an imputation theory of free will.

We have seen that the chief objection to basing freedom on imputation is the supposition that free will can somehow be discovered or demonstrated apart from some actual individual's claim to be responsible. In showing this supposition to be mistaken, our argument indicated the necessity of introducing the self-assertive standpoint of a human agent as a precondition of alleging freedom as a fact about the will. In a similar manner, an imputation theory of determinism implies the equal need of showing that reference to causal necessity as a fact about Nature presupposes the activities of a self that seems to gain some kind of direct control over occurrences in the environment. Statements to the effect that "every event has a cause," or that "Nature is a region of determinism," are simply pronouncements of faith that every change in the environment which can be identified as a distinct event can be actually or ideally produced or prevented by a human agent.

Whatever may be thought of the imputation theory of free will, the present writer takes satisfaction in pointing out that what is here called an "imputation theory of determinism" is no wild-eyed novelty. The anthropocentric root of the idea of "cause" has been observed by a number of writers. R. G. Collingwood, writing on *Three Senses of the Word Cause,* makes the telling observation that "For a mere spectator there are no causes." Quoting Bertrand Russell to the effect that "physics has ceased to look for causes," he elaborates the claim that when Nature is thought of in such a manner as to omit in principle all reference to human intervention, experiment, and control, we can give neither consistent nor defensible meaning to "x causes y." Causal explanation demands an activistic focus upon particular aspects of events in such a manner that it becomes possible to say that "x is *the* cause of y." But this, as is well known, can never be asserted in the pure world of objects. It can be asserted only where an interested subject takes an active interest in the condition or conditions of an event that are capable of being produced or prevented at will. "For example," to borrow one of Collingwood's illustrations, a "car skids while cornering at a certain point, strikes the kerb, and turns turtle. From the car-driver's point of view the cause of the accident was cornering too fast, and the lesson is that one must drive more carefully. From the county surveyor's point of view the cause was a defect in the surface or camber of the road, and the lesson is that greater care must be taken to make roads skid-proof. From the motor manufacturer's point of view the cause was defective design in the car, and the lesson is that one must place the centre of gravity lower." In noting that each person takes *the* cause of the accident to be the condition he is best able to alter or prevent, Collingwood concludes to the principle of "the relativity of causes." He further concludes that it is a "nonsense proposition" to assert that "the cause of accidents like this is something which somebody else is able to produce or prevent, but I am not."

In his elaboration of the anthropocentric root of the idea of "cause," Collingwood has, I think, made the mistake of making it impossible to criticize or correct the ascription of causes by diverse agents possessing differing practical powers and interests. Even in connection with his own example, one might suppose that auto manufacturers would in most cases decide that the cause of turning turtle is driver carelessness even though car drivers themselves can do more to prevent such accidents than the manufacturers. But in rejecting the psychological "relativity of causes" on the ground that it denies the possibility of criticizing the ascription of causes in specific cases, we cannot revert to the position that "causes" can be ascertained in the total absence of imputation: The point still stands that apart from some reference to powers of local control, actually or ideally exerted by active agents, the concept of "cause" can be given no specific illustration in the world of objects.

In what has just been said, there is precise analogue with what we found to be the case in the ascription of responsibility, viz., that whereas particular imputations of responsibility may be subject to correction, it does not follow that one can discover the presence or absence of responsibility as a fact apart from all imputation. The fear of the anthropocentric has always been rooted in its alleged incapacity to satisfy our demand for what is objective and non-psychological. It is the old story of Plato versus the Sophists. A man-centered philosophy has traditionally resulted in depriving man of access to an ordered world and thus to the only region that could serve to identify and correct subjective illusion, psychological caprice, and individual vagrancy. But a pan-objectivism swallows up all individuated and local realities, thus destroying the very finite centers of imperfection and incompleteness from which the demand for objectivity arises. The present essay has focused upon the demand to be responsible, and has tried to show that it is from this demand that the other arises. One cannot start by assuming that one lives in or confronts an ordered environment and then look for evidences of free will. There are none. To suppose that there could be is like supposing that David Hume might really have discovered himself to be at home when he stepped out into the Edinburgh street and peered into his study window! No one is free until he claims he is. Such a claim is underived and absolute. Thus freedom is one of the categories, i.e., it is involved in all descriptions of what is. What I have called the "imputation theory of freedom" is consequently an expression whose value is chiefly heuristic, for in the end "imputation" is not a theory *about* freedom but an inseparable ingredient in its meaning.

The argument just concluded contains implications that are tempting to develop but which can be only lightly sketched here. It will be recalled that our limited purpose was to make a single application of a general principle. We tried to show that freedom as an attribute of the self has to be imputed before it can be asserted even to be an attribute. It was only briefly stated that all attributes of the self are in a similar case: their *being* true involves their being *asserted* as true. There is plainly implied in this standpoint a definite break with the prevailing empirical temper of contemporary philosophy. This temper is aptly described by Mr. Stuart Hampshire in his recent book *Thought and Action:* "Philosophers, and particularly modern philosophers preoccupied with scientific knowledge, have turned attention away from the kind of thought and knowledge that is intentional and non-propositional, and that is not essentially expressed in testable statements" (page 103). As a result, even in connection with a person's knowledge of himself, the tendency is "to adopt a spectator's view towards oneself" (page 108).

The phenomenalistic outcome of treating the knowing self as only a passive spectator is familiar to all students of the history of modern philosophy: neither the psychological empiricism of Hume nor the logical empiricism of modern positivists have been able to "find" the self. And, of course, the same elusiveness extends to physical objects, causality, other minds, God, and the state. Since these concepts largely comprise the subject matter of traditional metaphysics, it follows that empiricism has inevitably tended to be antimetaphysical. Furthermore, because of the empiricists' assumption that all nontautological statements must have the same form as statements about possible objects of sense perception, no questions concerning the self could be posed without assuming that answers would be sought in the same way that one would inquire into the attributes of a perceptual object. In his criticism of the spectator standpoint of empiricism, Hampshire uses the example of a person discovering the reasons for his own intended acts: "The knowledge of the future, which is my own intention to act in a certain way, is in no way an inference. . . . I cannot avoid deciding for myself what I shall count as a sufficient reason for an action, and therefore I cannot represent 'finding' something a sufficient reason as something that happens to me, as a mere event in my consciousness. I do not hopelessly encounter reasons for action; I acknowledge certain things as reasons for action" (*op. cit.*, pages 128–129).

Whether or not the author of these statements would welcome it, I cannot resist calling attention to the fact that to "acknowledge certain things as reasons for action" is a clear instance of something being true of the self only because it is asserted as true. Hampshire is very likely merely noting that introspective psychological knowledge is noninferential and hence subject to no empirical test. (The fact that he uses the word "acknowledge," which retains some of the very passivity that he simultaneously deplores, would seem to indicate something less than a radical break with empiricism.) But once it is granted that a pronouncement may be true concerning what does not "happen" and is not encountered "as a mere event in my consciousness," we are, I think, repudiating the central contention that has characterized empiricism from Hume to the present day. No right-minded empiricist is likely to tolerate the claim that there are some truths whose existence is inseparable from their being asserted. This would be to open the door to the traditional bogies of all empiricism, viz., self-evident truths and the ontological argument! If, however, one is unwilling to accept as criticism the bandying of expressions that possess derogatory connotations only from an exceptionable standpoint, the claim may be advanced *à rebours* that the ontological situation is present not only when one is dealing with problems concerning the self but whenever one is engaged in what our English friends refer to as " doing philosophy." To be thus engaged is to be concerned with the making and criticizing of pronouncements which are not properly described as empirical or tautological or meaningless, but metaphysical. This is an essay in Metaphysics.

LAWRENCE W. BEALS
Williams College

Existence—Self—Transcendence

1. Ways of Knowledge — 2. World and Person — 3. Existence Exhibited —
4. Existence and the Self — 5. Self-Consciousness — 6. One's Own Self —
7. Freedom and the Thou — 8. Selflessness — 9. Value and the Unfolding
of the Self — 10. View of Transcendence

1. WAYS OF KNOWLEDGE

In entering into a discussion concerning the existence of man, his
self, viewed primarily from the point of view of modern philosophy
of existence, one must remark at the outset that what we are concerned with here is not thing-like objects which, qua "existing things"
(vorhandene Objekte), could be unambiguously, quantitatively defined according to the method of the natural sciences. Notwithstanding the success of this method in its proper domain, such an attempt
would by-pass the essence of what is in question, and instead of
breaking through to a Law of the Person *(Persongesetzlichkeit)*
would stop short at objective lawfulness (the Law of the Thing,
Sachgesetzlichkeit). We are dealing here with spiritual, psychic
phenomena which are more than what is only visible, and thus we
must transcend the mere empirical and discursive *ratio* in favor of
spiritual insights and experiences in their phenomenological dis-
closure. As Rainer Maria Rilke, the forerunner of existence-philosophical sensibility, once said in a letter to W. von Hulewitz, we
"recognize in the Invisible a higher rank of reality."

But are we not already standing here at the limits of what can
be thought and defined? Can anything we say be still valid here,
especially since we are concerned with inward human existence
in relation to the self? Our efforts will be in vain unless we try to
make genuine propositions with definite meaning, to indicate what
is meant. Otherwise we could not even speak about these matters.
Jaspers himself admits that it is unavoidable "to make (the content
of our talk) an object, although it never becomes an object adequately" *(Philosophie*, II, 27, 1932). However, I am not speaking
here of objects qua things standing over against me, but of objects
in their intentional givenness which always contains a qualitative
meaning-content. This includes in any case a residue of determina-
45

tion, and does not remain purely formal or indefinite and merely relational without specifiable content. "It is hopeless to want to apprehend it [existence] in thought" (Jaspers). And yet we connect an immediate meaning with "unconditioned existence" or "being a self." This does not imply that the object, or, to put it better, the content of my talk becomes fully identical with what is meant. To a large extent we must be content, as also happens in the natural sciences, with an inadequate truth (Jaspers, *ibid.*, 33; also Scheler). And if this is objected to, in advance, on the basis of an uncertain skepticism, then for the sake of this decisive region of human *Dasein* we must repeat the words of Heraclitus: *Panta rhei . . . dos moi pou sto* (All is in flux; give me a point where I can stand).

Let us have therefore a greater confidence in the accomplishments of spirit, and then the question of meaning discloses itself as the primordial question of all philosophy. Heidegger himself begins his work *Sein und Zeit* with the "question concerning the meaning of Being as such" (pages 1, 19, 183, [1931]), and Jaspers says that "even without knowing meaning thoroughly, man cannot stop raising the question concerning meaning" (11, 36, 37). Without meaning all is in stationless (*ortlos*) flux for us, everything yields and we lose our hold on all. By "meaning" we understand then a qualitative content that rests in itself no matter how often the word is used in relation to aims and purposes.[1] Yet in its original connotation "meaning" includes a possible or actual fulfillment, and is closely related to "value" (*das Werthafte*), as, e.g., when we deal with a concretely lived, great human life, a great work of art, or an act of sacrifice in aid of someone ill. This is also the view of Eduard Spranger, who justly proceeds from here to the question concerning "ultimate meaning" (*Magie der Seele*, page 15, 1947). This question remains in the background of our exposition even though we ask more emphatically how we can conceive World, Person, Existence, Self, Transcendence.

2. WORLD AND PERSON

World means the limited, many-layered, centerless, uninterrupted, yet creative unity which encompasses us and in which we find ourselves. It becomes "my world" according to the view I gain of it, according to the rich relational structure by means of which I am anchored in all that is. If I try to define it without any reference

to personal, human relations, I aim at a "scientific word-orienta-
tion" (Jaspers). Yet my conscious ego belongs in this encompassing
world, and our consideration of it (the ego) discloses a wholly new
region of *Dasein,* a region open only to man as distinguished from all
other creatures. Because of this, man has become, as of old, a problem to himself. It was a great discovery when for the first time the
human *person* was seen as "one's very own." "Person" means subjective, mental, psychic living and acting, which consists in the unity
of its accomplishments and possesses its ontic (*seinshaft*) background. "Person" presents us with the image of human essentiality
(*Wesensein*) and its intimacy. In ancient times the notion of "person" was already formed, and subsequently Boethius hit upon the
well-known definition of "persona" as *naturae rationalis individua
substantia.* Let us characterize it (the person) as a spiritual-indi-
vidual reality which acts, in limited freedom, out of an authentic
inner fund of its being. It is more in accordance with our present
knowledge of man if the person is viewed—*pace* Boethius—in its
encompassing, total and also vital relationships in which all orders
and levels of all that is (*das Seiende*) are present. The person is,
as St. Thomas said, *quodammodo omnia.*

Where else would Being itself manifest itself more, as Heidegger
justly remarks, than in human *Dasein*? "Facticity" belongs to the
person, yet this is to say very little. In view of the potentialities
proper to man, Kant spoke of the dignity of the person which must
always be regarded as its own end and never as a means to an end;
already a social conception. When we speak of its most inward
potentiality to be (*Sein-Können*), we advance within the realm of
the human person to a further dimension of depth, which need not
already be developed in every man even if the endowment for it is
there. Here, then, lies the ground that justifies our speaking of the
authentic dimension of human existence, of a mode of Being which,
as Heidegger says, has not yet been recognized as such. By "existence" we do not mean "existentia" in the traditional sense, which,
combined with "essentia," forms a concrete being, and which could
be predicted of all that is real. Rather, we are concerned here with a
decisive human condition, a "conducting oneself situated in the
midst of all that is" (*ein inmitten von Seiendem befindlich sich
verhalten*) (Heidegger). We can give a preliminary exposition of
this existence best by first exhibiting a mode of behavior that is not

existential. This approach will open a path toward the self too, in a manner similar to the one in which we become fully aware of what tact demands of a man by first experiencing its disregard in tactless behavior.

3. EXISTENCE EXHIBITED

Through his vacuity, our all too intellectual and technical modern man has fallen, by and large, into a state of unessentiality, mediocrity, lack of genuineness, and alienation of self. He has lost an inward, self-responsible status, has no inner convictions, only repeats what he is told, and thus falls prey to the "one" of everyday life.[2] How easily he succumbs then to propaganda and mass suggestion, until he is finally ready to let a dictatorship make his own decisions for him! He wears a variety of masks, and it is a question whether there remains anything in him that is his own. Thus all inner probity is lost and a far-reaching erosion of "being a self" (*Selbstsein*) results. We simply live in an everyday unauthenticity, and Heidegger demands that we "let ourselves be summoned out of the absorption into the 'one'" (*sich-aufrufen-lassen aus der Verlorenheit in das Man*) (*ibid.*, pages 299–301), thus achieving a liberation from our external alienation, from our "decay of Being" (*Seinsverfallenheit*).

How seldom is it that a man stands up for his convictions—provided that he still has some! In such cases his genuine being could still manifest itself. At the core everything is fragile, perishable, even decayed, and we no longer want to be something on the basis of the self's own resources; all we want is "status." The great insight of all philosophy of existence is that it is no good to profess to self-acquired insights, values, and duties, unless this profession has become one's most inward possession through an existential attitude. Angelus Silesius (d. 1624) demanded: "Man, become essential"! On account of its unessentiality, Nietzsche characterized our way of life, full of unceasing, urgent activity, with the words: "Oh, dead-silent noise." The global catastrophes of the last two wars, through which a man could be deprived suddenly of all he possessed, made man aware of the vanity of all the clever contrivances of our present management of life and thus made the human situation obvious. Often a man came to lose all his external possessions and status, and in the face of imminent death he had no other support than what he had accomplished existentially (cf. Jaspers). Only what a man was for himself, *his most inward existence,* remained firm. It is in such situations that a breach may appear in the surface of unauthenticity, making an ascent to authenticity of existence possible, an ascent that demands something that is more than mediocre, something that is unusual and extraordinary. Here we finally fall back on our inner world, on the depth-dimension of our self; a dimension—already known to Eckhart (d. 1327)—that has become to a large extent a fossilized, functionless, and atrophied organ in us.

Thus we have grasped the notion that existence is, according to Heidegger, an overcoming of unauthenticity and ascent to authenticity, qua inward-human transcendence, qua *"Ek-sistenz,"* qua *"das Ekstatische des Daseins,"* in the sense of a "standing out into the truth of Being" (*Hineinstehen in die Wahrheit des Seins*).[3] This is an overcoming of the alienation of *Dasein* and a return to the primordiality of Being. Jaspers even goes a step further: "Existence means to be a self that relates itself to itself and thus to transcendence," a transcendence that remains a mystery both for Jaspers and for Gabriel Marcel. Therein lies the "demand to be out of the original ground of one's self" (*aus dem Ursprung seiner Selbst zu sein*) (*Existenz-philosophie,* pages 6, 17, 21 [1933]). Yet for Jaspers transcendence is already of a magnitude decisively surpassing the essence of man. Thus he combines internally existence, self, and transcendence, without essentially distinguishing between existence and self. Nonetheless, we believe that it is both possible and right to make such a distinction, inasmuch as it can be said that the self is an even deeper-reaching and more encompassing special structure that is the ground of existence. Because of this, these two phenomena of "being human," as well as their internal relations, must be given more consideration.

For my part I should like to conclude at this point that *human existence is the ontological rank of inner attitudes and decisions which have their origin—to different extents—in the center of a person of essence qua person of worth.* Existence is, however, not always related to everything and given in its totality, in the manner of the Older Stoa, according to which there were only wise men and fools; rather, as experience teaches, existence can be complete in a higher or lower, more or less encompassing, degree. In any case it represents—provided that it speaks—a confrontation with one's own self. This already disposes us to make definitive propositions concerning it, instead of rejecting all such propositions as wholly distorting objectivities (*Gegenständlichkeiten*). Although in an existential-philosophical sense we speak here only of what is transobjective, in my opinion we can still mean something definable and valid.

4. EXISTENCE AND THE SELF

Existence is thus the expression and attitude of *the deeper, more encompassing self*, "decision" originating in the "primordial ground of being a self" (Jaspers, *ibid.*, page 40). Self belongs to every man, though not yet in existential self-completion. The two—self and existence—are most closely related. Heidegger says: "(Human) *Dasein* always understands itself out of an existence, i.e., out of a possibility of itself to be itself or not to be itself." Yet it can also fail to be itself. Or again: "We call existence: Being itself to which *Dasein* can be related in different ways and is always related in one way or another" (*Sein und Zeit*, page 12). Only thus can we hold ourselves "open" for Being, the original ground of all (*Humanismus-brief*, page 80)—an expression often used by Rilke. This "openness" can be accomplished, by means of self-reflection, in a "new apprehension of myself," "of the authentic, infinite, true self" (Jaspers, *ibid.*, pages 35, 47). Kierkegaard had set out to say this inasmuch as he was of the opinion that only an "essential cognition" makes existence possible, an act of spirit, for "spirit is the self"; spirit understood here, of course, in a wider sense as *ratio*. [4] In German-speaking countries we have been speaking, for a long time, of the task of man "to come to himself." Every man must remain himself; this is what today's ruined man yearns for. This yearning, as Kierkegaard rightly remarked, must go beyond merely hoping, unless man is to submerge in anguish before the threat in *Dasein*, and so I insist on emphasizing the possibility of certain spiritual "illuminations" in this effort.

Of course, this involves daring to be oneself, i.e., a yea-saying to oneself in the face of the recognized nullity of finite *Dasein* which is thereby transcended. Such a choice of oneself, the decision to be oneself, cannot be considered a merely formal, empty one, for then it would be mere sophistry without much significance. (Cf. my *Beyond Existentialism*, pages 165, 168.) This affirmation of one's own self must be performed with complete honesty, and we must admit with Goethe: "How late do we learn that in forming our virtues we are also cultivating our faults" (*Dichtung und Wahrheit*, III, 3, 13). Thus we will not be able to avoid taking guilt upon us, as Heidegger also sees (*ibid.*, pages 269, 283 ff., 306). It is because of this, I think, that in this movement toward one's self we cannot disregard the decision between good and evil, although, according to philosophers of existence, this often happens on account of the difficulties of presentation. If so, we must succeed in giving an ethical answer that is an appeal to the insight of "conscience" and its "ought" (cf. Heidegger, *ibid.*, page 269), for a delving into one's conscience is a turning toward one's self; a self that is confronted here naked, as it were, and in full honesty.

All this adds up to the fact that the road from "person" to existence and thus to the self is the road to each man in his uniqueness and irreplaceability; this is a special demand of the philosophy of existence. The high valuation of individual personality is part and parcel of Western historical tradition; it is expressed in the Christian belief in the eternal worth of the individual human soul, and is especially stressed in the philosophy of Leibniz. Owing to this, as we shall see at the end of our investigation, the transcendence of the person cannot be interpreted as the transcendence that cancels and negates it. We find the demand for the hiddenness and uniqueness of man's essence in the contemporary psychologist C. G. Jung also: "Become a unique being, and, inasmuch as by individuality we mean our most inward, ultimate and incomparable uniqueness, become your own self." [5] In contrast to this we might mention the opinion expressed by Paul Mus, an expert on Asia, at the East-West Philosophers' Conference, Hawaii, 1960. According to Mus, Europe knows only individual consciousness but not the tension of the self which is—as elaborated by the participating Indian philosophers (Mahadevan *et al.*)—impersonal, transindividual, and transcendent. No doubt these are divergent evaluations, yet we have to ask what exactly these words mean. Does the Eastern, Asiatic world commit the error of interpreting "individual person" in the Western sense as the mere foreground of the egocentricity of the ego, i.e., as egoism, selfishness? For this is not meant by self at all, especially not in European mysticism when it speaks, e.g., of the self in the face of God. [6]

5. SELF-CONSCIOUSNESS

Let us, however, take a brief look at the treatment of self-consciousness in European thought. In Plotinus self-consciousness (συναίσθησις αὐτῆς) is the turning (μεταβολή) of the spirit toward itself (*Ennead* IV, 4, 2). Augustine speaks of the (self-) apprehension of mind by itself. "*Mens se ipsam novit per se ipsam*" (*De Trin.* IX, 3) resembles Thomas Aquinas' version. In William of Occam the intuitive element comes into the foreground, although it does not develop into an authentic image of the soul in the thought of his contemporary, Eckhart. Descartes knows self-reflection in his *Cogito ergo sum*, and Kant writes of a self-consciousness that is yet quite far from a cognition of one's self (*Kritique der Reinen Vernunft*, II, 1, 407: *Anthropologie*, I, 1). In Fichte "spirit (obtains) an immediate awareness of itself" through willing; it has an intellectual apprehension of itself (*W.W.* I, 1, 401). In most recent times Oswald Külpe lays emphasis on the "unity of self-consciousness" in the subject. (*Vorlesungen über Psychologie*, pages 99 ff., 1922.) Let us also mention R. B. Perry: "If self-consciousness means anything it means mind functioning in an elaborated, complicated way." It is the sum of our "bodily actions" (*Present Philosophical Tendencies*, pages 281 ff., 1925).

Of course, all this does not quite get at the self at which our investigation aims. It is not without justice that Paul Mus remarks that the European "philosophy of consciousness" has been concerned only with that self-consciousness which became the medium of self-reflection. This tendency was, if anything, strengthened by the "theory of actuality" of the soul which originated with Hume (cf. also Fichte, *Ich als Tathandlung*) and found a general though modified expansion in Scheler's thought. The human soul is a constantly novel activity, an actual performance in whose course a reflection or mirroring of experienced events takes place in the consciousness. Taken in isolation this theory of the soul throws doubt on the older notion of a deeper-seated self in the realm of ontology. Following Jaspers the philosophy of existence returns to earlier views inasmuch as it points out that the self can never be grasped through an objective self-reflection of self-consciousness. Such objective self-reflection can discover only the modes of the manifestation of the self which are not identical with the self itself. "The self is more than all that is knowable" (Jaspers, *ibid.*, pages 34, 41). This is a sentence we can agree with if "the knowable" is understood as an object rationally analyzed according to the method of the natural sciences; yet not if we are concerned with definitive propositions which could lead to it. The self has precedence with respect to the entire objectivity of self-consciousness; as a central source it underlies all that takes place in us, and is thus more than a mere "project" of existence. In view of this, Philip Lersch speaks today once again of the "authenticity and substantiality of the self," i.e., of an ontological subsistence (*Der Mensch in der Gegenwart,* page 110, 1947).

Let us return to Paul Mus's view that, strictly speaking, European thought knows only self-consciousness. Without some qualifications this statement is not right. Who does not know Socrates' often repeated words, γνῶθι σεαυτόν (Know thyself)? Especially since Augustine, there has been much attention paid to the inner being of man (*pars interior, superior*), to an inwardness in which man meets God immediately in the *scintilla animae* (Eckhart, *Wertgedanke,* 270). Blaise Pascal's *ordre du cœur* also belongs here, inasmuch as the answer comes from the interior of the heart so as to transcend, finally, the self in faith. Being a self thus obtains an ethical-personal sense, which A. Welleck develops in his thorough report on "Self-consciousness" in its epistemological and psychological significance (*Lexicon der Pädagogik,* II, 643 ff., 1951). Following Welleck, we speak of the consciousness of self-affirmation and of self-reliance. These are indications of modes of behavior that have their source in the center of our underlying personal being and which let us know how the latter is or ought to be disposed. Especially the *consciousness of one's worth* indicates that certain demands are made on the self which allow for a derivation of self-affirmation and self-reliance in various measures.

6. ONE'S OWN SELF

In the preceding we elaborated on the only way of knowing that is adequate to the problem at hand, and then found it necessary to distinguish the authentic being of the person from the world that presents itself to each of us. The present temporal situation and the *Dasein*-alienation of man led, as shown, to a new apprehension of inward existence qua the mode of being of man that is characterized by a "standing out" of the rank of other beings, the mode of being through which the self is manifested in Being. The two fundamental terms "existence" and "self" were found closely connected in the thought of philosophers of existence, and the question arose whether or not a relative distinction between the two was still called for. At the same time it became clear that, as far as our fundamental sensibilities and valuations are concerned, we are dealing here with an always unique and inalienable self-completion in selfhood, which we have no other means to illuminate than conscious self-reflection. Our spiritual tradition, however, does not only concentrate on what is locatable in the consciousness, but also manifests the intention to go deeper and to disclose the authentic ground of all our acts in one's own self. This approach makes ethical demands on our self-completion that is grounded in Being. These are the "aims of life" (C. G. Jung). Nonetheless the outcome of all this is not yet fully satisfactory, and we once again face the problem as to what this self really is. After what we have said it is clear that the self is not a mere aggregate of active occurrences in us, and it becomes evident that we need the help of psychologists to pursue our line of thought. It is equally evident, however, that the psychic occurrences which they alone are competent to describe also reveal ontological structures.

Obviously we are dealing here with the *deepest dimension* of man and we must work our way down to it, yet this must be done in such a manner that in the end all the "layers of personality" (Rothacker) found in us are grounded in and encompassed as a whole by the self. This shows at the same time that our self is not mere mind, present to itself in consciousness, but also represents something more embracing—precisely this unique *original ground in Being (Urgrund im Sein)*. In "becoming conscious of myself" (Jaspers) I try to gain access to this original ground in order to promote it to greater authority. It is easy to see that "self-comprehension" has its limits here, and all attempts at an analysis involve dangers. Now, Jaspers has pointed out with great sensitivity that we become fully aware of this inner substratum only in the limit-situations of man, in the face of death, of struggle, of care, of suffering and of guilt. In the self man confronts existential decisions in which he fully participates and for which he must stand up unreservedly, provided that he is still capable of such action. This is a "stepping forward out of our unique, self-sufficient Being." If thereby one brings about a genuine, mutual human encounter, a communication with the Other, the self-disclosure of another self must also have taken place, so that we can say, He has spoken.

His behavior is not tainted here by diverse externalities which have nothing to do with himself.

In this connection the word "depth-person" (*Tiefenperson*) is often used today. Yet "person," if we must speak of one, can in my opinion only mean that all underlying latent and efficient forces, intentions and desires are being utilized, indeed, that all the id-like spheres in man are subordinated to its (the person's) conscious-unconscious leadership and are colored by its own complexion. Graphologists know this, and modern medical scientists too, inasmuch as they speak of psychogenic diseases.[7] Thus when dealing with the depth-person of one's own self we are obviously concerned with the "center of gravitation" (C. G. Jung) that is occasionally possible for us and in which the particularity of each self, i.e., the integrity of the ego, presents itself as the point of departure for the formation of personality. This ego can assert itself, or to put it better, it can succeed, only if the forces emerging from the unconscious are integrated into its entire being. It is from "being a self" that we first gain our unclouded answers, for it is the center of human value-resonance (*Wertresonanz*) and its attitudes.

This means that our self is our "center," the "focal-point and junction" of all our inner events, activities, sensual and spiritual passions.[8] There is much talk today about man's "loss of center," and I am fully in agreement with this line of thought. The center is the inner contact point of our intellectual, rational accomplishments with the realm of instinctive forces. Today these two strata often stand unrelated side by side, and the modern alienation of Being promotes this state of affairs. We are confronted with a world of seeming that is structured, logically constructed, and serviceable for practical use. Yet the authentic human realm of psychic experience, the inner relationship to the abundance of cultural values, is to a large extent decayed, and thus we are often internally empty. Owing to this situation the vital forces become more and more superficial, receive additional support from the great successes of the rational faculty, and invite us to violate and disregard what is authentically human. We ought to become once more students of Plato, who recognizes a central connecting link between the λογιστικόν (understanding) and ἐπιθυμητικόν (instinct) and highly values the θυμοειδές (spiritual elevation), the ascent of the soul to the fundamental ideas of the Good and the Beautiful qua measure (μέτρον) and ultimate aim of knowledge (μέγιστον μάθημα). This is the center of man that has been called, as of old, "temper" (*Gemüt*) in German. In this manner the mind will not omit anything vital, but it will admit the senses into the spirit, and it will fraternize with them in order to purify the whole into elevated strata of human fulfillment of *Dasein*. Unconscious instinct and mental receptivity must be combined in order to overcome the contrast between the consciousness of the ego and the acts of will which are often opposed to it. The vital ego must be raised to a higher level in the inner region of tensions, and a eugenia of the body as well as a eugenia of the mind will follow. Yet this is only possible if this center of man, the self, is preserved, and all our acts, dispositions, tendencies, and directions of life are illuminated and determined by it. Thus man is weighed in the balance so that in contrast to the appetites a decision may be taken in favor of what is in accord with his inward, positive essence.

At last *person, existence, self* are united. Self is the most encompassing of the three; it embraces the conscious, unconscious, mental, physical *Dasein* that gives rise to existential behavior or decision. "Person" also refers to the whole of the human being, yet under the aspect of the mental characterization and formation specific to man, which is given its penetrating force by what we call existence. The self is therefore that ground of unity, proper to the person, which in a manner lends its unity to all endeavors of man; a unity that is in internal accord with the whole of the vital psychic and mental reality of man.

7. FREEDOM AND THE THOU

I have said that a self pertains to every man as such. Yet the question is whether it is innerly developed and rightly structured. Thus we are not satisfied with the simple assertion of the self; we also try to determine more exactly what properties belong to it when it attains to a higher self-realization.[9] Jaspers regards as the decisive characteristic of the self the fact that it experiences its "authentic freedom as transcendence-given," and thus distinguishes itself from all "blind" occurrences as a possibility in Being, granted only to man (*ibid.*, pages 41, 49). This is the prerequisite and essential trait of the self. By virtue of its freedom it can overcome its directionlessness, instability, and indigence, and it can become whole. We know immediately when we meet such a man. His obviously not arbitrary possibilities are decided by the worth of the inner self, the growth of the unity and genuineness of the character and thus also of the loyalty to himself. Without these traits the other leaves us cold. It goes without saying that the personal self need not be accomplished always and completely. The self can also become shallow and inclined to what is negative and objectionable. We have had sufficient political experience recently of this abuse of freedom. Theoretically, as we have said, we could restrict ourselves to affirming the self and exhibiting its persistence. Yet since the self is what we are most concerned with in our *Dasein,* nothing requires more care and cultivation, and we feel we are called upon to subordinate it to an *ethical imperative* in *self-evaluation* and the *responsibility to oneself.* (Cf. also C. G. Jung.) What can move, address, and appeal to the self? If it is occupied and possessed by something, it will adhere to that in a positive and negative sense. This is known to every man who has ever undertaken a pedagogic task and recognized that mere rational reflection does not suffice for education, but that, on the contrary, self-appropriated ethical aims have the greatest inner moving force.

Before we pursue this thought any further it must be pointed out that the self (*Ichelbst*) is never isolated but is constantly related to others; this is the prime source of its obligations. A full accomplishment of oneself is thus attainable only if there is a *possibility to love* other persons, to enter further communities, and to assume worth-while tasks. Yet we love in another whatever makes him lovable, i.e., his kind of coined humanity, inasmuch as it bears positive and not lesser traits, even if the latter are always present in some way. That is why we find our self wholly real only in devotion, for in giving we receive, in forgetting ourselves we discover our self. "To want to evade authentic communication means to relinquish my being a self," "to lose the authentic self." "I am desolate when I am only I" (Jaspers, *ibid.,* pages 56, 58). The ego becomes a social ego. The center of man is moved only in the I-Thou relationship which manifests itself in the Thou of God too. (Cf. my *Endlichkeit,* page 450; Martin Buber, *Ich und Du,* pages 465 ff., also Wisser, *op. cit.*) Yet the I can approach the Thou only on the basis of freedom as a possible fundamental trait of being a self, for without freedom the relationship is clouded and disturbed. The ability to be addressed by a Thou is an existential *Wesensbezug* of the person, grounded in the disposition of the self. For our human understanding of *Dasein* the personal element is so deeply rooted in us that an impersonal, id-like sphere yields its place to it; this is an original condition which extends subsequently into areas of metaphysical and religious transcendence.

8. SELFLESSNESS

Yet is the above mentioned "self-oblivion" consistent with what we also asserted about a "concentration on the self"? This is indeed a critical question which must be answered. In order to answer it, however, a more elaborate discussion is required which may give us the first key to the evaluation of the self. Goethe used the word "selfish" (*selbstisch*) to designate the mode of behavior in which our ego is merely *self-seeking*. This is, up to a point, an ego related "only" to itself; a rationally calculating ego, divorced from all other claims made on it, seeking only what is in accordance with its own interest and its own will to status and power. Of course, our own self can be such, yet when it is it provokes our disrespect and we have to say with Jaspers, "Well, so this is what you are." Once again we can see in this subtle problem that it is impossible to define the self without taking an attitude of evaluation. We have to show that the self is fully developed only when the positive possibilities lying in it have reached fulfillment; otherwise, with its growth arrested, the self remains self-seeking.

Goethe had wrestled with this problem. He opposed the negative *Verselbstung* to the positive *Entselbstung*, although both are necessary for life. (*Dichtung und Wahrheit*, II, 8). The first of these is only narrowing, a concentration on oneself, the second a broadening into wholeness. Individual separation is a fall from the purifying search for a wide horizon, for divine order, a fall from the endeavor "to devote oneself voluntarily, out of gratitude, to something more exalted" (*Marienbader Elegien*). He even says: "Vice and crime adhere to the individual and ruin him; all that is good and virtuous draws us into the Universal." Nonetheless Goethe sees the "greatest happiness" in the lived, individual personality. How can we reconcile or answer this? It cannot be done by waiting for a *dissolution of the self* into impersonal being, a kind of self-annihilation, although there is a tendency in our times toward depersonalization, probably as a reaction to a one-sided individualism and the failure to achieve self-completion. Nor would I agree with Heidegger's view: "Es ist das Sein selbst, das den Menschen in die Ek-sistenz des Da-seins als ein Wesen schickt," inasmuch as everything comes to be from and through Being, whether we combine this Being inwardly with being a self, or perceive in it the address of a divine voice whose call man obeys. In the latter case it is supposed that we are determined no longer by *egoism* but rather by *altruism*.

As of old, this famous formula has been taken for the solution of the problem of ethical-personal behavior. Yet it is absolutely inadequate. Is there such a thing as complete *selflessness?* All our activities, the devotion to some cause not excepted, are in the end related to our self, so that Nietzsche could even speak of an egoism of *Verströmung*. Sought-for loneliness, and selflessness as well, may be the most intimate forms of self-enjoyment, provided that they are intended to fulfill my being. "Self-sacrifice is one of our most exquisitely contrived delights" (Heinrich Heine; cf. my *Endlichkeit*, pages 223 ff.). Thus we must state that selflessness as such does not in the least guarantee that something good is taking place; men can devote themselves with a fanatic selflessness to inferior aims that are misunderstood, unjustifiable before one's own most inner forum, and conducive to criminal behavior. We have experienced this in the political history of the recent past. There are idealists of the Inferno.

In our opinion the word "selfless" is used meaningfully only when applied to an identification of one's own ego, in devotion, with acts and aims of high worth, and thus with an overcoming of unjustified desires directed "merely" toward one's profit and advantage. It is man's natural and God-given right to see his own being transfigured through deeds, successes, and the Good, and justified to his own inner satisfaction. Even Kant, the ethical rigorist, says in his second *Critique* (Part I, II, 2 ad. 2, 117) that man may find "pleasure in his existence . . . (a pleasure) that must necessarily accompany the consciousness of virtue." Thus we come to the conclusion that this problem can be solved, not by means of the formal concepts—egoism, self-directedness, and altruism-selflessness—but by raising the question concerning the value-quality of action and endeavor. We have to consider what finds an echo in the heart of man himself and what kind of aims he is devoted to. What is he ready to identify himself with? What is he willing to adopt? What can fulfill his life and enrich his self? In this manner the self always points beyond itself in order to attain to its authentic *perseitas*, to use an ancient term.

The self transcends itself in the service of the Whole, in the service of another; this is the old problem of "German idealism" which lets the self originate in its relation to the community and does not oppose the isolated individual, egocentrically, to the crowd. In a modified and expanded form this problem reappears with the modern demand—already present in "German idealism" and romanticism—to transcend the *subject-object diremption*, a diremption that is to a certain degree unavoidable. This means that we have to deemphasize the fragmentation of the unitary reality of being (*Seinswirklichkeit*) into a thinking subject, which posits its objects according to its own criteria, and a world of objects which remains alien to him. After all, subject and object are akin, and in a similar manner the self and the *transcendence* of its mere self-relatedness toward something transsubjective belong together. The identification with this transsubjectivity thus does not yet imply a union with it, for identity does not necessarily cancel all difference.[10]

9. VALUE AND THE UNFOLDING OF THE SELF

Now we have come far enough to see that the self is always characterized by a "double movement." This (movement) originates in its sphere of intimacy, overflows and grows beyond itself, opens itself to others in communication and devotes itself to action. In this sense Heidegger can say "Im stiftenden Gründen als dem Entwurf von Möglichkeiten seiner selbst liegt . . . dass sich das Dasein (des Menschen) überschwingt," in order to attain to existence, and, we could also say, to self (*Vom Wesen des Grundes*, page 104, Husserl *Festschrift*, 1929). At the same time this encounter with others and the *devotion* to a meaningful world involves a reference back to myself, to my self-affirmation and the inner sanctuary of my efforts. This reference can be directed toward different strata in me, for man and his self are multidimensional. All depends on how this multidimensionality is structured, and on whether only the lower, instinctive strata or also the higher mental-psychic levels in me are open to be addressed. But thereby we make a plain value-distinction, and this is done quite consciously, for it is in the behavior of the self that the inner stores of value in man manifest themselves. It is through their broadening that the person ultimately appeals to itself when it is ready to be carried away by something worth while, and thus to enter a new, valuable field of force.

In order that our self-unfolding be possible, the self must be spacious so that all that has a claim to value can enter; it must be large, not small, so that it is open to every ever so unusual, genuine effort; it must be strong rather than weak, so that it can bear all burdens, remember the source of its own order, and never deny either itself or the order of things. Value is therefore a qualitative content which may fulfill life, on its own, by virtue of its rank, and to various degrees. Thus *self-disclosure* becomes *value-disclosure;* insight into the depth of value becomes insight into the depth of the world. In this manner the self is the source of self-coined value-expressions, the source of our value-answers. In another place I have tried to show that in existence, according to the philosophy of existence, there are, at least implicitly, assumptions of value and demands for value, inasmuch as, e.g., in Heidegger, man is called upon to raise himself out of his state of fall and unauthenticity to the level of authenticity, or, in Jaspers, a heightening of existence takes place in the communication of love (*Endlichkeit,* page 167 ff.).

How can this come about? Out of what horizon can this emerge? If we turn our gaze only to the burdensomeness of *Dasein* we become merely disconsolate and feel that the world is no good; consequently we devote ourselves to that which is superficial or adventurous, or we simply fail because of a lack of courage. This will not do. There is much too much emphasis in the philosophy of existence on gloom and the fundamental mood of dread (Heidegger). Unamuno was right when he said that the tragic sense of life is an essential characteristic of existential philosophy. Just think of the "absurd tragedy" of Camus! No wonder that instead of dynamic activity our self is prone to a melancholy which Petrarch had spoken of as a plague to the soul. Maritain put it convincingly: "Nothing is easier for a philosophy than to be tragic. All it needs to do is to deliver itself to its human burden." Even existential *despair* has been viewed as a prerequisite to attaining one's own self, gaining existence.[11]

I do not believe this, for "existential despair" cannot be creative on its own account—not unless there remains in it a residue of knowledge about values or unless one relies on otherworldly powers. Only then are we justified in saying that the noble forces in man must first be weighed down, then they will soar. Otherwise an excessive overload may destroy all value-reserves, for the inner meaning necessary to a positive departure is ruined. Nevertheless a positive orientation is essentially required for man. A dissatisfaction that is felt to be final does not create values, and it undermines the liberating possibility to find the way to one's own self. That is why I believe that this "fundamental mood of dread" in the face of nothingness (although Heidegger's recent words in the face of Being have a more affirmative sound) may be supplemented, transcended, and dissolved through the equally original mood of joy. (Bollnow speaks of "exalted moods.") Let us not therefore consistently forget all that makes us happy and gives us delight, merely because the present situation is full of menace. Inner joy transcends dread and makes it appear unessential. All that is great is born of joy, not of misery, hardship, and privation, and the former lends the soul the power to endure the latter. Joy is something other than happiness, just as experiencing value is something other than experiencing pleasure. Joy has more content than menace; it gives things perspective; it alone makes the self grow and enriches man inwardly. It has an eminently positive, trustful, and liberating character instead of merely provoking attitudes of defense in the face of dread. There is another decisive function it fulfills, inasmuch as it is only in joy that love can become value. And love possesses a cognition-illuminating force (cf. Augustine, Pascal, Scheler) that grants us our deeper insights, opens us to other men, and is capable of penetrating the self to its most inward core. It is then that we are fully justified in speaking of an existential love.

10. VIEW OF TRANSCENDENCE

Now we come to the last and concluding thought: There is joy over the highest values which can, however, never be fully attained, in an absolute sense, within the temporal scheme. They are thus a promise that can never be fulfilled in our finitude but that rather define its limits and deliver us from it. Joy points toward true timelessness; it points to the threshold of transcendence (*Endlichkeit*, 431). The human self that ever knows of this, and is qua person inwardly capable of accomplishing an existential ascent to it, will apprehend itself, on the basis of an ultimate ground-giving Being, as belonging to this unconditioned level of transcendence. All that is felt to be valuable in itself points us in this direction. In Kierkegaard, the ancestor of existence-philosophical thought, we find the impressive words that the self is a "really infinite concession." There is in it something "unearthly, supratemporal . . . which thus exists," i.e., something transcendent (*Krankheit zum Tode*, pages 10, 18, 52). Today, in German-speaking countries, there is a turn to transcendence in the philosophy of existence, especially in Jaspers. He voices the conviction: "As I am not *there* without world, so I am not my *self* without *transcendence*." But "without existence transcendence would have no meaning" (*Von der Wahrheit*, page 79, 1947).

Before I turn to what "transcendence" means, I should like to return once again to the notion of value, inasmuch as this, qua transition, gives us a vista into transcendence. In every value-fulfillment within the finitude of space and time we are aware of a dissatisfaction, an incompletion, an insufficiency. The fulfillment is fragmentary. We keep discovering limits. We can never fully actualize the value of the good, the beautiful, the pure, and of love. Value always retains an unattainable depth-dimension, for there is no insight profound enough to exhaust it. As Jaspers formulates it: "The thought, which, on the basis of the incompletability of every communication and the failure of every form of truth in the world, properly grasps transcendence, is like a proof of the existence of God" (*Vernunft und Existenz*, page 68, 1935). Thus, more positively, I would say that every value-characteristic has the tendency to point toward the unconditioned, the supertemporal, for no absolute enhancement is given in finite *Dasein*. Only in our most inner self can we perceive it, and because of this the self, as expressed in the existence of a person of value, and transcendence belong together.

This is not the place to discuss all the possible meanings of transcendence. In any case transcendence is an overcoming of self-enclosure in pure temporality, an ascent to timelessness and to indestructibility. Its "persisting value-contents" (*Endlichkeit*, page 181) are free of the instability of temporal change. Nevertheless it would be self-deception to regard transcendence as an imaginary quantity, a projection of our thought into the unconditioned, without assuming a metaphysical ground of Being. It would be more honest to give up the notion altogether. On another occasion I have pointed out that Jaspers' distinction between unauthentic and authentic transcendence as the "Encompassing of all Encompassing" delineates no fixed boundaries, and Heidegger's transcendence is, in the end, only one that is human-immanent and innerworldly, for Being and Time coincide in his thought. Now I regard it justified to use the word "transcendence" with full validity in reference to an ultimately metaphysical level that transcends finite *Dasein,* in reference to a "wholly other" dimension that is not immediately amenable to us.

The problem of authentic Being, which is, as far as we are concerned, the problem of our own self, is ultimately the problem of transcendence. Only thus does Being manifest the goodness that makes it the true object of genuine love. This goodness is for Albertus Magnus a *resonantia dei in mundo* (Eth. 1, 2, 4, Borgnet 7, 23b). The meaning and value of human *Dasein* can thus be extended into the sphere of the unconditioned so as to encounter its last depth. This direction of extension has always been proper to, and deeply rooted in, man; it indicates that the human spirit has what Fichte calls an "eternal destination." Out of this aspect of transcendence man can gain his essential inner light, as Eckhart says. Returning to what was presented at the beginning of this essay, we can now assert that human existence can attain to a full understanding of meaning, and to a supporting meaning-reference, only through this view of transcendence.

It is true that we arrive here at the limits of philosophy. It is understandable that there are philosophical trends which refuse to go on to a consideration of metaphysical transcendence. Yet if we dare to venture on this adventure of spirit, the prescribed task is an extension of what is amenable to thought, and this can be essayed responsibly and by means of an exposition of self-justifying insights. For millennia European thought has proceeded on this road by doing rational metaphysics; today this effort is deemphasized in favor of other endeavors. Thus we arrive at the borders of *religion* that is nourished by other sources. If we understand rightly the present struggle of the philosophy of existence about communication, about Being, and about the sway of transcendent forces, we can say that this struggle has a religious flavor. Yet an essential qualification must be added. If in a reflection on the self it is in the self that we see the possible culmination of human existence and of "being a person," then even transcendence will not lead to a dissolution of the self's most inward essence into something id-like, impersonal. Rather, as man himself is fulfilled only in the I-Thou relation, this places him, in a Christian sense, before the Thou of the highest absolute value, of God, and indicates to him the direction of an exaltation that transcends his own possibilities of value.

FRITZ-JOACHIM VON RINTELEN
University of Mainz, Germany

Self and Introspection

1. PROBLEM

Professor Pratt attempted a final formulation of his epistemology and metaphysics in his *Personal Realism* which appeared in 1937. He hoped that this book would show, among other things, why the position which he had subscribed to seventeen years earlier in *Essays in Critical Realism* was not an inherently naturalistic one. In his preface to the later work Pratt states that Critical Realism really points to a "conception of the partial independence and spontaneity of mind and of the reality of a substantial self." And in the same place he also says: "It is my belief that the only trustworthy defense of the reality of self, of a metaphysically grounded individualism, must be based upon a realistic epistemology." Pratt evidently felt that his own "Personal Realism," which diverged sharply from the naturalistic position of other Critical Realists like Roy Wood Sellars, depended largely upon a special view of the self.

The conclusions Pratt reached as to the make-up of the human being are those of traditional dualism. A person is neither simply a physical body nor a sum of experiences; rather, a person is a peculiar union of the body with an intangible, invisible substance called "the self." The relation between self and the body which it "owns" is that proposed by traditional interactionism. The self, for Pratt, is a wholly nonphysical type of substance which interacts with the body. It is what, in one of its uses at least, is denoted by the first personal pronoun. Pratt's arguments in support of this concept of the self are familiar ones.

In voluntary actions, for example, it is surely not one's physical body which makes decisions. It is not one's body which motivates movements in that body when the deed is voluntary rather than reflex. What is responsible is *something* other than the body: call it "the self." Another significant feature of human experience reinforcing belief in an immaterial, substantial self is its *continuity:* I

66

remember and anticipate. How can this be unless "I" stands for something which endures from moment to moment as pretty much one and the same thing? And it seems incredible to think of one's body as doing the remembering and anticipating. So the self must be conceived as a type of thing; it is a *doer*. Not only does it give the body directions, but it also is responsible for the *unity* that characterizes our experiences. The self cannot be equated with feelings or sensations, since it is instead that which "owns" them or to which they "belong." Without such "common ownership" the unity possessed by our experiences would be unthinkable. As the center to which all facets of one's experiences get referred as "mine," the self is unique. According to Pratt, "The self is *sui generis* in possessing a unity of an inherent sort which no other substance possesses. . . . It is true that the root and the leaves of the rose plant cooperate, and that we justly find in them together a unity in variety. But it is just as true that they are *two* as that they are one. The only being that is *essentially* one is a self." [1] Presumably this is what other philosophers have meant in describing the self as a "simple," uncompounded entity.

Furthermore, on a more phenomenological level it is possible to have a vivid sense of one's self in opposition to other things. Even as one stares at one's own body, one can begin to regard it as something which one (sometimes resentfully) "carries around" with oneself. The difference between "looked at" and "looker" can be increasingly felt, and the "otherness" of one's own body becomes a literal datum of one's experience. In such ways there develops a sense of self, a sense of being essentially a *nonbodily something*.

Thus far the view reads like a familiar oft-repeated page from the history of philosophy. But the account assumes more interest when we consider how Pratt answers the question, What kind of awareness, if any, can one have of one's self? There are passages in *Personal Realism* which suggest that the self is to be regarded as a postulate or inference designed to explain or "make sense of" the facts of our experiences. For instance, after quoting the famous section from Hume's *Treatise*, Pratt says: "There can be no doubt of the correctness of Hume's report on his introspection. The self is not to be found among the objects of consciousness." [2] Or consider this: "We know *that* the self is, and we know *what* it is by observing what it does. And this we know because every theory of the inner life which fails to recognize a knower and actor does violence to the facts of experience. If this is the case . . . the fact that the self cannot be directly found is irrelevant: in fact it is exactly what, upon our theory, we should expect to be true." [3] Other examples of this sort could be cited, thus creating the impression that, for Pratt, the substance-view of the self is strictly a matter of theory—a strictly theoretical postulate; so far as experience is concerned, the self is, in Ryle's phrasing, "systematically elusive." [4]

But the impression is misleading and is corrected in a later passage in *Personal Realism* where, somewhat surprisingly, Pratt quotes approvingly McTaggart's contention that the self can be directly apprehended or introspected, and he goes on to say that there is less contrast between Hume's and McTaggart's positions here than one might believe.[5] If I am not mistaken, Pratt's effort to remove what he himself realized to be an apparent contradiction—confessing to simultaneous agreement with both Hume and McTaggart—is almost entirely contained in the following quotations:

The self is not part of the conscious content found directly as feelings and sensa are. But in every case of knowledge we are directly aware of the "datum" not merely as a thing but *as a datum,* i.e., as something given. . . . The datum is something given to us, it is an object of our awareness or of our thought. *All experience contains the implications of a subject.* . . . The self, indeed, cannot be found in the way Hume sought to find it, but the reason is that it is too near to be seen. It is, of course, the very finder, and we can never get away from it.[6]

To perceive or find the self as such, apart from its states and activities, is quite out of the question, and had this been all that Hume intended, his denial of self-knowledge would have been entirely justified. But to perceive the activities and the states of the self is *in a real sense to perceive it.*[7]

. . . I believe that we have a *certain kind of direct intuition* of the self, and this gives us a knowledge of it which, like any other knowledge of acquaintance, is incapable of being completely stated in descriptive terms. . . . It may be said that we do not know the self; but at any rate we do experience it.[8]

. . . experience, consciousness, of the human sort, no matter what the object of its awareness, is the sort of thing that *naturally points to* and inevitably presupposes an existent subject.[9]

Confronted by the question, Do you introspectively "find" something to be called "the self"? many a philosopher, I suspect, has at one moment been convinced that Hume was correct in giving a negative answer, only to be convinced at some other moment that McTaggart was correct with his exactly opposite answer. Professor Pratt, as I read him, was quite ready to admit that he himself vacillated here, and his eventual "solution" designed to mitigate the felt contradiction between the views of Hume and McTaggart seems to be this: Hume is correct in holding that, so far as what is *ordinarily* known as introspection is concerned, our selves are not objects of introspection. We cannot be aware of our "selves" as we can of our feelings, moods, activities, etc. Nevertheless, we *can* have a "certain kind of direct intuition" of our selves: it is unusual, out-of-the-ordinary, *sui generis* in character. Certain of our experiences, when reflected upon, "naturally point to" (almost make us aware of) ourselves. In an out-of-the-ordinary way we can have a peculiar awareness of "the self"; from the point of view of ordinary introspection, it is an "almost" or "on-the-very-brink" type of awareness that is sometimes available. I trust this is a fair statement of Pratt's conclusion, and, whatever one may think of it as a solution to his problem, I think the discussion in *Personal Realism* is admirable for its clear description of that problem, and deserves rereading by anyone wishing to get the "feel" of its puzzlement once again.

How confident can one be that something resembling what Pratt and others have called "the self" is or is not introspectible? I think this is not really an easy question to answer, and, in any case, the fact that philosophers have responded to it with such uncertainty requires some attempt at explanation. One remembers Hume's lack of assurance in this matter, and the difficulties of the topic were sufficiently realized by James to make "The Consciousness of Self" the second longest of the twenty-eight chapters comprising the two volumes of his *The Principles of Psychology*. What, for example, do one's own introspections disclose toward an evaluation of the following claim? "The conscious feeling of having a *personal identity* is based on two simultaneous observations: the immediate perception of one's selfsameness and continuity in time; and the simultaneous perception of the fact that others recognize one's sameness and continuity. What I propose to call ego identity concerns more than the mere fact of existence, as conveyed by personal identity; it is the ego quality of this existence." [10] It seems to be characteristic of our introspective findings that they leave us mainly uncertain about how we should judge such claims, and this, to repeat, is a puzzling fact of some philosophical importance.

2. AGGRAVATIONS

In this section of the discussion I want to mention some of the factors which make the results of introspection seem so hazy in what they disclose about the existence of a self; or in what they disclose about the reference of the first personal pronoun. Since my interest here focuses upon the process of introspection, I do not intend to assess the relative merits and demerits of philosophical arguments designed to show a need for postulating or inferring the existence of a substantial or other type of self. Whether a special conception of the self is needed for theoretical and explanatory purposes is not of central interest here, but the matter of introspective testimony is. Since I cannot pretend to an exhaustive account of the complicating factors in this brief treatment of the topic, I can claim to notice only a few, often overlooked facts aggravating the already acknowledged difficulty of trying to be confident as to what introspection discloses on certain occasions.

Certainly there has been a steady decline of respect, during the first half of this century among philosophers and psychologists, for introspection as an important source of knowledge. Behaviorism and Freudian psychology have undermined former confidence in introspective reporting. And how could one, after all, place much confidence in a method which notoriously produced so many conflicting results? The following anecdote related by Boring makes the point: ". . . there is always to be remembered that famous session of the Society of Experimental Psychologists in which Titchener, after a hot debate with Holt, exclaimed: 'You can see that green is neither yellowish nor bluish!' And Holt replied: 'On the contrary, it is obvious that a green is that yellow-blue which is just exactly as blue as it is yellow.' That impasse was an ominous portent of the fate of introspection. When two distinguished experts could disagree vis-à-vis about so basic a matter as the nature of hue, some other method of approach was needed." [11]

Wherever possible, introspection is shunned in philosophical discussions, since the conflicting testimony of introspective results is just as embarrassing for philosophers as for psychologists. One remembers, for example, how Moore arrived at the "act-object" distinction within sensation on the basis of what introspection seemed to reveal, how on the same basis Ayer denied Moore's distinction, and how Russell, appealing to similar evidence, switched positions on the point. And, besides, introspection has been shelved on the grounds that it is usually irrelevant for philosophy. One effect of Wittgenstein's *Philosophical Investigations,* it would seem, is to encourage the belief that introspection is of little value in exploring the nature and source of philosophical problems. In one example after another Wittgenstein tries to show how far one misses the mark if appeal to introspection is substituted for a study of linguistic expressions and the occasions where such expressions are typically used. If introspection is so uncertain, and if one recalls the strange, *sui generis* nature claimed for the self, perhaps it is natural that one's introspective findings concerning the self should be so tentative. But there are even further aggravating facts to be noted.

"Suggestions"

One sometimes has the feeling, mentioned earlier, that one is on "the very brink" of inwardly glimpsing something deservedly called one's "self." I think this feeling is partially explicable by recognizing the distinction, often ignored in our use of expressions like "introspection," "introspectible," "based on introspection," etc., between what is *given to* introspection and what is only *suggested* to or by introspection. A headache, for instance, is *given* to introspective awareness; it has, so to speak, a "thereness" about it in occupying the focus of our attention. But consider this example: Suppose I am in a shop staring at some curtains, am trying to decide whether they match those at home as to color and size, and I finally conclude "on the basis of introspection" that they do match. So far as I can tell, even when vivid memory images are present, there is *nothing given* to introspection which is describable as either "the matching" or "the apparent matching" of the stared-at curtains with those being recollected. My conclusion that "these curtains seem to match those at home" is not itself introspectively verifiable as is "I have a throbbing headache"; we may say that it is *suggested* by what we introspect. It is also a fact, however, that the character of the memory images as well as of the inspected curtains may so strongly suggest or indicate their matching each other that we come to regard (mistakenly) their "apparent" matching at least as something given to introspection.

Introspective "suggestions" fall between, as it were, what is merely inferred, at one extreme, and what is actually given to introspection, at the other. Our belief in what is introspectively suggested involves some element of inference or taking-for-granted which goes beyond what is given to our awareness; at the same time, it may be so strongly suggested or indicated by what is given to our introspective scrutiny as to cause in us the feeling that we have an "almost" or "on-the-very-brink" type of direct acquaintance with it. Many of the features we ascribe to our moods, states of mind—even to sensations like headaches—are in fact suggested rather than given, and this explains why we can sometimes be in doubt as to the precise nature of something that we may be introspecting. Possibly, then, certain philosophical conceptions of the self are to be viewed as introspective suggestions strong enough to cause in the authors of such conceptions a feeling of having an "almost-acquaintance" with a self. The fact that not only what is *given* but also that what is *strongly suggested* are often both referred to as "introspectible" or as "based on introspection" helps to explain, I believe, why some thinkers have believed themselves on the brink of self-awareness and why others have simply felt uncertain on the basis of introspection. It does indeed aggravate the task of approaching the "problem of the self" via introspection, if in order to be certain that one's introspection reveals *nothing* about a metaphysical self one must first be certain that nothing like a self is suggested by introspection. A confusing peculiarity of an introspectively suggested self, it should be remembered, is the accompanying suggestion of its being given to introspective awareness.

Vagueness

There are numerous descriptions of the self or of what "I" refers to. Examples are: "a thing that does," "a relation of experiences," "a momentary I-quality," "owner of experiences," "a *sui generis* unity," "the center from which experience radiates," and so on. One would be correct, surely, in charging these descriptions with being highly vague; yet, if taken no further the accusation falls short of identifying the way in which vagueness is a genuinely aggravating factor in trying to decipher what introspection discloses.

For instance, some philosophical conceptions are occasionally dismissed as unintelligible because they are said to be so vaguely described that even their authors would not be able to recognize their instantiation if encountered; their authors cannot even state "what it would be like" to find instances of their own invented conceptions. But, even when this is the situation, the charge may be less than fatal for the following reason: a characteristic of some words in our language is that, until one has certain experiences whose features provoke or seem to warrant the application of such words to those experiences, the words remain too skinny or vague in their meaning for one to anticipate the proper occasions for their employment. This is true of many words used to describe moods, emotions, etc., but an artificial example will make the point more neatly.

Suppose I invent the term "perjealustration" to denote a type of experience which I've not in fact had but which I vaguely describe as involving "a peculiar mixture of perplexity, jealousy, and frustration." *Some* meaning has indeed been given to the expression, but it does not enable me to state now what it would be like to be perjealustrated. It does not enable me to say of a given experience that I *recognize* it as an instance of perjealustration, the reason being that I cannot say of the experience, "*This* is what I meant by 'perjealustration' all along," or, "The last time I was perjealustrated, it too felt exactly like this." What I can say is that the experience "sufficiently fits" the minimally specified connotation of my invented term to warrant its being brought under that label. I can argue that there is a "sufficiently close" matching of meaning with experience to justify my decision that I'm now, say, "perjealustrated." In short, the initially hit-upon instances of the new term's denotation are like any borderline cases of ordinary vague words ("heap," "bald," etc.); they are *legislated* (for reasons not entirely arbitrary) as falling under the term's range of application rather than being simply recognized as such. What is recognized, if anything, is that the occasion gives sufficient excuse for an initial application of a highly vague term; with such application, of course, the connotation of the term becomes relatively more fixed. Not surprisingly, some terms properly receive clarification through repeated applications rather than via verbal definitions.

Accordingly, a believer in a metaphysical self can meet the charge of vagueness by saying that "the self" is like "perjealustration"; some given experience or introspective scrutiny may give sufficient excuse for applying the term, may disclose something "deserving" to be called "the owner of experiences," "the special I-quality of experience," etc. One can now think of another explanation for the uncertainty of one's introspective conclusions: in seeming not to find a self, one has simply not recognized how to bring an invented, vague (or metaphorical) term into play, how to give it initial employment. One has failed to recognize within one's introspective contents "a sufficient excuse" for applying "I" or "the self" to it. The vagueness of these expressions can in a peculiar way aggravate our efforts to assess our introspections. The vagueness, that is, of "the self" can now be regarded as perfectly proper, even inevitable; any uncertainty felt about an alleged self-awareness can be ascribed to a failure to recognize introspectively when a sufficient excuse exists for relating a vague (or metaphorical) term to one's experience. Clearly, I think, we make introspection a still riskier procedure when we demand that it reveal "sufficient excuses" for applying certain vague expressions. We seem to be increasing the number of things that introspection may *overlook*.

Captioning

Consider these remarks: "In Wittgenstein's version, it is clear that the 'I' of solipsism is not used to refer to anything, body or soul; for in respect of these it is plain that all men are alike. The 'I' refers to the centre of life, or the point from which everything is seen." [12]

I find these remarks useful for making a special point in a moment, but, since no discussion of his own thinking behind the quoted comments is intended, whatever is said here should be regarded as strictly apart from and irrelevant to Wittgenstein's own views. Many people, I suspect, would find attractive the suggestion that what "I" refers to is not a thing or entity of some sort but rather "the centre of life, or the point from which everything is seen." Those holding that an "I-quality" or an "I-ness" is introspectible within one's experience might consider the suggestion an amplifying description of these allegedly introspectible items. Yet, if asked whether introspection provides a convincing test of the applicability of the description ("the point from which everything is seen") to one's experience in performing at least one important role of "I," honesty might very well force them to confess uncertainty. Also, something other than vagueness and metaphorical formulation may be the aggravating source of that uncertainty.

In saying that what "I" refers to is "the centre of life, or the point from which everything is seen," one may be saying that the function of "I" is to refer to whatever distinguishes one's experiences as *unique*. If so, we are not tempted to search introspectively for a referent of the metaphysical use of "I," since ordinarily our conclusions as to what makes our experiences different from those of everyone else are not established by introspection. On the other hand, if one takes the description "the point from which everything is seen" as phenomenologically based, as supplying a phenomenological description of what "I" refers to, does one really find within one's experience something—a quality, "feel," "atmosphere," etc.—answering to that description? To repeat, candor may force an uncertain reply to this question.

A reason why one may be in the situation of (*a*) believing that the description "the point from which everything is seen" is the best elucidation yet offered of the metaphysical use of "I," (*b*) believing that something corresponding to that description is introspectible within one's experience, and yet (*c*) finding the truth or falsity of (*a*) and (*b*) left uncertain by one's introspecting, is this: one's thinking that the description "the point from which everything is seen" is the most accurate elucidation of "I" as well as the most accurate description of an introspectible referent for "I" is due to one's mistakenly treating what is in fact a *caption* as if it were a description. The distinction I have in mind requires more elaborating than is possible here, but even a very brief explanation is sufficient to show its relevance to the topic of this discussion.

Besides describing episodes, situations, human actions, etc., we sometimes *caption* them somewhat as we caption cartoons. Captioning is not describing; a complete description of all the ascertainable properties of a cartoon, for example, would not include the possible captions one might give it. Acquaintance with the relevant descriptions is usually presupposed in captioning. In describing we aim to say something "true," whereas in captioning we aim at saying something "apt," "appropriate," or that "has point." A caption cannot be said either to profit or suffer from being vague or metaphorically formulated, but it either has merit or not in respect of being relevant or irrelevant, original or banal, appropriate or inappropriate, and so on. Ordinarily there are tests for the application of descriptions; there are no such tests for giving captions, although some people are more skillful than others in explaining why they think a particular caption is or is not apt. Finally, whereas a description must mention some identifiable or inferable property of what is described, this is not required of a caption. Nothing more than *some* basis of association between captioned and caption is needed for it to be judged as appropriate.

A fact I want to emphasize about captions is this: "the point" they make (as in cartoons) or the basis of their aptness is not a literally perceptible property of what has been given the caption. (This is part of what is meant, of course, in saying that captions are not descriptions.) One can see all there is to see in a cartoon, for example, without getting the point, and simply looking more intensely will not ensure getting it. Indeed, it can be misleading to speak of a caption's "point" as being something one can look for. And one can feel the aptness of a given caption without being able necessarily to pinpoint any particular aspects of the cartoon or episode as supplying the basis of the caption's aptness. The relations between caption and captioned in virtue of which the caption is said to "apply" can be quite elusive—which is also true very often of the relations between our introspected experiences and the descriptions we give them.

In trying to find a phenomenological reference for philosophical descriptions of the self and of certain metaphysical uses of "I," one may be casting about, then, for an appropriate caption rather than for a true description with which to dub his experience. Evidence that such is often the case is found in the fact that one can and does find that the process of trying to introspect the basis for a certain philosophical description of the self is often like looking into a vast emptiness; nothing pertinent swims into view. Yet that description may seem to "fit the facts" of one's experience better than the others proposed. The basis of the description or the point it makes is, however, not literally introspectible. One may suspect that those who claim to introspect such a basis have become impatient with their prolonged state of uncertainty, and claim more than they are entitled to. They may resolve the uncertainty of their introspective scrutiny by deciding that they are describing when in fact they are only captioning.

That we do very often offer captions rather than descriptions for our experiences as introspected does seem to me a plausible explanation of why, in certain instances, introspection produces typically

uncertain verdicts. But I don't know how one could establish it to the
satisfaction of anyone convinced that he was describing rather than
captioning in applying "the point from which everything is seen"
to his introspected experience. It's not merely that the point of
captioning our experiences is often elusive to introspection; indeed,
even the distinction itself between describing and captioning is,
on occasion it seems, forever elusive to introspection.

3. PROPOSALS

If the preceding section has contributed toward explaining why
philosophers, including Professor Pratt, have been justly puzzled
about the amount of illumination afforded "the problem of the self"
by introspection, it may also have created certain misleading impressions. I do not, in particular, wish the previous discussion to be
taken as a wholesale attack on introspection; nothing so absurd
is intended, since introspection, of course, must be appealed to in
reaching some of the conclusions of this paper itself. Nor do I want
to be thought denying that people sometimes have experiences of
such a nature that they *seem*, if not really, to be introspectively
aware of something answering to a philosophical conception of "the
self." Indeed, if they did not, I would have to regard this discussion
as largely wasted. But, after noting certain kinds of difficulties for
the claim that introspection acquaints one with one's "self," what
conclusion are we to arrive at? Are the mentioned difficulties sometimes surpassed, so that one can say confidently that the self has
been introspectively encountered? That no such encounter really
ever occurs? Or that the question is doomed to uncertainty?

In proposing my own conclusion, I must first make it clear that
the only types of philosophical theories which we are trying to test
introspectively are those maintaining that there exists a "something"—substance, quality, process, event, etc.—which is discernible
introspectively and is revealed as fitting adequately enough some
traditional description of the self like "the immaterial entity enduring identically from one moment to the next," or "the central
I-quality upon which all my experiences converge," etc. Further, such
theories would seem committed to the claim, if they are to avoid
being extremely exotic, that the self is available to *repeated* introspections. If, as it were, one once gets the hang of it, then one
should be able to summon up introspective acquaintance with the

self more or less at will. It should assume a certain character of familiarity and recognizability. My own belief, based partly upon my own introspective efforts and partly upon the available testimony of others, is that no encounter with such a self ever really occurs. I can find nothing, I feel certain, within my own introspections that meets the requirements of these philosophical theories. But this is by no means the main conclusion I wanted to reach here, as the following observations should indicate.

Where traditional theories of the self do the greatest violence to the facts of experience, perhaps, is in encouraging the belief that one can set out more or less at will to introspect something called "the self." (Just as one can stop and look at the waiting view, so one can pause and introspect the waiting self.) It is not merely the substance theory we are questioning, it should be noted, but any theory maintaining that a *recurrent* "something" fitting one of the usual descriptions of the self is available for one's voluntary introspections. The type of person that is especially misled by such theories is the one who, on one hand, is convinced that his "sense of self" *is* somehow the result of his being a sensitive, introspective individual, and, on the other hand, is baffled (to the point sometimes of chronic uncertainty) by the repeated failure of his deliberate introspecting to yield what is wanted. I will try, in concluding the discussion, to explain more exactly why this type of person is described as "especially" misled and why, it seems to me, the burden of doubt falls upon anyone who confidently asserts his ability to introspect at will a constantly available self.

Because of the testimony available, it seems only sensible to suppose, whatever one's own experience may have been, that experiences appropriately called instances of "self-awareness," "self-consciousness," "sense of self," etc., do occur. Further, it is likely that these experiences sometimes strongly "suggest" to introspection some philosophical or metaphysical conception of the self. It is the occurrence of such experiences that leads one to consider "the self" as more than a postulate, much less a fiction. But it is equally likely that these experiences, which apparently provide introspectible support for the concept under discussion, are extremely heterogeneous and are not to be considered as all instances of one type. They are not all instances of an "I-type" experience. An examination of the descriptions that a person might give his different experiences sug-

gesting a self would show, I believe, more striking disparities than
similarities between those descriptions. What is needed, in fact, if
introspection is really to be relevant to the traditional "problem of
the self," are more actual specimens of introspective descriptions of
those experiences suggesting existence of a self. This might enable us
to appreciate more clearly what sorts of things impress people
as providing introspectible support for some of the traditional views.
More attention should be paid to such statements as "If I were to
put that particular experience into words, I would describe it
like . . . ," "On occasions of that sort, I feel like . . . ," and so on.
I think we would, as a result, obtain a much clearer picture than we
presently possess of what and why people, on the basis of introspection, think of themselves—metaphysically as well as psychologically.
But traditional theories of the self tempt us into supposing that the
suggestive experiences are all instances of one type, and hence we
set out to find the "I" which they in common are thought (mistakenly) to indicate. The result can only be defeat or uncertainty,
and it is especially baffling for one whose attention has been dis-
tracted from the particular experiences which originally suggested
acquaintance with the self. One's "sense of self" will only be restored,
we may guess, by paying attention to certain experiences when one
has them; one can set out to have such experiences and be suitably
rewarded, but when one sets out to introspect an "I" there's only
disappointment ahead.

In this discussion, let it be emphasized, there has been no attempt
to prove or disprove the existence of a metaphysical self. Professor
Pratt, for instance, offers in *Personal Realism* a number of distinctly
philosophical arguments designed to show the plausibility of the
belief in a substantial self, even if introspection is conceded never to
disclose such. An exhaustive treatment of the "problem of the self"
would, of course, have to assess the merits of those arguments. Our
topic here, however, has been restricted to uncovering some of the
reasons why introspection so often leaves one's thinking about "the
self" tentative and uncertain. The main, positive conclusion arrived
at has been this: if we want illumination via introspection on the
problem as it vexed Pratt and has puzzled numerous other thinkers,
we either need to find or provide for ourselves more concrete
descriptions of those experiences where we seem "most involved with
ourselves" or most "self-aware." We need a closer introspective

scrutiny of the relevant experiences; insofar as they contribute to the belief in a self, an amplified description of them should bring, if anything can, an amplified understanding of the possible connections existing between one's experiences and philosophical conceptions of the self.

In suggesting, as it were, that the metaphysics as well as the psychology (in one of its aspects) of the self would profit from adopting this proposal, I do not mean to intimate that no metaphysical problems would remain. Putting into words our experiences as we seem to introspect them is, as was declared in the middle section of this paper, a most complex business. It is extremely difficult to know, on the basis of introspection, whether introspective language describes or, as we expressed it earlier, rather embroiders on our experiences by giving them captions. One writer makes a very similar observation when he says, *"Language is not a mirror of thought.* Language is only as fine a tool as the discriminations it contains; it can only report observations that have previously been made by members of the culture and formulated in words. Thus we find the introspective method giving rise to a science of verbal metaphor."[13]

So, proposing a more intensive introspective scrutiny of those experiences where a sense of "I" is especially suggested presents its own thorny problems. In example after example one would meet, if attempting to execute our proposal, the perplexing question, Does this particular introspective report "really" or only "metaphorically" describe the experience reported? And how does one resolve conflicting answers that people give to this question on the basis of their respective introspectings? One must argue, and defend, it would seem, even one's introspective reports, as long as uncertainty exists as to their exact relation to the experiences introspected. Trying to assess the adequacy of introspective reporting is to have embarked upon a "metaphysics of the inner life"; a doubt can always force reassessment. But—with Professor Pratt—I don't see why, for that reason alone, the enterprise can or should be side-stepped. For reasons already mentioned, I think it is a type of inquiry directly relevant to the traditional "problem of the self."

GERALD E. MYERS
Williams College

Part II
PHILOSOPHY AND RELIGION

Theology*

James Bissett Pratt was a teacher to whom I owe a great deal. The polemical tone of much of my writing, including the following piece from a work in progress, may obscure that fact; for he was generally mild and kind—more so in speaking of religion than in combat with philosophers. He often seemed serene; and when he sometimes said with a sweet smile that he was not a Christian but a Buddhist, most of his students agreed that he had some of the Buddha's qualities.

It was under Pratt's guidance that I first read extensively in *The Sacred Books of the East*. In a two-semester course in comparative religion—for a generation, one of the finest courses offered in any American college—we had to write ten papers; and in my senior year I wrote several more in Pratt's small, but equally exciting, course in the psychology of religion. It was under his supervision that I first wrote hundreds of pages on religion, on topics set by him. We sometimes disagreed, but there was never the slightest lack of mutual affection and respect; and even today the agreement seems to me much more important and extensive than any difference.

Pratt's sympathetic, but never uncritical, approach to religion was essentially untheological. He made us study ancient scriptures and he led us to consider varieties of religious experience in books by modern writers; but theologies were usually ignored, unless some system was presented as a fascinating oddity. His whole approach was pluralistic and empirical, and it never even seemed to occur to him that he might employ one set of standards when considering his own traditions and another when we studied the religions of the East. His admiration for the Buddha was obviously no mere matter of temperament: he felt a profound attraction for Gautama's antitheological agnosticism.

* With some slight changes and several substantial additions, this chapter forms part of Walter Kaufmann's book, *The Faith of a Heretic,* to be published by Doubleday and Company in 1961.

It would be impertinent to claim Pratt's agreement with an essay that he never read. But it does seem pertinent to emphasize my own sense of a striking continuity with Pratt's teachings and writings, and to take this opportunity to voice my gratitude.

1.

What is theology? Certainly not what *Webster's* says it is when the dictionary gives one of its meanings as the "critical, historical, and psychological study of religion." This definition is introduced with the words, "More loosely"; but any definition which would make Gibbon's *Decline and Fall of the Roman Empire,* Nietzsche's *Antichrist,* and Freud's *The Future of an Illusion* exercises in theology is not only loose but absurd.

The same dictionary, which is known as "the supreme authority," defines a theologian as "A person well versed in theology" or a "writer on theology." This would not only turn Gibbon, Freud, and Nietzsche into theologians; any *critic* of theology being a "writer on theology," would himself be a theologian.

This usage has no basis in the etymology of the word or in judiciously spoken English, though such thoughtlessness occasionally finds expression in the language. The Unabridged furnishes a motive for this misuse of "theology" by immediately following it up with a quotation from the *Encyclopaedia Britannica*: "Many speak of *theology* as a science of religion [instead of "science of *God*"] because they disbelieve that there is any knowledge of God to be attained." In other words: some people, believing that theology involves deception and that such great theologians as Aquinas and Calvin were impostors, prefer not to say so outright and instead appropriate such words as "theologian" and "theology" for something else which is respectable.

This comfortable ambiguity obviates any criticism of theology, but such criticism is badly needed. To be sure, the early positivists rejected theology as meaningless; but they rejected so much else as no less meaningless that theology was in good company: it was not singled out for criticism and examined closely.

Then one began to note that the early positivists had used "meaningless" in a rather unusual sense: what was meaningless as they employed that term was really quite "meaningful" in the usual sense of that word; so one cared even less. When it was widely recognized that some of the positivists' prose was meaningless by their own standards, their initial repudiation of theology came to be considered an amusing episode, no more. And after the Second World War some of the heirs of the later Wittgenstein reversed the line of his early followers and tried to rehabilitate theology. Wittgenstein had talked of language games and urged his students to discover the meaning of words by considering how they are actually used in various contexts; so one began to discuss the language of theology in an attempt to see how this or that phrase functions in the discourse of the theologians. Thus ineffectual criticism gave way to appreciation, and philosophers came to confirm the common notion that theology is intellectually perfectly respectable. But is it really?

Much depends, of course, on how we define theology. Webster's main definition is all right but takes up fifteen lines, and then is followed by the loose one which has been discussed. But the most complete dictionary of the English language, the twelve-volume *Oxford English Dictionary,* is brief and to the point when it defines theology as "The study or science which treats of God, His nature & attributes, & his relation with man & the universe." Further, it defines: "*Dogmatic theology,* theology as authoritatively held & taught by a church; a scientific statement of Christian dogma. *Natural theology,* theology based upon reasoning from natural facts apart from revelation." It allows that "theology" sometimes means "A particular theological system or theory" and that it may be "Applied to pagan or non-Christian systems." Finally, it lists two obsolete meanings: "Rarely used for Holy Scriptures" and "Metaphysics."

2.

There are, then, two types of theology: natural and dogmatic. Natural theology purports to tell us about God, his nature and attributes, and his relation with man and the universe, on the basis of reasoning from facts of nature, without relying on revelation. But from the facts of nature one cannot even infer God's existence; much less "his attributes and his relation with man and the universe"; still less the qualities which theologians, as we generally use the term, ascribe to him: omniscience and omnipotence, justice and love, perfection and infinity.

From the facts of nature one can infer further facts of nature, but one cannot with any certainty infer anything beyond nature; not even with any probability. At most one can say that there are some events one is not able to explain by means of any hitherto known facts; and at such points one may possibly elect to postulate some occult entities or forces, pending further research. Past experience indicates that all such invocations are extremely likely to be dated by a new advance in science. Indeed, even as one writer postulates some unknown entity outside of nature, some scientist elsewhere is likely to be able to dispense with it. Moreover, even if it were permissible to infer something suprascientific from the facts of nature, it is never really the facts of nature that determine what precisely is invoked at that point, but some preconceived ideas mediated by religion. *At the crucial point, natural theology falls back on dogmatic theology.* It is the teaching of the theologian's own religion, not the facts of nature, that decides whether, where other explanations fail, he should invoke one god or two, or more; a god of love, a god of wrath, or one of each, or several of each, or one who loves some and hates others, or perhaps a god of perfect love who permits, or insists upon, eternal torment.

To be sure, there are those who believe that God's existence can be proved from facts of nature. They may be referred to Kant's *Critique of Pure Reason,* which contains the classical refutations of what Kant considered the only three basic types of alleged proofs. I shall not discuss these proofs here, having dealt in detail with the five proofs of Aquinas and with Plato's argument, Kant's "postulate," and Pascal's "wager," as well as the question whether God's existence can be proved, in my *Critique of Religion and Philosophy.*

Most Protestant theologians admit that God's existence cannot be inferred from facts of nature and that knowledge of "his attributes and his relation with man and the universe" has to be based on faith and revelation. In sum, they repudiate natural theology. Many Catholic theologians believe that God's existence can be inferred from facts of nature; but they, too, base their alleged knowledge of "his attributes and his relation with man and the universe" on faith and revelation. In sum, they repudiate natural theology. What people in the twentieth century generally mean when speaking of theology, whether they are Catholics, Protestants, Jews, or agnostics, is what the *O. E. D.* calls *dogmatic theology* and defines as "theology

as authoritatively held & taught by the church." What this definition overlooks is merely that there are *many* churches, and that each
has its own theology—or rather *many* theologies.

The rest of this essay will deal entirely with dogmatic theology,
and the criticisms offered will not depend on any disbelief in God's
existence. If it were granted that God exists—even that the Bible
was revealed by him—almost all of the following objections would
retain their full force.

One preliminary consideration that suggests the state of dogmatic
theology at a glance is that, although it purports to tell us about
God's "attributes and his relation with man and the universe," most
modern theologians avoid any clear and unequivocal answers to
questions about hell. But few questions about God's attributes and
relation with man could be as important for us as who is doomed to
eternal torment, and what we must do to avoid such a fate. The
impatient retort that the theologian does not believe in fire and
brimstone or howling and gnashing of teeth does not come anywhere
near settling the problem whether those who would avoid eternal
punishment must beware of following the example of such celebrated heretics as Luther and Servetus, Kierkegaard and Tolstoy,
Spinoza and Russell, to name just a few. We must press two questions: If even the answers to these most crucial questions are not
known, can anything of comparable importance about God's "attributes and his relation with man" be known? And if these questions
about hell *can* be answered to some extent, then how exactly does
one proceed to find the answer?

3.

The first point to note about theology, as the term is generally
understood, is that it is denominational. And a theologian is a man
or, rarely, a woman who does not merely expound the beliefs, particularly those about God, held by his denomination, but who also
offers a sympathetic exegesis and, in fact if not expressly, a defense.
Neither Presbyterian missionaries nor agnostic anthropologists who
offer careful expositions of the beliefs of the Navahos would be
called Navaho theologians. To be called a theologian one must be
committed to the beliefs about God, or gods, of which one offers
an account. By betraying a lack of sympathy, or by evincing

hostility, a writer makes clear beyond a doubt that he is not a Navaho theologian or a Christian theologian, even if he should be very "well versed" in Navaho or Christian theology. A man may be well versed in theology without being a theologian; and he may be a theologian without being well versed in theology.

To understand theology, one has to understand commitment to an institution. As a first example of a very educated and intelligent writer whose books cannot be well understood unless we keep in mind that he has voluntarily committed himself to an institution, consider not a theologian but a Communist: Georg Lukacs. Many Western writers, including Thomas Mann and Herbert Read, have hailed him as the most intelligent Marxist critic and historian of ideas, and his erudition is amazing.

In *From Shakespeare to Existentialism*, I have attempted a quick sketch of Lukacs and quoted passages in which he links me with Eisenhower, McCarthy, the pope, and Cardinal Spellman. In the present context only three points matter.

First: no dead writer who has not specifically been condemned by the Party is safe from being enlisted as a comrade who all but took the final step. Second: Lukacs adopts a peculiar language which shows at a glance that one is reading a committed Communist. Third: he continually cites authority to back up what he says. Points are proved by quoting Marx, Engels, Lenin, and, depending on the Party line around the time of publication, sometimes, but not always, Stalin.

Confronted with all this, two reactions are possible. One may say: How perceptive and erudite this writer is! How liberal, really! He almost agrees with me! Of course, he puts all his points in rather odd ways; but, being a Communist, he is doing the best he can. Or one can say: If he is so liberal, why does he not draw the consequences? Why does he not come out into the open to say what he thinks? For years he did not have to be a Communist; why, then, did he write as he did? The answer is clear: because of his commitment.

The parallel with many Catholic intellectuals is obvious. They, too, assimilate to Catholic doctrine the most divergent materials and enlist all kinds of writers as searching souls who all but took the final step. They, too, adopt a peculiar language. And they, too, back up their views by constantly quoting authority. And here, too, one

may exclaim: How erudite! How liberal! The man almost agrees
with me! Of course, he puts his points a little oddly; but, being a
Catholic, or a Thomist, he is doing the best he can. Or one can ask
why such writers do not draw the consequences and say freely what
they think without encumbering every utterance with such an involved ritual.

Instead of laboring this point, let us consider Protestant theology.
For the point suggested here is easier to see, and has been noted
much more often, in connection with Catholicism, and millions of
English-speaking people would readily grant that Catholic writers
are vulnerable to such charges; but few indeed have noticed that
Protestant theology is in the same boat.

The choice of a peculiar language and the quoting of authority
stare us in the face; and the leading Protestant theologian in the
United States, Paul Tillich, counts the Hebrew prophets among the
greatest Protestants of all time, assures us that Marx, Freud, and
Nietzsche were the most outstanding Protestants of the last hundred
years, and considers Picasso's art deeply Protestant, too.

The point here is not merely that the same three points which we
have noted among Communists and Catholic intellectuals are found
among the Protestants as well. But to prepare for our central criticism, let us explore two examples in more depth.

4.

Toward the middle of the twentieth century, no Protestant
theologian in Germany attracted more attention than Rudolf
Bultmann. Long known as an outstanding New Testament scholar,
he published an article in 1941 in which he urged that the New
Testament must be "demythologized" in order that its central
message, unencumbered by the myths of the first century, might
reach modern man. His article was widely debated, outside
Germany, too; more and more of Bultmann's books were translated
into English; and eventually he was invited to give the Gifford
Lectures in Scotland and various other lectures in the United States.

Of the many criticisms of his call to demythologize, few, if any,
annoyed Bultmann as much as an essay by Karl Jaspers, widely
known as one of the two leading German existentialists, although he,
like Martin Heidegger, repudiates this label. Jaspers' critique of

Bultmann is open to many objections, but it has the great merit of having stung Bultmann into making a staggering admission. (The two essays, together with Jaspers' reply to Bultmann's reply and Bultmann's laconic response to Jaspers' second essay, are available in English in a paperback, *Myth and Christianity*.) In his initial reply, Bultmann says of Jaspers: "He is as convinced as I am that a corpse cannot come back to life and rise from his tomb. . . . What, then, am I to do when as a pastor, preaching or teaching, I must explain texts . . . ? Or when, as a scientific theologian, I must give guidance to pastors with my interpretation?"

Up to this point, Bultmann had generally referred to "the Easter event," and students had debated just what, according to Bultmann, had happened at the first Easter. Now Bultmann let the cat out of the bag, not only concerning one particular belief but regarding the whole nature of theology. Here we have an excellent formulation of the dilemma which Bultmann shares with Catholic as well as Protestant theologians, and with men like Lukacs, too.

The retort to his rhetorical questions need not be the answer he intends. Again, one might well say: If you are convinced that the beliefs in terms of which the institution to which you commit yourself defines itself are false, why don't you draw the consequences and renounce your allegiance to the church, the Party, or St. Thomas, as the case may be?

The matter of the Easter event is no isolated instance. Here is another illustration. In the wake of Bultmann's challenge, there was a great deal of discussion about demythologizing hell. At the German universities the debate raged around such questions as whether the fire in Luke 16 is a physical fire. Surely, this is a relatively trivial question. Even the Nazis were able to devise subtler torments and, for example, made a woman's hair turn white overnight by falsely telling her that the screams she heard from the next room were those of her son under torture. If there were an omnipotent god, intent on inflicting piteous sufferings on some of his creatures, he could certainly improve on physical fire. The serious question which one would expect the theologians to discuss is how they propose to reconcile eternal torture with divine perfection. Most American Protestant theologians refuse to consider this question: they prefer to talk about the kingdom of God. And German theologians prefer to discuss whether the fire is physical fire. Even when asked outright about the other problem, most theologians manage somehow to change the subject quickly.

Catholic theology may seem to be more forthright in this matter, but certainly not so forthright as most people suppose. An involuntarily amusing editorial in the Chicago diocesan newspaper, entitled "Yes, Professor, There Is a Hell," is not unrepresentative. Taking issue with an article that a professor had contributed to "a well-known magazine," the editorial makes a great point of the fact that it "is by no means the position of the Catholic Church" either "that 'the great mass of mankind' will be tormented for all eternity" or that "only those who are a part of the Christian communion will find salvation, whereas 'the rest of mankind (will) suffer eternal torment.'" As it happened, the professor had not said that this *was* "the position of the Catholic Church." But be that as it may, the editorial ends: "There is a hell, professor, and the easiest way to find out is by not believing in it, or in God." This is a mere editorial, full of misrepresentations, and it would be foolish to saddle the Church with it. For that matter, notwithstanding the notion many people have of the supposedly monolithic nature of Catholicism, there is no single theologian, not even St. Thomas Aquinas, whose views can simply be attributed to the Church. What is typical about the editorial is merely the alternation of protestations of liberality with threats. One does not usually find both so close together; but the two strains are almost omnipresent in contemporary Catholicism.

On the one hand, scholarship insists that "though a few individual teachers of the Church may have held this, it has never been regarded as a matter of the Church's teaching"; on the other hand, homiletics requires threats and promises. As we listen to the preacher or the missionary, everything appears to be as clear as could be; but under the scholar's or the critic's questioning this surface clarity gives way to endless complications and uncertainty.

St. Thomas Aquinas, who will be considered in due course, was on the whole exceptionally clear; but the Catholic Church is not committed to his views. In his encyclical *Aeterni Patris,* Pope Leo XIII, in 1879, said: "As far as man is concerned, reason can now hardly rise higher than she rose, borne up in the flight of Thomas; and Faith can hardly gain more helps from reason than those which Thomas gave her." He cited many previous popes who had spoken similarly of the saint: "Pius V acknowledged that heresies are confounded and exposed and scattered by his doctrine, and that by it the whole world is daily freed from pestilent errors." And "The words of Blessed Urban V to the University of Toulouse seem to be most worthy of mention: 'It is our will, and by the authority of these letters we enjoin you, that you follow the doctrine of Blessed Thomas as true. . . .'" And the encyclical cites "as a crown, the testimony of Innocent VI: 'His doctrine above all other doctrine, with the one exception of the Holy Scriptures, has . . . such a truth of opinions, that no one who holds it will ever be found to have strayed from the path of truth. . . .'" From all this one might conclude that the pope, speaking *ex cathedra* on matters of faith and morals, and therefore infallibly, had taught us that we shall not stray from truth if we accept St. Thomas's view that the blessed in heaven will see the punishments of the damned so that their bliss will be that much greater. Or that one angel can speak to another without letting other angels know what he is saying. One might even suppose that his views on scientific matters are invariably true. But Leo XIII also says, in the same long encyclical: "We, therefore, while we declare that everything wisely said should be received with willing and glad mind, . . . exhort all of you, Venerable Brothers, with the greatest earnestness to restore the golden wisdom of St. Thomas, and to spread it as far as you can. . . . We say the wisdom of St. Thomas; for it is not by any means in our mind to set before this age, as a standard, those things which have been inquired into by Scholastic Doctors with too great subtlety; or anything taught by them with too little consideration, not agreeing with the investigations of a later age; or, lastly, anything that is not probable." In a similar spirit, Etienne Gilson, one of the most outstanding Thomists of the twentieth century, says at the outset of *The Christian Philosophy of St. Thomas Aquinas*: "Personally, I do not say of Thomas that he was right, but that he *is* right." But this does not prevent him from admitting now and then in passing, without emphasis, that Thomas was *not* right.

Bultmann, asked about eternal torture in a conversation, said that on that subject he agreed with Lessing. He had every right to expect that a younger colleague, no less than a student, would proceed to the nearest library and begin reading through a set of Lessing's works, in search for the crucial passage. After the first ten volumes, he could safely be expected to give up. Encouraged by my

American training, however, I asked, "And what did Lessing say?" The great theologian hesitated, then allowed that Lessing had once said somewhere that if even a single soul were in eternal torment he would certainly refuse to go to heaven. It would seem, then, that Bultmann disbelieves in *any* form of eternal torment, but he does not make a point of this. In his huge *Theology of the New Testament*, hell and eternal damnation are simply ignored.

This refusal to let one's No be a No is one of the central characteristics of theologians no less than of committed Communists. One does not emphasize one's points of disagreement with tradition or the scriptures; instead one emphasizes points of agreement and side-steps embarrassing issues by raising questions of exegesis. As a consequence, the agreement among committed believers is, to a surprisingly large extent, apparent only: they proclaim their allegiance to the same scriptures and traditions, but the very passages which are to one man the superlative expression of his faith are to another a source of embarrassment and an unexampled challenge to his exegetic skill. And two men who love the same sentence are likely to interpret it quite differently.

One need not even run the full gamut of Christian views from the first century to the twentieth, from Presbyterianism to Catholicism and the Greek Orthodox Church, from the Armenian Church to Christian Science, from superstitious peasants to scholarly professors, to see how little agreement there is among Christians who profess the same beliefs. Dr. Billy Graham and Dr. Paul Tillich are both twentieth century American Protestants; indeed, there are few other spokesmen of mid-century American Protestantism who are so well known and so influential. Yet it is at least arguable whether Paul Tillich is not closer in his views to the writer of this exercise in heresy than he is to Billy Graham. The same question about Reinhold Niebuhr might be difficult to answer. But as soon as we compare what men like Tillich and Niebuhr actually believe and disbelieve with the beliefs not of Billy Graham but of avowed fundamentalists, or of Martin Luther and John Calvin, or of St. Augustine and St. Athanasius, or of St. Paul and St. John the Evangelist, the question ceases to be hard to answer: the beliefs and disbeliefs of at least two of our most celebrated theologians are much closer to mine than they are to those of millions of their fellow Christians, past and present.

5.

The most crucial criticism of theology ought now to be apparent: theology depends on a double standard. One set of standards is employed for reading and interpreting one's own tradition and its texts; another, for the texts and traditions of all others. Here, one is committed not only to make sense of everything but to make everything come out superior and profound and beautiful; there, one is not averse to finding fault and even emphasizing all that is inferior to one's own tradition.

Protestants are perceptive regarding the faults of Catholicism, and not inclined to make allowances for them the way they do for Luther's faults or Calvin's, or for those of their own articles of faith; those of the Westminster Confession, for example. Catholics can see plainly what was wrong with all of these, but approach their saints with a very different attitude. Pressed about eternal damnation, Protestant theologians point out that this doctrine impresses on us how important our choices in this life are; asked about the latest Catholic dogma, they do not exert themselves to find a profound meaning in it, but are quick indeed to disown it as sheer superstition. Christians stress the references to divine wrath in the Old Testament while ignoring or interpreting away the references to wrath, relentless judgment, and eternal torment in the New Testament; they point to the references to love in the New Testament, less to those in the Old; and they conclude, as if they had not presupposed it, that the God of the Old Testament is a God of justice, wrath, and vengeance, while the God of the New Testament is a God of love, forgiveness, and mercy. Moreover, one contrasts the realities and mediocre representatives of other traditions with the ideals and the saints of one's own.

Theology is a comprehensive, rigorous, and systematic attempt to conceal the beam in the scriptures and traditions of one's own denomination while minutely measuring the mote in the heritages of one's brothers. Of course, that is not all there is to theology. Theology is also a comprehensive, rigorous, and systematic avoidance, by means of exegesis, of letting one's Yes be Yes, and one's No, No: instead of saying No one discusses other matters, and in a pinch one "interprets" and converts beams into slivers, and slivers into gold.

And theology is also a continual attempt to force new wine into old skins. The new wine is not always the best available, and perhaps the old skins aren't either; but the whole point is to avoid a fair comparison of skins: into one's own one stuffs whatever looks good, while one associates the skins of others with an inferior vintage, going back, if necessary, a few centuries to find a really bad year.

Theology is antithetic not only to the Sermon on the Mount but to the most elementary standards of fairness. It involves a deliberate blindness to most points of view other than one's own, a refusal to see others as they see themselves and to see oneself as one appears to others—a radical insistence on applying different standards to oneself and others.

It is, no doubt, exceedingly difficult to be completely fair, but theology is founded on a comprehensive, rigorous, and systematic refusal to as much as attempt to be fair. It does not merely occasionally lapse into acceptance of a double standard: theology is based on a devout commitment to a double standard.

6.

One word that sums up much of the procedure of the theologians is *gerrymandering*. (See my *Critique of Religion and Philosophy,* Section 56.) That Aquinas carved up Aristotle, citing to his purpose what he could make fit, meets the eye. Even Thomist theologians will admit that. But it is hardly less obvious that he did the same with Scripture. The method of his imposing *Summa Theologica* is simple enough, though the amount of Gothic detail is staggering.

A question is asked and first of all answered in a manner that Aquinas considers false. This false answer is then buttressed with a few quotations that would seem to support it. Then a quotation is introduced which apparently conflicts with everything said so far. A tension is created but immediately resolved by Aquinas' concise *Respondeo,* or "I reply." He takes his stand with the immediately preceding quotation, gives his reasons, and then replies, one by one, to the objections raised before he stated his position. In this manner, every question is answered: Whether God reprobates any man? Whether God can do what he does not? Whether God can do better than what he does? Whether several angels can be at the same time in the same place? Whether the semen in man is produced from surplus food? There is never any hesitation, any slight lack of self-confidence, any suspense of judgment. Thomas knows it all and proves it all—proves it in his own fashion, which amounts to quite the boldest and the most extensive feat of gerrymandering ever undertaken. Proof involves, and frequently consists in, the adducing of quotations—usually from the Old or New Testament, from Aristotle, or from pseudo-Dionysius (a fifth century Neoplatonist whom Aquinas and his contemporaries mistook for a contemporary of St. Paul and the Blessed Virgin). One of the few things all of these authoritative proof texts have in common is that Thomas was unable to read any of them in the original. But even if he had been a still greater scholar than he was, even if he had been able to read Greek and Hebrew instead of occasionally misconceiving biblical and Aristotelian passages, and even if he had known that the pseudo-Dionysius had not been converted by St. Paul himself, his method would for all that have been thoroughly unsound. Unlike historical and philological scholarship in the employ of conscientious efforts at interpretation, the theologian's method is not designed to uncover the original intent and meaning of the quoted passages. Rather, Thomas chooses what fits and ignores or rejects what does not fit; but some readers fail to realize what goes on because at the beginning of every question he sets up a few straw men whom he can knock down a page later with the aid of rival quotes—if necessary, from the pseudo-Dionysius. This was the greatest theologian of them all.

To be sure, Thomas has to be seen in the context of his time if one wants to arrive at a fair judgment of the man. What appears monstrous in the perspective of a later age is always apt to have been commonplace when it occurred. But the whole point of the present discussion is that Thomas' method is by no means *exceptionally* unsound. On the contrary, he is a splendid representative not only of his time but of theology in general. What distinguishes him is not that he was arbitrary. What is exceptional is rather his unflagging patience, his attempt at comprehensive coverage, and his amazing clarity which shows us at a glance what he is doing. Faithful throughout to the same simple method, he takes up question after question, stamping out his treatment with a stencil, as it were—or, metaphors apart, dictating relentlessly, only stopping occasionally, we are told, to pray.

On major points, the conclusions are predetermined, and Thomas himself makes a point of this. In the Second Part of the Second Part of the *Summa Theologica,* he insists that we "ought to believe matters of faith, not because of human reasoning, but because of the divine authority." But he writes theology because "when a man has a will ready to believe, he loves the truth he believes, he thinks out and takes to heart whatever reasons he can find in support thereof." Only when faith is primary and seeking understanding, only when we are finding reasons for what we already believe, instead of basing our faith on reason, "human reasoning does not exclude the merit of faith, but is a sign of greater merit" (Article 10).

On lesser points, of course, the conclusion is not always predetermined by tradition or authority, and Thomas has some freedom to develop a position of his own. Like most theologians, however, he blurs this distinction, backs up controversial stands, too, with citations of authority, and thus gives the appearance that his system is not only singularly comprehensive and consistent but the gospel truth. In fact, the tightly woven structure is a doubtful asset: if a few key concepts are based on confusions or if a few basic suppositions are no longer plausible or tenable in view of some advance in knowledge, the whole edifice may topple.

Thomas's vast erudition, clarity, and noble simplicity have perhaps never since been equaled. But his bold air of omniscience and his gerrymandering have been matched time and again. In twentieth century Protestant theology men like Heidegger or Nietzsche have taken the place of Aristotle, and Marx (in the thirties) and Freud (in the forties) that of the pseudo-Dionysius. The Bible, however, is gerrymandered as artfully as ever.

To balance these remarks about the greatest Catholic theologian: how many of those who cheer Luther's declaration that he would not recant unless refuted from the Holy Scriptures are aware of his repudiation just a little later of the Epistle of St. James in the New Testament as "an epistle of utter straw"? Or of Luther's saying that one might even call John the only true evangelist? Who recalls his bold interpretation of Jesus' moral teachings as commandments that were meant to teach us our utter inability to do good works and please the Lord that way?

The Christian denominations have little in common except that all of them have managed to get around the apparent rigor of Jesus' moral teachings without repudiating Jesus. This stunning feat has been the prime accomplishment of the Christian theologians. And at times an outsider, lacking grace, gets the impression that the Christian theologians place the object of their legitimate love on higher and higher pedestals the less faithful they are to him. Luther even said outright that there is no greater enemy to ardent faith than the continual effort to be faithful, and that a good whopping sin breeds the most ardent love and reverence.

It would be an interesting exercise for students to construct from the same scriptures half a dozen or more different theologies: Catholic, Lutheran, Presbyterian, Anglican, Greek Orthodox, and Baptist, for example. Or to give Neoplatonic, Kantian, Aristotelian, Spinozistic, Pragmatist, the Liberal interpretations. This might make them see the utter arbitrariness of the procedures used without the least self-consciousness by theologians. It might also keep them from writing and talking, as most theologians do, as if the sole alternative to what they offer were some sort of crude, insensitive materialism. It would thus deprive theology of one of its foundations: the loaded alternative.

The reason why the theologians gerrymander should be obvious. They set themselves an impossible task which cannot be solved with sound methods: to offer an interpretation of the whole New Testament, indeed of the whole Bible, all at once. The books of the Old Testament were written over a period of roughly one thousand years, and when we add those of the New Testament the total span comes to over 1,300 years. Moreover, Luke introduced his Gospel by remarking that others had written lives of Jesus but that it seemed good to him to write another version "that you may know the truth"; and the Book of Acts gives a detailed account of some of the disagreements among Paul and Peter and James.

It is exceedingly difficult to give an account of Plato's views, or Aristotle's, or of various pre-Socratics; but the task the Christian theologian sets himself is rather like an effort to interpret "the message of the Greeks" in a single treatise: if he must offer a single message, he simply has to gerrymander; and it stands to reason that different theologians will come up with different messages. If they were determined to be fair and to employ the methods used by conscientious historians and philologists, they would have to admit that there is no single message; that there are many different views; and that an honest and careful interpreter must often be unsure even about the views of single authors, such as Paul or John, Matthew or Luke—not to speak of Jesus.

7.

Another instance of the double standard is also understandable as the result of a quixotic task. The theologians have a way of redefining terms in rather odd ways, and frequently engage in something best called *double-speak*: their utterances are designed to communicate contradictory views to different listeners and readers.

Some instances of this have already been noted, but the rationale of this procedure has probably been stated best by Tillich in his little book *Dynamics of Faith*. In a little over one hundred short pages, he redefines such terms as faith and heresy, atheism and revelation. It turns out that the man who accepts the ancient beliefs of Christendom, the Apostles' Creed, or Luther's articles of faith may well be lacking faith, while the man who doubts all these beliefs but is sufficiently concerned to lie awake nights worrying about it is a paragon of faith. "Atheism, consequently, can only mean the attempt to remove any ultimate concern—to remain unconcerned about the meaning of one's existence. Indifference toward the ultimate question is the only imaginable form of atheism" (45f.). Other forms of atheism, not at all hard to imagine, are defined out of existence; and it turns out that millions of theists may really be atheists, while such avowed atheists as Freud and Nietzsche aren't atheists at all.

It becomes clear that when Tillich preaches, writes, or lectures, he is not saying what those who don't know his definitions think he says. If a large percentage of his audience is misled and thinks he means what he in fact does not mean, is this unintentional on Tillich's part? Apparently not. Taken literally, Tillich considers the Christian myths absurd; but "the natural stage of literalism is that in which the mythical and the literal are indistinguishable," and this is characteristic of "the primitive period of individuals and groups. . . .This stage has a full right of its own and should not be disturbed, either in individuals or in groups, up to the moment when man's questioning mind breaks the natural acceptance of the mythological visions as literal." When that point is reached, one can "replace the unbroken by the broken myth," saying frankly that

what was so far believed literally is, so understood, absurd—but
capable of reinterpretation. Yet many people "prefer the repression
of their questions to the uncertainty which appears with the breaking of the myth. They are forced into the second stage of literalism,
the conscious one, which is aware of the questions but represses them,
half consciously, half unconsciously. . . . This stage is still justifiable, if the questioning power is very weak and can easily be
answered. It is unjustifiable if a mature mind is broken in its personal
center by political or psychological methods, split in his unity, and
hurt in his integrity" (52f.).

It is clear that Tillich stands unalterably opposed not only to the
Inquisition, which tore people limb from limb, but also to
authoritarian methods that harm people's mental health without
touching their bodies. No man must be forced to believe. But
Tillich considers it all right to let people believe things which are
plainly false—things they would not believe unless the churches
made them believe at an early age, before "man's questioning mind"
discovers difficulties. And even when that point is reached, it is all
right, according to the passage cited, to put the believer's mind at
ease by reconfirming him in his false literal beliefs, "if the questioning power is very weak and can easily be answered."

One can picture the theologian's problem as he is confronted with
a doubter: Should the young man be initiated into the inner circle
of the broken myth, or is his questioning power weak and does he
belong in the second stage of literalism? It all depends on whether
he "can easily be answered." If the theologian were a bit crude, he
would throw an argument for God's existence at his questioner, or
possibly the wager of Pascal, or an appeal to miracles. If the questioner accepted that, this would be proof that his questioning power
was weak and that the second stage of literalism was just right for
him. But if the young man saw through the answer given him, then
one might pat him on the back, congratulate him on his acumen, and
let him graduate into the inner circle.

Tillich, however, does not favor the crude method of confronting
men with arguments which he himself considers bad. Instead he
redefines the crucial terms and cultivates a kind of double-speak.
Literalists thus feel reconfirmed in their beliefs and are pleased
that so erudite a man should share their faith, while the initiated
realize that Tillich finds the beliefs shared by most of the famous

Christians of the past and by millions of Christians in the present utterly untenable.

A rare reader will remark that any such account of Tillich is misleading because Tillich says publicly—in his *Dynamics of Faith*, for example—that he finds the central Christian articles of faith absurd, if they are taken literally: clearly, then, if anybody is deceived that is not Tillich's fault. But the reader arguing that way is usually a professor of philosophy and certainly one of the initiates. Students, on the other hand, including even bright young men and women studying religion and philosophy at leading universities, are generally quite unsure where Tillich stands: they feel confused and do not find unaided that Tillich says what the professor who defends him claims he says so plainly.

What is unusual about Tillich's little book is that it is so short and relatively simple and explains the rationale of methods used by other theologians, too. Here is a brief work of some stature that exemplifies some of the central problems theologians face and some of the devices they employ to cope with them.

Some of the other charges made here can be illustrated from this little book, too; for example, gerrymandering one's own religion to make it attractive while presenting other religions in a less favorable light. "Every type of faith has the tendency to elevate its concrete symbols to absolute validity. The criterion of the truth of faith, therefore, is that it implies an element of self-negation. That symbol is most adequate which expresses not only the ultimate but also its own lack of ultimacy. Christianity expresses itself in such a symbol in contrast to all other religions, namely, in the Cross of Christ" (97). Jesus' death on the cross is apparently to Tillich a reminder that Jesus was not really God—if he had been, he would not have died— but a symbol of God. The crucifix thus "expresses not only the ultimate but also its own lack of ultimacy." But instead of conceding that Christianity went further than many another religion, and especially Judaism, in mistaking a symbol for the ultimate and a human being for God, Tillich gives Christianity the benefit of his daring reinterpretation; and instead of admitting that Calvin no less than Aquinas would have favored burning him for so heretical a piece of exegesis, he proclaims that Christianity (with the benefit of his interpretation) is superior "to all other religions."

Two questions present themselves. First, could Tillich be unaware

of the vast difference between his own views and those of the
Reformers, not to speak of Catholics? At such points, regard for
history and facts simply evaporates, and on the next page (98) we
are told: "Doctrinal formulations did not divide the churches in the
Reformation period." As if Luther did not dispute over doctrines first
with papal representatives and later with Zwingli; and as if the
splintering of Protestantism had not been precipitated by doctrinal
differences over the sacraments.

The second question is whether other religions, given the benefit
of equally daring exegeses, not to speak of such a thoroughgoing disregard for inconvenient facts, might not be formidable rivals for
the faith the theologian champions. But other religions are gerrymandered in opposite fashion. And even Tillich, who has more
feeling for the Hebrew Bible and for Judaism than most Christian
theologians, suggests that in Judaism God "can be approached only
by those who obey the law" (65). One thinks of the Book of Jonah,
of ever so much of the Old Testament, and of dozens of famous
quotations from rabbinic literature—and would be stunned if one
had never read theology before.

This is the price the theologian pays for trying to perpetuate a
mass movement. If every preacher stated clearly where he stood on
virgin birth and resurrection; heaven, hell, and purgatory; various
miracles ascribed to Jesus; all the dicta in the Sermon on the Mount;
the remarks about "the Jews" in the fourth Gospel; Paul's theology
and John's, and James's Espistle; and Augustine and Aquinas,
Luther, Calvin, and the various creeds—no mass movement would
be left. It would be apparent that there are as many different views
as preachers, that such phrases as "the message of the New Testament" and "the biblical view" and "the Christian answer" are quite
hollow, and that the temporal and spatial continuity of Christendom
depends on ambiguity.

The preacher who insists on being forthright loses at least half
his audience: at best, he has the choice which portion of his parish
he would like to keep. If he wants to have a representative community that does not consist solely of intellectuals, he must speak
in a manner that makes sense at what Tillich calls "the natural stage
of literalism . . . in which the mythical and the literal are indistinguishable"; and he must also keep the interest and confidence
of those who have reached "the second stage of literalism, the

conscious one, which is aware of the questions but represses them, half consciously, half unconsciously"; nor must he antagonize those who spurn literalism as absurd. One only has to put oneself into the preacher's place to understand how his predicament quite naturally leads him to resort to those devices which we have discussed. There, but for the lack of God's grace, go I.

8.

Theology, of course, is not religion; and a great deal of religion is emphatically antitheological. At the very least, large *parts* of the Sermon on the Mount are antitheological: not only those alluded to above, but also passages like the following: "Think not that I have come to abolish the law and the prophets. . . . Till heaven and earth pass away, not an iota, not a dot, will pass from the law until all is accomplished. Whoever then relaxes one of the least of these commandments and teaches men so, shall be called least in the kingdom of heaven; but he who does them and teaches them shall be called great in the kingdom of heaven." Or: "Whatever you wish that men would do to you, do so to them; for this is the law and the prophets." Or the conclusion of the Sermon: "Every one then who hears these words of mine and does them will be like a wise man who built his house upon the rock. . . . And everyone who hears these words of mine and does not do them will be like a foolish man who built his house upon the sand. . . ." Parts of the New Testament seem to say that what ultimately matters is our conduct and not our beliefs, and least of all theology. But the claim that this is *the* message of the New Testament, however dear to many liberals, can be backed up only by gerrymandering.

If only implicitly, the teachings of the Hebrew prophets are much more consistently and radically antitheological. "I hate, I despise your feasts, and I take no delight in your solemn assemblies. . . . Take away from me the noise of your songs; to the melody of your harps I will not listen. But let justice roll down like waters, and righteousness like an ever-flowing stream." These words of Amos state one of the central themes of the prophetic books. Isaiah says similarly: "When you come to appear before me, who requires of you this trampling of my courts? Bring no more vain offerings; incense is an abomination to me. New moon and sabbath and the calling of assemblies—I cannot endure iniquity and solemn assembly. . . . Wash yourselves; make yourselves clean; remove the evil of your doings from before my eyes; cease to do evil, learn to do good; seek justice, correct oppression; defend the fatherless; plead for the widow." And Micah: "What does the Lord require of you but to do justice and love mercy and to walk humbly with your God."

In the prophets and in parts of the New Testament—though certainly only in parts—love, justice, and humility appear to be all that is asked of man, and questions of belief appear to be entirely peripheral, while precise formulations about God, "his attributes, and his relation with man and the universe" are altogether out of the picture. Perhaps the Book of Jonah goes furthest: here the wicked men of Nineveh are forgiven everything because they are sincerely sorry; they are pagans and they need not even be converted or acknowledge any new beliefs whatever.

The Buddha brushed aside all theological and metaphysical queries as "questions that tend not toward edification," and proclaimed that all we need to know to live good lives and find salvation are four simple truths about sufferings; its cause in human ignorance, desire, and attachment; its cessation when detachment is achieved; and the kind of life that leads to the cessation of desire. Around the same time, about 500 B.C., Confucius, in China, disparaged questions about the supernatural, and taught men to concentrate on this life and their relations to other human beings.

In the Confucian Analects we are told that "The Master would not discuss supernatural beings" (VII, 20); and when someone "asked about his duty to the spirits, the Master replied: When still unable to do your duty to men, how can you do your duty to spirits? When he ventured to ask about death Confucius answered: Not yet understanding life, how can you understand death?" (XI, 11).

The other great sage of China, Lao-tze, went even further in disparaging speculations, doctrines, and pretensions to knowledge. With a whimsical humor he extolled the virtues of a simple life.

An attack on theology, therefore, should not be taken as necessarily involving an attack on religion. Religion can be, and often has been, untheological or even antitheological.

9.

Whether Christianity can ever dispense with theology is another matter; for Christianity has always emphasized beliefs that must seem foolish to the uninitiated—a point already made in the oldest part of the New Testament, the Epistles of Paul. Shorn of these beliefs, Christianity ceases to be Christianity and becomes some kind of Reform Judaism or Unitarianism, or—to use a term which historians of religion use for the religion of those early followers of Jesus who, rejecting Paul, remained Jews—Ebionitism. Christianity defined itself less as a way of life than as a faith which, right from the beginning, involved assent to various propositions. Disputes over these beliefs and their correct interpretation led to establishment of different churches and denominations. Confronted with so many theologies, a Christian faces a variety of possibilities.

First, he can try to ignore this abundance, refuse to give himself any account of the meaning of his beliefs, and repeat the hallowed articles of faith without caring how they are interpreted. This is intellectually sloppy, and leaves open the question to which church he belongs and goes. If he goes to the nearest one, or to the one which other people of his social status generally attend, while turning a deaf ear to his minister's interpretations of Christian belief, he is likely to be a pillar of society; but he could hardly be said to take his Christianity seriously. It was against nominal Christians of this sort that Kierkegaard wrote throughout his long life. Though Kierkegaard is popular today, he is enlisted, much against his express will, as an apologist, and people overlook that the kind of Christianity which Kierkegaard attacked is precisely the kind of "religion" whose revival in the middle of the twentieth century we are asked to note with hope.

Second, a Christian can acquaint himself with more than one theology and then choose a denomination which makes sense to him, which he finds congenial, which says more or less in Christian terms what he believes in any case. And if the theologians of this church do not carve quite exactly what he wants out of the Gospels and Epistles, he may attempt some small adjustments of his own.

One might suppose that this is what most Christians do; but in fact the vast majority even of educated Christians fall into the first class and not into this one. Few Presbyterian college students or college graduates know what the Westminster Confession is; fewer have read it; hardly any have compared it with the basic documents of other denominations.

The present critique of theology would be grossly misleading if it gave the reader the impression that theology is generally more than window dressing. Theology moves no mountains; it does not even move people: it is something people put up with, something they do not take seriously, something good manners require one to respect—and not to think about.

How little people think about theology, how much it is a mere epiphenomenon of organized religion, has been shown in some detail by Richard Niebuhr in *The Social Sources of Denominationalism*. As long as Protestant denominations have existed, social status rather than theology seems to have decided in most cases to what church a family belonged. Whether this analysis by a man who is often claimed to be a theologian is excessively colored by Marxism—the book first appeared in 1929—and gives a picture that is just a little too extreme in emphasizing economic factors while reducing ideologies to ineffective superstructures, is a question for sociologists. What matters in the present context is not the precise percentage of unthinking Christians who, while they resent all critical reflections on theology, cannot be bothered to inform themselves about beliefs of which they claim to think that they may seriously affect our posthumous careers. Statistics offer a welcome escape from self-reflection. It is another irony of the alleged revival of religion that contemporary apologists insist that the many millions who crowd our churches can't be wrong, while their Holy Scriptures insist constantly that there is no safety at all in numbers; on the contrary.

In the end, a Christian may choose to reject theology—for some of the reasons given here, and for others besides. But in that case he gives up Christianity, though in some laudatory senses of the word he may be a better Christian than some theologians. But in that way many Buddhists, Jews, Confucianists, and atheists are also better Christians than most Christians.

After all, Christianity is inescapably a theological religion, and those who give up the ancient formulations of alleged knowledge about "God, his nature and attributes, and his relation with man and the universe" break with Christianity. They may still admire

Jesus, as some agnostics, Jews, and Hindus do, too; but they are no longer Christians. But could one remain a Christian and retain the ancient formulations without employing any double standard, without gerrymandering, redefining terms, or double-speak?

One can avoid all this by the simple expedient of refusing to think about one's religion. But if one does that, is one a Christian? Or one can say: I accept everything, though on the face a lot of what I am accepting appears mutually contradictory—which only shows that reason is, as Luther said, "the Devil's bride" and "God's worst enemy." Again, one refuses to think about one's religion. But if one insists on thinking about it without either gerrymandering or redefining terms, and without any double-speak, one has to say: this I accept, this not; this I believe, this not; this I admire, this not. And if one employs no double-standard, one will have to add: in other scriptures and religions, too, I find things I accept, believe, admire, including much that compares very favorably with ever so much in my own tradition. Still, one may conceivably conclude, it is my own tradition that I love best, though I really agree with no more than a fraction of it. And if that is what one does, is one a Christian—or a heretic?

10.

My conclusions can be briefly summed up. Natural theology involves fallacious reasoning. Dogmatic theology—and it is only practitioners of this that are generally called theologians—depends on a devout commitment to a double standard, and its methods are a model of unsound procedure and special pleading.

To show what is wrong with theology in the ordinary sense of that word, one does not require any positivistic theory of knowledge: the faults of theology can be seen with the naked eye. To show that these charges against theology can be sustained against the best theologians, one must consider the works of a few outstanding theologians, taking up one man at a time. (This I have tried to do in my *Critique*, Chapters 5–8.)

The rejection of natural and dogmatic theology does not involve the repudiation of the critical, historical, and psychological study of religion. On the contrary, such a study is most valuable. Those who want to improve their thinking about the important questions of life and become more conscientious should surely consider the divergent answers to these questions that the great religious figures of the past have given. Nor need one ignore the theologians. But *instead of studying theology one should study theologies.*

The committed study of a single theology—or a single philosophic system, for that matter, or the views of a single scientist whose theory happens to differ from the views of most of his colleagues—is a training in unsound method, in partiality, and in the gentle art of paralyzing intellectual integrity. Instead of being taught how some one theory can be indefinitely patched up if one happens to allow it privileges which one would deny all others, students should be exposed to a variety of views and led to discover what is to be said for and against each.

That many philosophers, past and present, are open to charges here pressed against theology may readily be granted. A philosopher who criticizes theology is surely under no compulsion to defend all philosophers. On the contrary.

That these charges are not applicable to all men who happen to be teaching at a seminary or to all historians of religion, is, of course, part of the point of this critique, which is emphatically aimed at what the *Oxford English Dictionary* calls "dogmatic theology."

The most odious feature of this criticism is the charge that the "dogmatic theologian" is "unfair." The charge is, of course, not that all such men are "unfair" all the time, regardless of what they are doing. The question is whether they are fair to rival points of view when they do theology. The claim that they are not does not raise the remote presumption that such men are likely to be found unfair in games. As a matter of fact, the present essay, in its formative stage, gained from extended and intense discussions with several groups of Protestant theologians, ministers, and students of theology some of whom asked me to address them and discuss with them; and the faculty and students of Georgetown University invited me to present the final draft in an open lecture and gave me the benefit of two hours' exemplary discussion. Such conversations without reservations are among the most exhilarating and worth-while experiences a teacher or a writer can have; and in questioning a speaker many students and teachers of theology yield to nobody in fairness.

One practical conclusion remains to be drawn. Theological

seminaries create many of the problems which their products are expected to resolve. For years the students at most seminaries are trained to see their own denomination as they see no other one; then they are supposed to go out as spiritual leaders, teaching people how to love their neighbors as themselves, sitting down with representatives of other faiths in mutual respect and understanding. Having been trained to see Catholicism as the Catholics do not see it, Judaism as the Jews do not experience it, and other Protestant denominations as they do not look to their own members, the young clergyman is expected to collaborate with priests and rabbis and to busy himself in the ecumenical movement, doing his best throughout his professional career to heal breaches which, but for the training which he and the other ministers, rabbis, and priests received, would long have disappeared.

My point of view is not that of a disciple. But if a man were a true disciple of the Buddha, of the prophets, or of Jesus, could he fail to be against theology? Could he help becoming a heretic?

WALTER KAUFMANN
Princeton University

Religion as a Pursuit of Truth

1. RELIGION, SCIENCE, AND METAPHYSICS IN A COMMON KEY

In the history of humanity up to the present, religion, science, and metaphysics have again and again met with different kinds of opposition, and they have also conflicted with one another. But they have continued their winding courses, overcoming all obstacles till the present day. One of the vital forces which has made this progress possible is what can be called sincerity. Sincerity, which produces earnestness, strength, and courage necessary for the pursuit of truth at all sacrifice can be said to be the common key underlying progress in religion, science, and metaphysics. Paradoxically enough, it has been both the source and solvent of conflict among these three major pursuits of man.

Sincerity as the unconditional devotion to truth opposes all compromise with untruth and resists deception and duplicity in thought, action, and emotion. Therefore, it fosters conflict between the habitual loyalty to the accepted and the nascent loyalty to truth newly perceived, espousing the case of the latter. But the conflict is solved if sincerity is real, persistent, and effective enough to be able to overthrow the yoke of superseded truths. Just as sincerity opposes the persistence of falsified beliefs in our cognitive life, it resists the sway of unjustified devotion to false ideals in emotional life, and also tries to reform the life of action by changing old ways rooted in exploded ideas and ideals. Sincerity helps, therefore, to remove the gap between thought and emotion, thought and action, and emotion and action. The sincere man is prompted to cultivate and discipline his emotions in accordance with the truth as he perceives it; he tries to live in the truth, and he acts as he genuinely feels. Sincerity thus makes for an integrated personal life, evolving and harmonizing conflicts.

110

In interpersonal behavior, too, sincerity plays a similar and important role. While the sincere person comes into frequent conflict with others because of his uncompromising attitude toward untruth, he also raises the moral level of society, to the extent that he can maintain his devotion to truth.

The greatest conflicts that sincerity has engendered, and has also been called upon to solve in the history of mankind, are those between two persons or groups, or a person and a group, who are both apparently sincere but who firmly hold, as true, two opposite beliefs about things which cannot be easily or completely verified. The trial of Socrates, the crucifixion of Christ, the holy wars, the summoning of Galileo to the Inquisition, are but a few records of such conflicts. In most of these cases the vindication of truth and right has come through temporary discomfiture, suffering, and death, and by the ultimate verdict of distant posterity. In some cases no clear verdict has been pronounced by history. Yet, one thing is clear from history. The conflicting claims of truth are not settled by force of verbal conquest, legal authority, or lethal weapons. Where force temporarily silences the fair claim of truth, posterity, attracted by the sincere sacrifice of the condemned, reopens the case more sincerely and more dispassionately than the contemporary could, and bestows retrospective justice, and even raises the impugned sometimes to the rank of martyrs or prophets.

We must distinguish, then, between genuine sincerity and sincerity vitiated by motives other than truth. Unconditional regard for truth helps the genuinely sincere person rise above passions and biases which otherwise warp judgment. The earnest desire to know and live the truth makes the genuinely sincere man aware of the vastness, complexity, and profundity of truth, and helps him realize his ignorance and limitations. He thus feels humble and eager to look at things patiently from all points of view and to learn as much as he can from others as well. He acquires thus a spirit of tolerance and regard for others. Genuine sincerity, with its characteristic humility, patience, and selfless regard for truth, can more easily disarm suspicion, overcome opposition and resistance, and win the respect and confidence of others. Genuine sincerity can thus resolve conflicts in most cases; on the contrary, inadequate sincerity prejudiced by extraneous motives, manifests itself in obstinate dogmatism, undue certainty, overweening self-righteousness, or aggressive fanaticism. It provokes antagonism and impassioned counterclaim instead of resolving conflict.

It should be clearly understood, however, that there may be cases at issue where two genuinely sincere and equally wise persons dispassionately bent on the discovery of truth can logically arrive at opposite conclusions. So the conflict cannot disappear if truth must be upheld. But in such a case the persons should be able to discover, after patient scrutiny, that they start from different data or assumptions, equally permissible, or occupy different possible standpoints. They would then agree to differ, allowing each other the freedom of choice regarding equally permissible alternative premises and conclusions. Such ultimate differences, gracefully recognized, create neither bitterness nor mutual recrimination, but generate deeper understanding and appreciation of alternative possibilities.

2. THE COMMON FAILING

But such a dispassionate regard for truth is rare to find even among scientists who are reputed to be most objective, and is found much less among partisans of religious and metaphysical theories, and still less sometimes among the advocates of so-called scientific philosophy. That religious and metaphysical controversialists are often swayed by forces other than regard for truth is commonly recognized. But to realize that scientists of even the present day are not exceptions, we have only to remember the influence of Marxism on scientific controversies regarding the biological role of heredity and environment, the influence of anti-Semitism and color prejudice on ethnic and anthropological researches, the controversies between Japanese and American scientists regarding the effects of atomic explosions in the Pacific Ocean, and controversies among medical authorities regarding the baneful effects of certain narcotics, medicines, foods, contraceptives, etc. Ideological, political, cultural, sectarian, mercenary, and self-protective motives—and more often the subtle element of prestige—creep in and warp even the scientist's judgment and cloud the perception and expression of truth.

As for those modern Western thinkers who are known as scientific philosophers, they start with the presupposition that empirical knowledge, based on the scientific methods of observation, experiment, measurement, induction and deduction, forms the whole field of genuine knowledge. This partial outlook, influenced by the phenomenal achievements of science in the knowledge and control of outer nature, ignores the possibility and importance of other spheres of human knowledge and experience. "Science" and "Scientific" become words to conjure with, delude the unwary into an implicit faith, just as "scriptures" and "scriptural" used to be in ancient times. Controversies among the logical positivists or scientific empiricists have revealed during recent times that they themselves are hardly in agreement about the meaning, scope, and methods of science, the meanings of meaning, law, truth, probability, etc., which are the fundamentals of science. Many of them even hold that only tautological propositions are certain. Yet they seem to feel certain that all knowledge and value rest in science and that metaphysics is meaningless, religion is an illusion, and so on.

The foregoing considerations would show how necessary it is to cultivate genuine sincerity and the accompanying moral qualities of humility, patience, and regard for the views of others who may afford some neglected aspects of truth. Religion, science, and metaphysics equally need these moral qualities, and by recognizing them these human pursuits acquire a higher level of perfection and also help one another. Even science, as the pursuit of truth in a limited sphere and a limited way, learns from genuine religion the spirit of unconditional devotion to truth, self-effacement, and a humble openness to the unknown so necessary for the gradual widening of the horizon of science. And from metaphysics whose speculation extends over the whole realm of reals, possibles, and illusions, science has always obtained many of its basic ideas and hypotheses (e.g., about space, time, matter, energy, etc.) as materials for stricter observational, experimental, and mathematical investigation.

It is instructive to note that the attempts to exaggerate the claims of science, and to belittle the scope and value of religion or metaphysics, have scarcely come from any of the great scientists (who possess the proverbial sincerity and humility of Newton and know their limitations), but mostly from those protagonists of science who move on the borderlands of science and philosophy and do not happen to have gone deeply into either. They have mostly sought to produce an effect on philosophers by talking over their heads in terms of science and mathematics which they condescend to interpret in behalf of science for the benefit of philosophers. The most instructive situation arises when some of them (e.g., Stebbing) try to warn philosophers against philosophical interpretations of science by the great scientists themselves, such as Eddington, Jeans, and Whitehead. As in religion, so also in science, the disciples often claim more than the master, and they rush in where he would fear to tread.

3. RELIGION NEEDS SCIENCE AND METAPHYSICS

Genuine religion as a sincere and total endeavor to live in the truth needs the light of truth from all available sources. For the efficient and ideal management of his body, his mind, and the objects and persons that surround him, the religious man has always depended on the knowledge about them made available to his generation by the respective sciences. Scientific knowledge often adds so indirectly and imperceptibly to the general stock of knowledge of the community that the individual is not often aware that his food, clothes, shelter, medicine, implements and utensils, etc., have evolved from continued and systematic investigation by countless generations. Such systematized empirical knowledge, however crude or imperfect it may be, is the science of his age and country on which he always depends. Science is constantly progressing, and the science of today becomes the superstition of tomorrow. Yet a religious man, more than others, has to utilize the scientific knowledge of his times, as much for the knowledge of the world as for successfully working out his fuller destiny in and through the world. In India the earnest spiritual seekers realized the importance of the body, as well as of the mind, as a vehicle of spiritual progress, and they themselves carried on some valuable scientific investigations about food, medicine, the nervous system, physical and mental exercises, etc.

The conflicts between religion and science, as previously noted, arise from the side of religion when it blindly clings to superseded science, and from the side of science, if it dogmatically denies the value and validity of knowledge and pursuits other than the empirical. The extreme partisans of both sides belie the genuine spirit of their respective disciplines. It is realized now at this distance of time how immaterial it is to genuine Christianity whether the earth moved round the sun or vice versa, whether the world was created six thousand years ago or not. A similar dispassionate judgment regarding the achievements of science should reveal

that the knowledge attained and the methods adopted are so limited
in their scope that even if Newton lived now he could still say,
"We are but little children picking pebbles on the shore of the vast
ocean of knowledge."

Science throws no light on the ultimate cause beyond or behind
the space-time world, and neither proves nor disproves God and
Soul. Mechanical explanation of phenomena is a methodological
postulation made by science, and implies nothing about the presence
or absence of a purposive cause. It is by forgetting its limitations
that Freudian psychology tried to rush from its investigations about
abnormal minds in a patriarchal Jewish-Christian society to the
sweeping psychoanalytical explanation of religion as an illusion and
of God as the father image. The Marxist explanation of religion as
a product of the fear of the unknown—which is thought now to have
been dissipated by science—is equally oblivious of the insufficiency
of the data and the hypothesis. Incidentally, it should be observed
that science has been bringing to light the existence of so many
distant regions of space and periods of time, and so many new
mysteries of the atomic particles, that it is equally possible to say
that science is generating an increasing sense of mystery of the
Unknown, and must also be strengthening the religious consciousness, if it be based only on the fear of the unknown. The new fear
of total destruction to which science itself has exposed humanity
may also incline some to invoke the help of a benign divine power.

Religion needs, even more than science, a metaphysics which
inquires into the nature, ground, limits, and validity of all kinds of
knowledge—empirical, scientific, as well as of other types (e.g.,
aesthetic, moral, noumenal, mystic). Metaphysics investigates the
most universal structural elements of the known universe (e.g.,
cause-effect, substance-quality, space-time, subject-object, and ap-
pearance-reality, etc.), and attempts to reach the most comprehensive view of the known and the unknown, though it may sometimes
end in skepticism or agnosticism. Religion needs metaphysics
especially, because it is metaphysics which speculates most rationally
about God, self, immortality, and the like. Every religion has some
metaphysics, good or bad, at its back in at least an implicit form.
The more explicit and rationally examined this metaphysical background, the stronger is the religious faith. And if it is thought that
reason or any metaphysical system constructed by it is involved in

contradictions or is incapable of throwing any light on ultimate things, this conclusion should be established by reason, as is done, for example, by some Advaita Vedantins or Madhyamika Buddhists who secure thereby their religious faiths with a formidable battery of destructive dialectic. On the other hand, religious experience has often tried to express itself, with reason, in metaphysics and make itself acceptable to others. It should be admitted, however, that religion has reason to complain against dogmatic and cocksure metaphysics which forgets its limitations and the possibility of other equally cogent metaphysical systems based on other postulates and standpoints—each of which may be the basis or support of a different kind of religious faith.

Religion can even profit by linguistic analysis in so far as it clarifies the meanings of ambiguous words which convey religious ideas. For example, before we try to answer questions like: Is God one? Does God exist? it is useful to clarify the meaning of "God," "one," "existence," and remove any such ambiguities. But here again it is the exaggerated claims of semantic analysis as a substitute for metaphysics which unnecessarily create troubles. A sincere and realistic sense of limitations and the resultant humility can obviate conflict and promote concord among the different disciplines, as history has shown again and again.

4. RELIGION AS LIVING IN THE TRUTH

Religion, as we conceive it, is living in the truth. It is an all-round dynamic sincerity—sincerity in thinking out a consistent view of Reality and attaining a coherent system of beliefs, and sincerity in letting our beliefs mold our emotions and actions. Religion is thus an all-round integral uplifting of life in the light of truth as envisaged and accepted by the individual. The contents of the system of beliefs may differ from individual to individual, and differ particularly with cultural traditions or local and temporal influences. Reality may be conceived to be one or many, indeterminate or determinate, conscious or unconscious, or some blend of these various types. There may be belief in the soul or not, in immortality or not, in one soul or many. The world may be conceived mechanistically or teleologically. There may be belief in one god, many gods, or even none. Yet each consistent system of belief sincerely molding the entire life can rise to the status of a religion.

This conception of religion would appear on the one hand to be so loose and wide as to verge on atheism, and to be, on the other hand, so narrow as to exclude even the institutional religions lacking in sincerity. Regarding the first point, we have to remember that the word "religion" is now applied to all the faiths of the world, e.g., Christianity, Islam, Zoroastrianism, Hinduism, Jainism, Buddhism, Confucianism, Taoism, Shintoism, to say nothing of the less-known faiths or of the newly founded ones like the Positivist Religion of Auguste Comte and the naturalistic ones sponsored by some philosophers (e.g., Lloyd Morgan, Samuel Alexander, and George P. Conger). If this wide denotation is to be preserved, then the connotation of "religion" must necessarily be very limited.

Most Western theologians define "religion" in the light of Hebrew-Christian theism as a belief in a personal deity with its attendant expressions in thought, emotion, and will. They would exclude, therefore, Buddhism, Jainism, Taoism, Advaita Vedanta (belief in an ultimate, indeterminate absolute), and even the faith of a Spinoza or a Hegel or a Heidegger, from the denotation of "religion." But some open-minded Western thinkers—among whom we find the late Professor James Bissett Pratt—have been recognizing the possibility and value of other types of faith, like Buddhism, which are not theistic, and yet deserve to be esteemed as genuine types of religion.

What then would be the connotation of "religion" taken in the widest sense? We suggest that an all-round dynamic sincerity, expressed in the serious effort to live in the truth as envisaged by the individual concerned, may be regarded as his or her religion. Every kind of faith (including even Comte's Humanism) can be called a religion if it is found to possess the sincerity mentioned before. But would not this conception make religion too narrow, make it a matter of personal life, excluding religious institutions like Judaism, Christianity, or Hinduism? This is the second objection, previously raised, that demands an answer. We must confess that this objection holds if it is thought, as it *is* very often, that religion is a matter of verbal profession, or mere theoretical belief, or mere external formality, or affiliation to an organized church. But if genuine religion is to be distinguished from these outer expressions, the sincerity spoken of must form at least a part of the core of religion. A person has religion if he has this requisite sincerity, and not only by belonging to a church or professing a faith.

This inner view of religion as a sincere endeavor to live in the truth can be found in the different historical religions in spite of their widely differing metaphysical backgrounds. One of the early Indian (Vedic) prayers is: Lead me from a-sat (unreal, untruth) to sat (real, truth), from tamas (darkness, ignorance) to Jyotis (light, knowledge). Sat (Real) and Satya (Truth) are almost synonymously used as the nearest expressions, pointing to the Inexpressible Infinite, Reality—the Brahman. "The universe is grounded in Truth," says the Mahabharata, the great Indian epic. "Truth prevails, not untruth," says the Mundaka Upanishad. Truth-fulness (satya or sunrita) comes to be regarded as one of the supreme virtues. Sincerity (arjava) consisting in the practice of truthfulness in thought (manas), in speech (vachas), and in action (karman) is an integral part of religious discipline in every one of the time-honored paths of India—nontheistic (e.g., Sankhya, Buddha, Jain), theistic (e.g., the various Vaishnava types), and supertheistic (e.g., the Advaita Vedanta). One common truth ac-cepted by all of them is that every living being (jiva) is a center of value and potentiality for perfection. The sincere practice of this truth involved a "regard for life" and others (ahimsa—noninjury to life in thought, speech, and action) as another basic virtue like truthfulness. Sometimes Ahimsa is regarded even as the supreme virtue (parama-dharma). Logically deduced from it are the three other virtues: (1) nonstealing (asteya), not to deprive anyone of the rightful means of living; (2) control of passion (brahmacharya), and (3) nongreed (aparigraha). These five, called the five great vows and variously formulated, have been recognized, from the era of the Vedas to the more recent teachings of Gandhi, as essential for all the great paths. These virtues, along with others derived from them, are called distributively *dharmas,* and collectively *dharma* which is now used for "religion" in Indian language.

We can distinguish in Indian thought three deepening notions of truthfulness (satya): (1) speaking the truth, (2) speaking gently what is true and also good, and (3) practicing what is true and good. The first is simple veracity. The second (also called "sunrita") incorporates gentleness and goodness in a richer truthfulness. The third sense makes "satya" (truthfulness) equivalent to virtue in general—all forms of true and good living. It is in this comprehensive sense that the Mahabharata (in Shantiparvan) describes the thirteen virtues (veracity, equanimity, self-control, nonjealousy, sense of shame, endurance, nonenvy, sacrifice, concentration, nobility, fortitude, compassion, and harmlessness) as but the thirteen forms of truthfulness (satya). In this last and comprehensive conception, satya becomes equivalent to dharma, religion. Truth, cultivated with sincerity (arjava, as the epic calls it) enlightens the will, controls passions, rouses good emotions, strengthens the character, enables the individual to sacrifice his attachment to the lesser perishable goods made attractive by ignorance and infatuation. Truth emancipates the self from infatuating ignorance (moha) and leads to immortality (amrita), says the epic. It declares: "The secret of the Veda is truth, that of truth is self-control, that of self-control is emancipation." And it is by emancipating the self from ignorance, selfish passions and attachment to the perishable that truth, effective in life, raises the self above perishability, that is, to immortality.

We find in modern India the reappearance of this line of thought in the socio-religious political leader M. K. Gandhi, who comes to adore truth as God, endeavors sincerely to live in the truth, in every sphere of life, and invents a truthful and nonviolent method of redressing all wrongs. This method he names Satyagraha (sticking to the truth). He describes his own life as *My Experiments with Truth*. He aims at spiritual emancipation through a truthful life of selfless service. He regards morality as the essence of religion, though personally he was a devout theist.

In Zoroastrianism, the other cognate Aryan faith, morality has the highest place. Ahura Mazda, the God of light and righteousness, enables the religious man to overcome the forces of evil through pure thought, pure word, and pure deed. The Vedic Rita (righteousness, truth) becomes here Asha (symbolized by fire), truth and right, the ideal of a religious man.

Turning to the Hebrew-Christian tradition we can find ample evidence of the great importance given to truth and sincerity for religious life. The Old Testament shows the model of sincere faith in the character of Job who patiently suffers the terrible ordeals of bereavement, impoverishment, dire bodily affliction, and social humiliation, and yet budges not from the truth he accepts. The life and death of Christ provide the classical example of abiding in the truth at all costs—including the sacrifice of life itself. He teaches the redeeming power of truth: "And ye shall know the truth, and the truth shall make you free." In the *Confessions* of St. Augustine we have again the luminous example of a religious soul reveling in sincerity. In more recent times we have in Kierkegaard the revolt of sincere faith against all formal and external religiosity: "I want honesty, neither more nor less. I stand for neither Christian severity nor for Christian mildness; I stand solely and simply for common human honesty."

In Islam, God is also called the Truth (Haq), and the importance of truthfulness is taught by the story that a man who tries to deceive a horse into captivity by the false show of grain is deemed unfit to become a disciple of the prophet. Sufism aims at a mystic union of the self with the Truth (An al Haq).

Both Confucianism and Taoism lay exclusive emphasis on truth, sincerity, and fidelity; the former teaches man to be true to his own human nature (jen), and the latter teaches him to be true to the Way (Tao), the eternal principle underlying the entire cosmos. The Zen Buddhism of Japan lays aside all formality, and goes straight to the inner nature of man, trying to regenerate it for immediate realization of truth.

In every one of the historical religions we find two parallel streams—a surface one abounding in dogmas, doctrines, ostentations, rituals, and ceremonies, and, on the deeper level, a mystic current of inner seeking and genuine becoming. The latter expresses the revolt of sincerity against formality. And there is a wonderful similarity among these mystic phases of all great religions in spite of their doctrinal differences. Sincerity, honesty, humility, firmness, and the wealth of inner transformation are the common possession of all mysticisms. We are reminded again and again that genuine religion consists in sincere living in the truth, however it may be formulated.

5. THROUGH TRUTHS TOWARD TRUTH AND BEYOND

Religion as the individual's sincere endeavor to abide in the truth has necessarily to start with the limited aspects of truth, or truths as grasped by him under peculiar physical, mental, and cultural conditions. These latter define for every individual his own unique religious life. Again, as sincerity cannot be imposed from outside, religion must necessarily grow from within. Religiosity is not religion; as a kind of insincerity it is inimical to religion. But in spite of this uniquely personal and internal nature of religion, it has also a universal tendency born of its regard for truth. The inner dialectic of sincerity makes the religious soul constantly strive for fuller and purer views of truth, correcting the sources of self-deception, and learning from other devout souls. The dialectic of religious experience acquires momentum and self-correcting power in so far as the entire personality—intellect, emotion, and will—is thrown into the effort, so that no truth is satisfied unless it can satisfy the entire personality. The inner evolution of an earnest and sincere soul has always been in restless pursuit of a perfect deity that would satisfy the ideals of truth, love, and goodness.

The Infinite and the Perfect have always been, therefore, the lure of the religious soul; and, though unattained, the uplifting effort for the ideal has proved the most exhilarating task, the pang of separation the most enjoyable of all bereavements, the insolubility of ultimate problems the most sacredly guarded mystery. Humanity has nothing but cause for gratitude to the few genuine religious persons it has produced. For wisdom, honesty, humility, love, firmness, courage, sacrifice, and other similar virtues which make for human progress and survival have been exemplified most by these few. They remain the undying sources of inspiration to the major part of humanity. But the inner prize which sustains them in their all-absorbing uphill enterprise is best known to them. To denounce religion because it has been used as a cloak and pretext for shameful vices is to denounce truth because it has been the mask under which falsehood and deception have ever stalked the world. Shams are found out and shed on the way. Religion in pursuit of truth—infinite and perfect—goes on forever.

DHIRENDRA MOHAN DATTA
Santiniketan, West Bengal, India

Comprehending Zen Buddhism

When critics of Buddhism happen to be of the Christian faith, they are generally apt to regard Buddhism as a rival religion or as one not worthy of serious scholarly study. Thus, what they have to say about it is usually of little value. Dr. Pratt was an exception. His attitude was singularly impartial, and, as he remarked in his preface to *The Pilgrimage of Buddhism,* he strove "to make Buddhism plausible . . . and to enable the reader to understand a little how it feels to be a Buddhist." According to him, therefore, he tried to catch the emotional undertone of the religion he proposed to study and expound. His is a legitimate attitude toward a religious faith other than his own. This is the way scholars should approach Buddhism to make their followers listen to what they wish to say. Preconceived judgments are most harmful, particularly in respect to the study of religion.

I wish to say in this paper a few words about the Zen form of Buddhism, which was the subject of our talk when Dr. Pratt visited Japan in 1927. He found it difficult to comprehend fully, but he knew why this was so as regards Zen. Zen expresses itself frequently in a startling manner, apparently ignoring both logic and common sense. He knew, however, that Zen is experience and not the mere juggling of words at the conceptual level. Though I have tried in my books to explain that these Zen contradictions or paradoxes are not at all beyond human comprehension, and that they are not altogether irrational, I wish to give my own interpretation of the "Ten Ox-Herding Pictures" which are well known among Zen followers and also to a certain extent to Western readers who are interested in Zen.[1] I have no memory now whether I spoke of these pictures to Dr. Pratt. They illustrate the stages of progress one makes in the study of Zen, and are helpful in many ways for those who are trying to understand the discipline and teaching of Zen.

The first question Zen would ask is: How do we get the idea of the infinite or of zero? Everything we see around us is finite, and we are always dissatisfied. However many times finite numbers are multiplied, infinity can never be reached. But we cannot stop at any number so long as it is finite. There is something in us that compels us to go on persistently toward an end which never ends. The cosmos as we know it is spatially limited; the astronomer cannot survey beyond certain points. But we cannot rest content with this limitation; the human mind is much too inquisitive. Why is it so?

The above is true with the conception of time. Buddhists often use such expressions as "since the beginningless beginning," or "a Kalpa that knows no ending," or "the wheel of causality revolving endlessly." Where do we get the idea of infinity or eternity? The very idea of finitude or finality is derived from the idea of infinity, however incomprehensible the latter may be. Indeed, existence itself loses its meaning when this incomprehensibility is ignored. We say that our existence is subject to birth and death, but death cannot mean the end of existence. If it ends, we ask, what comes after the end? The idea of the end is inconceivable. Teleology is only possible in time, and has a sense in time, while time itself has a sense only in reference to eternity. We cannot solve this dilemma as long as we stay on the level of sense-experience and logic.

Zen philosophy tells us that the answer to this dilemma lies just where the dilemma comes out. The dilemma is solved when it turns to itself for the solution instead of going out of itself.

Expressed in religious terms, we all have "God" within us, and it is this "God" that makes us feel uneasy about "this world" or "this life" as finite, limited, and subject to change. The "God" in us wants to be discovered by us who contradict him in every way, and we cannot rest until this is done.

In the "Ten Ox-Herding Pictures," the "God" is symbolized as the "ox" or "cow," and the man or boy is ourselves. The Pictures depict the Buddhist pilgrim's progress in quest of the Infinite, that is, of "God."

The ox is shown here as being trained by the man, but in reality it is the man and not the animal that is trained. When the man trains himself to follow the way of the animal, the latter may appear as if he is following the man. But the fact is just the reverse. When the man thinks he is breaking the animal to follow his way, he is, con-trariwise, obeying the animal. A harmonious relationship is thus established between the two, and the time finally comes when each forgets the other: the adjustment is so perfect that what one feels the other unconsciously shares. Here we see in full realization what Meister Eckhart says in his sermon "The Just Live For Ever": [2] "What is life? God's existence [Wesen] is my life. If my life is God's existence, then God's being is my being [sein] and God's is-ness is my is-ness [Istikeit], neither more nor less." From this it follows that God's will is my will, for I have none of my own. Picture VII symbolizes this situation.[3] The perfect unconscious unification wipes out the whole universe together with its moon and mountains and rivers, grasses and trees, including the man himself. This is Picture VIII, where $O \equiv \infty$.[4]

Psychologically, it may be represented by a circle with no circumference, which Bankei of late seventeenth century Japan depicts as:

> The old bucket
> Has lost its bottom,
> Through and through:
> And throughout the triple world
> Not an inch of the encircling hoop
> Is to be found anywhere!

Picture IX [5] is the reverse side of Picture VIII, for the two together make one complete circle with no circumference:

$$O \equiv \infty, \quad \infty \equiv O$$

Picture VIII is not a complete circle in itself; it always has Picture IX on the other side. The Enlightenment experience is never satisfactory unless it has VIII and IX as one. Human psychology and logic separate the one from the other, as if each could stand independent of the other. When this partitiveness is effaced, Picture X inevitably follows.[6] If we call VIII and IX the *prajñā* (Wisdom) interpretation, X is the *karunā* (Love). When we have one of the three, VIII, IX, and X, we have the other two, showing that the experience is indivisible.

As long as we stop at VIII and IX we are merely a philosophical mystic and a recluse and not yet a Zen man. The latter must have X supplemented by VIII and IX, or VIII and IX must go on to X, thus completing the course of ten.

One point in my interpretation of the Ten Pictures that is somewhat jarring to the Christian as well as to the Buddhist ear is the use of the term "God" here. The Christian reader may object to my symbolizing Him by the ox or cow and being shown as whipped and dragged up and down, this way and that; a desecration indeed! But the "God" here referred to does not mind being represented in any situation, for he is the controller and contriver of every possible means *(upāya)* to execute his final end, which is universal Enlightenment.

The Buddhist objection will be the use of the term "God" itself. Buddhists, they would protest, have nothing to do with God as is usually understood, that is, as a figure in the Judaeo-Christian mythology. My answer is: God is a symbol as Buddha is. The famous Joshu says, "Do not stay long where there is a Buddha; pass on quickly where there is no Buddha." Buddha is a fine name, but when we are attached to it it begins to smell, as the Zen masters would say. Rinzai's strong admonition, therefore, is: "Kill Buddha or patriarch whenever you meet one." God, Buddha, patriarch, the eternal, the holy, the good, the almighty—they are one and all mere concepts, mere names, mere sounds, and have no reality in them. The masters persistently tell us not to do anything with them, but go straightforwardly to "It," which is represented by a circle with no circumference. It is difficult to depict all this in the Pictures, and so I must point out that VIII and IX make one picture, $O = oo$, $oo = O$.

Western people live under the delusion that we are controlling or conquering nature; particularly in the field of science do we hear this claim. What we are actually doing is following the laws of nature. To think otherwise is a delusion, and as long as we continue under this delusion we shall surely end in destroying ourselves. The sooner we awaken from this myth, the sooner we shall be more comfortable, free from mental uneasiness. The boy in the Pictures may also be living under the same delusion that he is training the ox, but the fact is he is training his own wild nature, not the animal's. When he realizes this, the "God" or "Christ" within him will be revealed in the death of Adam. However, the Zen masters will warn you: "Do not get attached even to your 'God' or 'Christ'; do not make a fetish of him, which will surely drive you to thralldom." The ultimate goal of Zen discipline is to make one free from ties. As long as there is even a modicum of anything that will keep one from enjoying freedom, one is not a master of oneself.

In this connection let me quote Eckhart again, for his sermon on "Modicum" is highly illuminating in regard to the attainment of spiritual freedom or Enlightenment. Eckhart thinks that Reason (*die Vernunft*) is the most important instrument in detecting and knowing "God." The following is given as the first property of reason:

. . . it is detached from the here and now. "Here" and "now" are symbols of place and time. "Now" is the smallest element of time. It is not a bit of time nor a part of an end of time. But no matter how small it is, it must vanish. All that touches time must vanish. Furthermore, the intellect is separated from "here." "Here" is a synonym for place. The place where I am is indeed small, but however small, it must vanish if one is to see God.[7]

Eckhart wants to see even a little bit of time and space vanished, that is, reduced to a point, to a zero, to "emptiness" (*sūnyatā*), and God will come into your consciousness. "God" stands here for the infinite manifoldness of things (or "the ten thousand dharmas"). We must remember, however, that what is meant here is not that zero is reached and that God then comes out and is seen. We ought not to have any idea of time intervening here. All is done as if in a flash of lightning, and as soon as we utter a word or emit a sound to express ourselves all is lost: time is back, space is back, and we find ourselves again in our old world. Reason (*die Vernunft*) or *prajñā* functions in this formula: $O \equiv oo$, and $oo \equiv O$. The Buddhist notion of "emptiness" thus is shown to be filled with infinitely inexhaustible virtues (*sarvaguna*) or functions or potentialities, in which there is neither increase nor decrease (*abhangin, fuzō fugen*). Here again the word "filled" or any word of a similar meaning is, if possible, to be avoided. First, a vacuity, and then something comes to fill or occupy the vacancy—this is not Eckhart's idea, for then again we have time and space. The Enlightenment experience is that emptiness which is fulfillment; substance is functioning, being is becoming, zero is infinity, and infinity is zero. Language is conceptual and temporal, and we must never forget that language is not the moon, but merely the finger pointing at it.

DAISETZ T. SUZUKI
KAMAKURA, JAPAN

What Metaphysics Is Good For

1. Metaphysics — 2. Speculation — 3. Conceptual Analysis — 4. The Method of Knowledge in Metaphysics — 5. Metaphysical Positions Distinguished from Metaphysical Hypotheses — 6. Dogmas, Religious and Other — 7. What Light Metaphysics Can and Cannot Throw on the Truth or Falsity of Dogmas — 8. Example: The Religious Dogma of Life After Death — 9. Example: The Religious Dogma of the Existence of a Deity or Deities

The questions to be considered in what follows are whether metaphysics—"speculative philosophy as distingushed from conceptual analysis"—has any utility; if so, then what specifically is it good for; and in particular what if anything can metaphysics contribute toward a solution of the doubts which arise in critical minds concerning such dogmas of religion as that there is for man a life after death, or that one or more deities or other "spiritual" beings exist.

Responsible answers to these questions are not possible unless and until our understanding of some of the terms employed in them has been made more precise than the common rather vague one, which is adequate only for the purposes of their use in stereotyped conversational or literary phrases.

1. METAPHYSICS

The first of the terms whose designation needs to be clarified is Metaphysics. Aristotle's treatise, to which this name was eventually given by Andronicus of Rhodes, deals with questions that are "prior" —prior for us (πρότερον πρὸς ἡμᾶς) and prior by nature (πρότερον φύσει). It is the science of being as such (τὸ ὂν ᾗ ὄν), and inquiries into the ultimate grounds of the existence of whatever exists: the substratum or material cause of it, the essence or formal cause, the moving or efficient cause, and the end or final cause.

The two traditional branches of metaphysics, Ontology and Cosmology, have their roots in Aristotle's conception. Ontology inquires into the nature of reality as distinguished from appearance: Is matter, perhaps, alone real and mind only appearance? Or the converse? Or are both of them real? Or is reality something else, of

127

which matter and mind are but parts or aspects? The questions Cosmology considers, on the other hand, are whether the processes of the universe are all blindly mechanical, or whether they are somehow all ultimately purposive, or whether pure chance has some part in them.

Epistemology, which inquires into the nature of knowledge, its content, its objects, its forms, its methods and its criteria, has been regarded sometimes as another of the branches of metaphysics, and sometimes as a distinct philosophical discipline.

But many questions, more specific than those mentioned above, would generally be regarded as anyway belonging to metaphysics. Instances would be: What is causality? Is it universal? Is it uniform? What is purposiveness? What is mechanism? What is substance? What kinds of attributes may substances have? What does it mean, to say of something that it does, or does not, "exist"? And what exactly is that, about which it is relevant to ask whether "it" does or does not exist? What is matter and what is mind, and how are the two related? What is time? What is space? Are they finite or infinite? etc.

At this point, I shall not attempt to identify the characteristic shared by all these questions, that differentiates them from questions belonging to ethics, aesthetics, logic, or other branches of philosophy. Rather, I shall assume that the above list is representative enough to mark adequately for the present the class of questions termed specifically metaphysical.

2. SPECULATION

In the statement of our initial question, speculation is contrasted with conceptual analysis and is assumed to be the method of inquiry distinctive of, or specially appropriate in, metaphysics. In fact, however, speculation is simply invention of hypotheses, one or another of which one hopes may be the right answer to some question one is considering. Speculation is thus the first of the three steps of the scientific method of discovery which W. S. Jevons termed "the Newtonian method"; [1] the second step of it being explication of the implications of the hypothesis; and the third step, comparison of those implications with the relevant facts, which, if the implications accord with them, confirm the hypothesis, and if not, disconfirm it. Speculation is thus an indispensable part of a process by which, in all fields of inquiry alike, valid explanations are discovered.

It is true that, in the speculations of the natural sciences, care is taken to formulate as precisely as possible the hypotheses invented, and not to accept them without having tested them both in respect of internal consistency and of accord of their implications with the relevant independently known facts; whereas in metaphysical speculations the hypotheses invented have too often been formulated in vague or ambiguous terms, and been assumed by their inventors as somehow known to be true notwithstanding that, in the case of hypotheses so loosely formulated, rigorous testing of them either for internal consistency or for consistency of their implications with known facts was hardly possible.

But these defects are not necessary characteristics of speculation, which ought to be just as capable of being purged of them in metaphysics as it largely has been in, for example, physics. Certainly, even such metaphysicians as might contend that speculation is the proper method in metaphysics would not in so saying mean speculation epistemically defective in the respects mentioned above, but much rather speculation free of those defects.

3. CONCEPTUAL ANALYSIS

Whether in philosophy or in the natural sciences, analysis of the concepts employed in formulation of the hypotheses speculation invents is what makes those concepts and those hypotheses precise instead of vague and makes rigorous explication of the implications of the hypotheses possible; this in turn making possible definite confirmation or disconfirmation of the hypotheses when their implications are compared with the relevant known facts.

What, then, is a concept? A concept is a complex consisting essentially of a "word," in the broad sense of a discursive entity, and of its meaning.[2] The meaning of a word, however, may be known only *ingenuously*, or else *analytically*. One knows it only ingenuously if one is able to use the word correctly in, and to understand correctly, the common more or less stereotyped phrases in which the word occurs, but not able to give an explicit correct account of its meaning. On the other hand, one knows its meaning analytically if one is able to give such an account, and hence able to draw remote yet demonstrably valid inferences from particular substantive or adjective employments of the word.

Conceptual analysis, then, is the activity in which we have to engage when our purposes on a given occasion make it necessary for us to know more precisely than we do at the time either which subjects we are *talking about* when we use a given word substantively, or what we are *saying about* something when we use the given word adjectively and predicate it of that thing. In the first case, the analysis called for is *analysis in extension* and is possible at all only in so far as we somehow already know the intension of the term concerned. In the second case, the analysis we need to make is *analysis in intension,* and we can undertake it only in so far as, correspondingly, the extension of the given term is somehow already known to us.

In the case of metaphysical speculations, the terms whose meaning we need to analyze are ones specifically philosophical; and *philosophical terms* are either:

(*a*) terms designating psychological processes that are conative (telic), valuative (axiological), or significative (epistemic); i.e., comprehensively, terms designating psychological processes that have objective reference (intentionality); or

(*b*) terms in terms of which is worded the analysis of the designatum of the terms that come under the (*a*) heading.

The terms coming under the (*b*) heading are *metaphysical* terms as distinguished from terms belonging to ethics, aesthetics, or others of the branches of philosophy. And the facts, against which is to be tested the validity of the analysis of the meaning of a given philosophical term (whether it be one specifically metaphysical or not) are *philosophical facts.* These consist of paradigm statements or phrases in which the term concerned is employed, as the case may be, substantively or adjectively. Those statements or phrases are paradigmatic, i.e., standard, in the same sense as that in which is so the statement that when a certain platinum-iridium bar in the International Bureau of Weights and Measures in Paris is at a temperature of 32° F., the distance between a certain two lines on it is "one meter."

4. THE METHOD OF KNOWLEDGE IN METAPHYSICS

Metaphysicians generally offer arguments or evidence of some sort in support of their assertions. This indicates that the status they tacitly seek for these is that of *knowledge,* as distinguished from groundless opinions, arbitrary pronouncements, articles of faith, or mere conjectures. And this in turn means that, at least on those occasions, metaphysicians tacitly acknowledge responsibility to the generic canons of scientific method; that is, to the methodological requirements which, no matter in what field, inquiry must comply with if what it yields is really to be knowledge, even if only of probabilities.

In the light of what was said above concerning speculation and conceptual analysis, it is evident that, no more in metaphysics than in other fields of inquiry, are speculation and conceptual analysis alternative methods, one or the other of which is the right one for solving the problems of the particular field concerned. Rather, as we have seen, analysis is a means and the only means by which the concepts employed in the hypotheses speculation invents can be made precise enough to permit the testing of them as regards both internal consistency and consistency with facts known.

5. METAPHYSICAL POSITIONS DISTINGUISHED FROM METAPHYSICAL HYPOTHESES

The question whether reality is ultimately material throughout, or on the contrary mental or spiritual, or of both or of neither of these kinds, has been extensively debated by metaphysicians, and the barrenness of their discussions of it has tended to bring unwarrantedly into disrepute the whole field of metaphysics.

The fruitlessness of the controversy over the nature of reality has had its root in the failure of the metaphysicians who engaged in it to distinguish between *existing* and *being real*, and in their consequent erroneous assumption that the conflicting ontological positions were *hypotheses*; hence true or false; and hence capable in principle of being proved or disproved.

But in fact, what the metaphysicians who believed themselves to be offering evidence that reality is of one rather than another particular kind were instead doing unawares was only attempting to induce their readers to adopt as basic terms, in which to phrase descriptions of man and of the world, the same terms which the particular metaphysician concerned was in the habit of employing when himself so occupied.

For what is formulated by a statement of the form "Only what has character C is real," or "To be real is to have character C" (for instance, "To be real is to be material"), is not a hypothesis, conjecture, or supposition, but a *position,* i.e., a *positing.* What it formulates is the utterer's *prescription, adoption,* or *acceptance* of the character C *as basic,* i.e., *as origin,* for the purpose of descriptions of man and of the universe. This means that, for the metaphysician addicted to employment of character C as basic for that purpose, anything that does not *patently* have character C has to be conceived as being some "function" or other of the things that have it —an "appearance" of them, perhaps, or an "effect," or "epiphenomenon," etc., of them.

To have or occupy a particular ontological position, then, is to be addicted to the use of a particular rule for the interpretation of whatever is observable or imaginable. And a rule is not the sort of thing capable of being true or false, but only capable of being adopted or relinquished; complied with or disregarded either steadily or temporarily; by Tom but perhaps not by Harry; and capable of being fruitful or barren of some particular kind of value for a given person who adheres to the particular rule concerned.

Ontological positions are thus to some extent analogous to the various positions in space at which an observer may elect to place himself and thus to take as origins for his descriptions of what he observes. At each position, he is in relation to everything in space, but his relation to a particular object in space will be different according to the particular position in space he himself occupies. From any given one, certain of the objects in space will be patent to observation and certain others not—the latter then being describable only in terms of their relation to those observable. The view from a mountaintop and that from the heart of a jungle will be different; and each is one he will be able to have at will if moving from the mountain to the jungle, or *vice versa,* falls within the range of his power to change his own position in space. But none of the very different views he will obtain by thus changing his point of view will be characterizable as "the true" view of the world, or as "truer" or "less true" than any of the others: each will simply be *the* view which is to be had from a particular point of view by a person having such eyes as he happens to have.

The views obtained from certain of the possible positions in space, however, will for a given observer be greatly superior aesthetically, emotionally, or pragmatically to some of the others—some beautiful and some ugly; some sublime and others depressing; some interesting or intriguing and others indifferent or tedious; some useful or useless for a given purpose. And all the above, which is true of the views obtained from different positions in space, is analogously true of the different *Weltanschauungen* corresponding to different onto-logical positions. None of them is a "truer" world-view than the others; but one will be more congenial or more rewarding to a given metaphysician than will another, according to his particular psy-chological make-up.

Moreover if, as Dr. Lawrence S. Kubie has convincingly argued,[3] the essence of psychological health is flexibility as contrasted with rigidity—that is, capacity to act not blindly in stereotyped manners, but intelligently in ways relevant at the time to the circumstances and to one's purposes—then the healthy ontologist will be one who remains capable of being a materialist in the morning, an idealist in the afternoon, a dualist in the evening, and a neutral monist per-haps the next day, as may be most appropriate at the time to what his ends and the circumstances happen to be. In short, ontological health will consist in "ontological liberalism"—the name which was suggested by Josiah Royce as appropriate for the contention that ontological positions are neither true nor false, when the present writer submitted it to him in 1912.

Besides ontological positions, however, which as we have seen are neither true nor false but have values of other sorts, there are also ontological hypotheses; and these, when stated with precision, are capable of being confirmed or disconfirmed by comparison of their implications with empirical facts of the kinds relevant to them.

The statement of an ontological *position* would take some such form as that "Only what has character C *is real*"; but the ontological *hypothesis* similar to it in form would be that "Only what has char-acter C *exists*"; for instance, "Only material things and events exist." And whereas the materialistic ontological *position* is neither true nor false, the *hypothesis* that only material things exist is demonstrably false since, besides material things and events, there exist also thoughts, feelings, desires, hopes, etc., which are events of the kind denominated "mental" not "material," and therefore *are* mental not material for the same reason that a boy named "John," not "James," by his parents *is* John and not James.

It might be, of course, that every mental event is an effect of, or perhaps an appearance of, a material, or more specifically a cerebral, event; but even if this should be so, the fact would remain that being effect of, or being appearance of, etc., are relations radically different from that of being identically the same as; and indeed that either of the mentioned former precludes the latter.

If, on the other hand, it were contended that a thought or a feeling —e.g., pain—*is, identically*, a motion of molecules in the brain, or perhaps a particular form of verbal or other bodily behavior, then the sufficient reply would be that, as regards what *pain itself* is, nothing remains to be discovered by a person who has experienced pain; for no matter how ignorant he may be of what the causes or effects of pain may be, what *pain itself* is is then known to him *perfectly;* and his testimony that what he designates by the word "pain" is wholly different from what he designates by the words "a movement of molecules" or "a form of bodily behavior" is completely authoritative.

This cardinal point has been stated by no one more clearly than by F. Paulsen when he wrote: "I understand by a thought a thought and not a movement of brain molecules; and similarly, I designate with the words anger and fear, anger and fear themselves and not a contraction or dilation of blood vessels. Suppose the latter processes also occur, and suppose they always occur when the former occur, still they *are* not thoughts and feelings." [4]

Obviously, a precisely parallel refutation would dispose of the idealistic ontological *hypothesis*—the hypothesis that only minds and mental events *exist*. But, analogously, the refutation would leave wholly intact the idealistic ontological *position;* that is, the positing of minds and mental events as alone *"real"* in the sense of basic or central for one's purpose of describing the universe.

We have thus as existing, on the one hand material things and events, and on the other minds and mental events. And we have also the fact that neither can be "reduced" to the other, but that either can be described in terms of its relation to the other. It follows that the traditional metaphysical problems as to how minds are related to "their" bodies, and as to how minds gain knowledge of the material world, are not pseudoproblems like that of the "truth" of one or another of the ontological positions, but are genuine problems capable in principle of being solved through employment of the particular form of scientific method relevant to metaphysical problems.

6. DOGMAS, RELIGIOUS AND OTHER

On the basis of what precedes concerning metaphysics, speculation, analysis, ontological positions and ontological hypotheses, we
are now in position to consider directly the question put at the
outset, as to what contribution, if any, metaphysics can make
toward the resolving of doubts as to the truth of religious dogmas.
Let us, however, be clear first of all as to what a "dogma" is, and
then as to what determines whether a given dogma is specifically
a religious one.

A dogma is an opinion widely accepted as true, but the truth of
which has not been demonstrated. There are dogmas not only in
the field of religion but also in other fields. For instance, in aesthetics,
that the merit of a work of art is a matter of such beauty as it has;
or, in ethics, that unethical conduct ought to be punished and ethical conduct rewarded; or, in science, that the cause of a physical
event is necessarily always itself physical; and so on.

The beliefs that there is for the human individual a life after
death, or that there exist one or more deities, are dogmas in the
sense stated above. But whether they are *religious* dogmas depends
on what one conceives religion essentially to be.

The only conception of this, comprehensive enough to apply to
the religions both of primitive and of civilized peoples, and to the
nontheistic as well as to the monotheistic, polytheistic, and pan-
theistic religions, would seem to be the conception that defines
religion in terms of certain functions, social and personal, which
religion can verifiably perform; these functions being as follows.
The social one, to provide the believer of the dogmas with a motive
for subordinating his personal interest to the demands of the social
welfare in cases where the two conflict and where other motives
are not effective enough for this; and—the personal function—to
give the believer who abides by the precepts based on the dogmas
confidence and peace of mind even at times when nothing else
avails for this.

This conception of religion entails that the two dogmas specifically in view here will be religious dogmas only in so far as belief
of them operates in the manners just described. But whether it
does or does not so operate will depend on whether certain additional beliefs are coupled with the two dogmas now under consider-

ation. For evidently, belief in a life after death provides no motive for conduct just or altruistic instead of selfish or malicious unless that belief is coupled with the belief that—whether automatically or at the hands of a divine judge—felicity in the life after death will result from conduct of the first kind in the present life, and misery on the contrary from conduct of the second kind. Without this additional belief, the belief in a life after death no more operates to perform the functions of religion than would, for instance, a belief merely that one will eventually move from, say, New York to Chicago, or perhaps from America to Australia.

Similarly, the belief in a God or gods provides no motive for socially beneficial and against socially detrimental conduct unless coupled with the belief that the deity believed in rewards the first and penalizes the second in the life after death even if not always in the present life. Nor is the belief in the existence of a deity a source of comfort and strength in adversity or of humility and temperance in prosperity unless that deity is believed to be aware of the individual's situation; is also believed to be benevolently concerned with the purification of the individual's soul; and is also believed to be wise and powerful enough to send him such trials or temptations as ultimately best promote his purification. For in the absence of these additional beliefs, the mere belief that a God exists would no more operate to perform the functions of religion than would belief in the existence of some wise and holy king on the planet Neptune.

Those various additional beliefs, then, are intrinsic even if tacit constituents of the dogmas of life after death and of the existence of a deity, qua *religious* dogmas.

7. WHAT LIGHT METAPHYSICS CAN AND CANNOT THROW ON THE TRUTH OR FALSITY OF DOGMAS

The clarifications resulting from the remarks presented up to this point make it possible now to state what metaphysics, or more exactly what a metaphysician as such, can and cannot contribute to the ascertainment of the truth or falsity of dogmas. In the present section, this will be described in general terms and, in the next two sections, illustrated by application specifically to the two religious dogmas we have had in view.

The first thing which a metaphysician, in his capacity as metaphysician, is likely to be able to do is to perceive such ambiguity as may be present in the statement of an ethical, religious, scientific, educational, or other cultural dogma; and then to state explicitly each of the two or more interpretations to which an ambiguous statement of the dogma is open. But once the metaphysician has done this, the person who (we are assuming) applied to him for aid must then decide for himself which of these alternative possible interpretations of the statement of the dogma is the one he personally adopts and the truth or falsity of which he desires to ascertain.

When the inquirer has decided this, the metaphysician then can scrutinize the selected interpretation for possible internal contradictions and for possible contradictions of external facts known; for his metaphysical equipment, consisting as we have seen it does of analytical knowledge of the meaning of philosophical terms, is likely to have made him sensitive to inconsistencies or incongruities that pass unnoticed when one's knowledge of the meaning of those terms is only of the ingenuous kind. Any such defects, which the dogma turned out to contain would, of course, suffice to show that the dogma, anyway as interpreted by the inquirer, is false.

If on the other hand, it appears to be free of logical defects, then the metaphysician's analytical knowledge of the meaning of the philosophical terms appearing in the statement of the adopted interpretation of the dogma is likely to enable him to specify what kind(s) of empirical evidence would, if possessed, suffice to prove, or to establish a positive probability, that the dogma as interpreted is true, or on the contrary false. But it is no part of his task *as metaphysician* to make himself the observations or experiments that would be capable of yielding the kind of evidence which he has specified as relevant to the end of proving or disproving the dogma.

If, however, he happens to be competent not only as a metaphysician but also as an observer and experimenter, then there is no reason why he may not if he wishes himself engage in the search for the desired evidence.

The essential point here is thus that although metaphysical knowledge as defined earlier is *necessary* for clarification and logical purification of the meaning of implicitly inconsistent or tautologous statements of dogmas, such knowledge is on the other hand *never by itself sufficient* to establish the *objective* truth or falsity of a dogma free of logical defects.

8. EXAMPLE: THE RELIGIOUS DOGMA OF LIFE
AFTER DEATH

Let us now see what contribution metaphysics can make in the search for an answer to the question whether there is for man a life after death.

Persons interested in this question generally assume that it admits of a Yes or No answer, even if finding out which of the two it should be is difficult or perhaps impossible. The fact is, however, that the question is highly ambiguous and that, until it has been made unambiguous, the person who asks it is in the position of not knowing what it is he wants to know; and hence of being unable to tell whether a piece of information presented to him, or one he happens to have already, perhaps provides the answer he seeks.

The principal respects in which the question as to life after death has to be made specific before attempts to find out the answer become possible are the following:

(*a*) Life after death, *for how long*? If it were for, say, only ten minutes or even ten days, such survival would hardly satisfy the desires which make survival desired; hence the question of survival would have little but academic interest.

If, on the other hand, *survival forever* is meant—immortality, life eternally—then no empirical evidence is conceivable that would be adequate to establish even a probability of it.

But, by "eternal life" might be meant life that is *timeless* in the sense that it involves no consciousness of succession or of duration of states. In this case again, however, it is hard to imagine what could constitute empirical evidence of post-mortem life eternal in this sense.

(*b*) "*Life*," in what sense, after death? If by "life" be meant what biology means by the term, then life of one body after its death could consist at most only of perpetuation of its germ plasm in the bodies of its progeny; and this is evidently not what is meant by the persons who ask whether there is a life after death.

The survival meant must therefore be survival, either discarnate or else reincarnated in a new body, of the *psychological* part of the personality, i.e., of the *mind* of the deceased.

(*c*) Survival of *which* of the mind's constituents? But the human mind is not simple. It is a complex of "dispositions," i.e., of capacities or abilities, some of which might survive and others not. For example, aptitudes alone might survive, but not acquired psychological skills. Or memory might survive, but intellectual initiative might not. And the further question would anyway arise whether such capacities as perhaps survive do so *only* in a dormant condition like that of many of our capacities during sleep and at other times when they are not being exercised; or on the contrary survive *and* get exercised.

(*d*) *Possible forms* of life after death. Such exercise might consist only of a single, changeless state of consciousness, whether blissful, painful, or indifferent. Or it might consist in a reviewing of the memories of one's past life, in an attempt to garner from them such wisdom as may be latent in them. Or it might consist in exercise of the creative capacities—mathematical, poetic, musical, or other—of the mind. Or it might include telepathic interaction with other discarnate minds. And evidently what would, if we got it, constitute empirical evidence that a mind lives discarnate in a given one of these manners would not automatically be evidence that it lives in some others of them also at other times.

(*e*) *Sameness* of a mind. But further, the question would have to be faced as to what kind and quantity of empirical evidence would suffice to show that a mind that lives discarnate even in the fullest manner is *the same mind* as that of a particular person we knew, who died; for its being the same mind is an essential part of what it means to say that *his* mind survives.

(*f*) *Relation* of the post-mortem to the ante-mortem life. Moreover, only if survival had already been proved, and only if in addition it had been possible to obtain details that showed that the felicity or misery of the afterlife of the person concerned justly corresponds to the virtuous or vicious manner of his past life, would survival as a *religious* dogma have been proved true.

What the metaphysician, as such, can contribute toward a solution of the question whether the religious dogma of survival after death is true is thus only what has just been sketchily done in the present section. That is, he can bring up the various questions that have to be answered *about that question* if its meaning is to be made unambiguous. And when they have been answered by the inquirer to suit himself, the metaphysician then can define what would or would not constitute adequate empirical evidence that that dogma, taken in the particular sense adopted by the inquirer, is true. But to provide or seek that evidence is not a metaphysical task.

9. EXAMPLE: THE RELIGIOUS DOGMA OF THE EXISTENCE OF A DEITY OR DEITIES

The metaphysician's contribution here would be of the same general nature. He would call for precise definition of what is meant by speaking of a being as "divine" or as a "deity." Also, for specification of what, beyond this, are the characteristics which differentiate from other possible deities the particular one or ones whose existence is being inquired into. He would point out that if, as commonly is the case, the deity in view is defined as one omnipotent, omniscient, and perfectly good, then, nothwithstanding the many would-be theodicies, the fact that evil does exist rules out the possibility that a deity of that particular description exists, though not the possibility of a deity or deities conceived in terms less megalomaniac.

The metaphysician also can point out the logical defects which invalidate the classical cosmological, ontological, and teleological purported proofs of the existence of that particular kind of deity.

Once a conception of a deity has been defined that is free of internal contradictions and is not inconsistent with any known facts, then the question arises as to what would constitute empirical evidence, probable or conclusive, that such a deity exists. The metaphysician's contribution here will first be to point out that so-called "miracles" do not necessarily provide the desired evidence. For "miracle" is only the name we give to occurrences inexplicable in terms of the knowledge man has won up to the particular time of the occurrence concerned; so that what was a miracle in a given epoch often turns out to be a commonplace in a later one. Moreover, no occurrence is known to be not only unexplained but inherently and ultimately incapable of being explained in a natural as distinguished from a so-called "supernatural" manner. Indeed, to invoke a "supernatural" agency as explanatory is not in the least to explain the occurrence concerned, but is only to *postulate* by that term, gratuitously, that the occurrence is one ultimately and absolutely incapable of being explained. For to say that it is caused by God would be to say only *who* caused it, not at all *how* it was caused; and only the latter would constitute explanation of it.

The metaphysician can point out, however, that proof of survival of a human mind after death would be proof that an intelligent and purposive being *can* exist as a "spirit," i.e., without a body of flesh. But if this is possible at all, it may then well be possible that intelligent and purposive beings *other than human ones* also exist without a body; and if so, some of them might be superior enough to man in intelligence, power, and benevolence to warrant terming them "divine." Others, of course, might have a similarly "spiritual" existence but be of a nature that would warrant terming them instead "devilish."

But once the specific capacities defining the nature attributed to such nonhuman spiritual beings had been stated, then empirical evidence of the existence of those beings would have to be of the same generic even if not of the same specific nature as in the case of the existence of discarnate human beings; for the nature of the possible evidence, in both cases equally, is ultimately dictated by the kinds of objectively cognitive experience of which man is capable.

C. J. DUCASSE
Emeritus, Brown University

Part III

PHILOSOPHY AND METAPHYSICS

Metaphysics and Empiricism

Metaphysics has been a kind of stepchild of modern philosophy. From Francis Bacon to John Stuart Mill philosophers have neglected metaphysics: some of them have denied its possibility, and a few have ridiculed it as a pseudoscience. There are of course certain exceptions to this statement, among whom Spinoza is notable. And, with the twentieth century, metaphysics shows signs of once more coming to the front of attention. But for the long period of the seventeenth, eighteenth, and nineteenth centuries only scraps of metaphysics crept into the speculations of most philosophers. And, as is normally the case when metaphysics is ignored or abjured, such bits of metaphysics as did creep in were bad metaphysics.

Many reasons might be given for this eclipse of metaphysics in modern times. Only one of these reasons is discussed in this essay. This reason is the growing authority in modern times from Bacon to Mill of the school of empiricism. And this is a strange happening. For metaphysics, as surely as any other science, can only prosper and reach successful formulation through the use of a strictly empirical method. But there is a big difference between use of an empirical method and enthusiastic allegiance to the "school of empiricism." And the history of modern philosophy manifests much more of the latter than of the former of these two quite different philosophical attitudes.

It is one of the ironies of intellectual history that development of empirical theories of knowledge should obscure rather than illuminate the direct, frank, open-minded observation of the world which, in metaphysics and of course in the other sciences and in many affairs of daily life, men wish to know. For the original intent of the founders of the modern empirical traditions was to provide a technique for the criticism of all prior philosophical systems and a program for a fresh and more unprejudiced report on the facts on which any adequate reflections about the world ought to be based.

The outcome, however, was not a fulfillment of the intent. The outcome was rather the formulation of one more system—a system which has come to have its own primary assumptions or first principles, its established doctrines, its internal dialectic—a system the advocates of which are prone to dismiss as meaningless any affirmation about the world which they can not derive from the manipulation of their own principles and doctrines.

I have begun my essay with a sweeping statement about the relation between the growth of a school of empiricism and the decline of competent metaphysical thinking. I cannot, indeed, fully substantiate this statement in this one essay. The statement defines a theme which historians might well find philosophically enlightening. In this essay, however, I do wish to give two points which will illustrate the kind of considerations on which my general statement is based. These points, I believe, are crucial. They are in a sense doubly crucial. They are crucial in that they exhibit defects in the position which empiricists have customarily maintained and still do in most cases maintain. And they are crucial also in that they refer to easily observable traits of nature which, however neglected in the speculations of professed empiricists, are yet fundamental for any empirically-minded metaphysics.

My first point is this. I maintain that we observe throughout the world around us the active operation of dynamic and efficacious agents. We are not empirical enough if we list the things we encounter in nature and omit reference to these things' forceful behavior. We find, to be sure, such things as bodies, air, water. But the bodies we find are, many of them, meteors that burst into flames because of friction with the air, trees that crash to the ground and smash bushes that grow beneath them, volcanic rocks that strike with immense impact upon surrounding fields. The air we find is never "merely" so much air: it is gentle breezes or violent winds or hurricanes or masses of air so imprisoned in a vessel that it resists the intrusion of water. The water we find may be thundering waves, floods that cut new channels through the countryside, gentle rains that patter sonorously on many a roof. This kind of comment on non-human agents like meteors and winds and waves can be made similarly on human agents too. Men pull on ropes, drive spades into the soil of their gardens, push one another out of the way, hug their sweethearts, throw balls, kick balls, and so on in a vast variety of forceful actions.

Sometimes the dynamic efficacy of the agents in nature is so violent that, relatively to our frail bodies and limited strength, it is dangerous and destructive. At other times it is so gentle that, relatively, to our finite facilities and imperfect sense organs, it is not immediately apparent at all. What is not immediately apparent, however, is not to be glibly dismissed as nonsensical. Empiricists have often wanted to treat unobserved things and forces in the same manner in which they are justified in treating fairies and goblins and chimeras. Or, if they are in a generous mood, they may yield enough to say that the reference to unobserved things and forces is a metaphorical way of predicting sequences among observable items of sense experience. Not all allegations about unobserved matters are sound, nor are all unsound. The allegations have, all of them, to be carefully checked. In some cases, when the allegations are checked, the inferences concerning unobserved matters may be shown to be without evidence or even contrary to evidence. In other cases, the inferences may have evidence enough to be highly probable or at least somewhat probable. The point of major importance here is that weighing of evidence is not the business of the epistemologist. It is the business of the scientist in whose field the inference properly lies. Members of the school of empiricists have denuded their world of too many things, taking their own range of perceptions as setting bounds to the possibilities of nature. References to the operation of agents may at times be mistaken. But such references are certainly not metaphors for sequences among sensations, even if such sequences may turn out to be highly useful as aids in proof or disproof of the truth of the references. Dynamic operation is one thing, and sequence of sensory items is quite another. We do immediately observe efficacious action in many cases. We infer it in many other cases. We know what we mean in inferring it, even when our inference goes beyond the range of the immediately observed. We mean the same kind of compelling drive, though on a quite different scale, which we *do* directly observe in the operation of many agents. We know what we mean because we have directly encountered elsewhere the kind of thing we are talking about. We know what we mean when, sometimes, we are mistaken and our inference is incorrect. But—and this conclusion can hardly be too much stressed—we have good grounds for saying that we are not always incorrect in our inferences beyond the immediately apparent.

The empirically-minded thinker must grant, so I am contending, that, over and over again throughout the world around us, we observe the active operation of dynamic and efficacious agents. I furthermore contend that the empirically-minded thinker, provided that he is familiar with the findings of carefully controlled inferences by competent scientists, must conclude that many other efficacious agents are at work beyond the range of direct sensory experience. And in this manner we are led to a genuinely metaphysical proposition; namely, that always and everywhere in nature active, pulsating, forceful, dynamic agents are operating. No more important a proposition, I believe, can be laid down for any empirical system of metaphysics.

This proposition concerning the efficacious operation of dynamic agents is almost always absent from formulations which come from members of the school of empiricism. Nor is its equivalent in any other language to be found in their discussions. Partly this may be due to the fact that members of the school are preoccupied with other matters. And of course not all philosophers are under obligation to pursue the study of metaphysics. But partly this is due to implicit denial that we can observe—even that there are in nature —any effective agents. The world as spoken of by members of the school of empiricism is usually far from being a dynamic world. From Locke to John Stuart Mill, and often down into the twentieth century, empiricists have treated items of sensory experience as the fundamental fact of which we human beings are or can be aware. The language in which the empiricists' position has been expressed has varied from one to another member of the school. Locke spoke of ideas. So did Berkeley. Hume spoke of impressions and ideas. Thomas Reid and Sir William Hamilton both sought to escape from, but eventually relapsed back into, the subjectivity of this "ideal theory." John Stuart Mill began with what he called "feelings or states of consciousness." And then we have many writers, contemporary with those mentioned and subsequent to them, who prefer such terms as mental states, sensations, or sense-data. Even when (as in Locke) these writers do not regard their sensory items as constituting the natural world, they do claim that the world appears to us solely in terms of these items. And often, as the centuries passed and the empiricists' school came to have its sanctioned orthodoxy, the claim was made that the sensory items are the basic facts of natural existence.

Now I am not denying that these various terms—ideas, impressions, mental states, sense-data—can be so defined as to designate empirically identifiable items in the world around us. But I do insist that the items so identifiable are far from being original data. They are not the first things we encounter as we move around in the world. They are rather more or less elaborately fashioned products of our analysis of the world. They are analyzed out of a world of which we are acutely aware before we begin the analysis. They are isolated from their natural context by means of ignoring the richness and complexity of that context. And put together again in even large numbers, they would never collectively give an adequate reproduction of the world from which they were derived. They ignore the efficacy of events. Quite properly so, for some purposes, but not for purposes of metaphysics. They ignore efficacy because they are, each of them, flat, static, inert items. They are end products which men in their ingenuity detach from the turmoil of events, hoping thereby to find tools relevant to and useful in the solution of the difficulties of moving securely among the dire forces of nature.[1] They are clues, and they are cues. They are clues to the interpretation of the complex events men have trouble in handling in the gross occurrence of those events. And they are cues to action which, coming after interpretation, may then be efficient. An automobile driver who paid attention to the entire panorama of intricate traffic on a crowded highway would soon meet disaster. But he may drive safely if he singles out a patch of green or a patch of red, using these items as clues to what the fuller situation is and as cues to action which in that fuller situation may yet be safe. The patch of green or the patch of red may be called an idea or a sense-datum or a state of consciousness, if, by that language, be meant that the item functions as clue or cue in the processes of reflection and of living.

The leading philosophers of the school of empiricists were great figures in the development of our intellectual traditions. I have no intent to disparage their positive contributions to theory of knowledge and to emancipation of the modern mind from prejudices and antiquated authorities. I confess that in some respects I should like to regard myself as standing in their camp. But a sound metaphysics can not be derived from sheerly methodological considerations. And such is what empiricists are prone to try.

What a vast difference there is between, on the one hand, thinking of the world in terms of dynamic and forceful behavior of vast organizations of bodies, and, on the other hand, thinking of the world in terms of collections and sequences of sense-data! The former gets down at once to something basic in the world—to the pulsing, compelling, coercing, urgent, powerful drive of each thing in its interactions with other things in the vast intricacies of nature's processes. The latter confines its view to the surface of things, to the ontological tinsel with which the depths of nature are sometimes embellished, just as a Christmas tree, even after it has been cut from its roots and is no longer growing, may be decorated with glittering and fragile balls. The evidence in favor of the former view is abundant and overwhelming. Coming-into-being and passing-away are phases of the history of any and every thing in nature —solar systems, planets, mountains and rivers, vegetable and animal organisms, even political regimes. These processes of coming-into-being and passing-away are not merely arrangements of now one state of affairs and now another. They are dynamic operations of efficacious agents. The dynamic efficacy of the agents is the generating and destroying factor in the events. By comparison with the recognition of the dynamism of nature the interpretation of the world in terms of collocations and sequences of sense-data seems pallid and effete.

My second point is closely connected with my first. It is so closely connected with the first that it has inevitably been already indicated in discussion of the first. But it seems to me to deserve special emphasis and so appears as a second point.

I now maintain that each and every operation of an efficacious agent is, in its individual occurrence, an instance of causal action. I wish to stress the words *each, every, individual, instance.* We have, to be sure, causal laws, in which a structure common to many events is singled out for attention. But causal laws are universal propositions. And causal events, I am maintaining, are, each of them, single, particular, individual. Each causal event would still be the causal event it empirically is, even if it were the only event of the kind that had ever occurred and could therefore never be grouped together with similar events under a comprehensive formula. Causal laws, of course, never cause anything: universal propositions do not act. Each causal event, however, is an action: it is an action in which an agent produces something. The agent, then, is the cause;

the something produced is the effect; and the process of production is the agent's causal act. The metaphysical position I am maintaining is that each dynamic occurrence in nature is a causal action.

The usual position of members of the school of empiricists is quite a different view. It is that we do not really find anything in nature which we can call cause or effect or causality. Causality is treated as a name for the fact that we can collect certain events with similar structure into a class and can then describe that structure in a common formula. It is a concept which applies to no event in its singularity; it applies only to collections of events.[2] If we ever do speak of a single event as causal, we are told that we can properly mean no more than that we are entitled to expect the sequential order of the single event to recur in other events we group together with it. Sequence, then, may be taken to be a natural fact: we find it in the world. But causality is a name for our human way of handling facts: we introduce it into facts when we arrange the facts in groups. Causality, so to speak, enters into our discussion of nature through the statistical tables which men manufacture in their laboratories. No wonder that members of the school of empiricists have made slight contribution to metaphysics!

There are both an atmosphere of enlightenment and a philosophical animus in the attitude of the school of empiricists toward the problem of causality. The animus is one against superstition—against the kind of superstition which ensues when an abstract word is taken to be sufficient evidence for the existence of a corresponding concrete thing. This animus has its healthy aspect. It keeps philosophy from becoming an affirmation of all sorts of transcendental nonsense. Members of the school of empiricists are not going to let themselves commit the fallacy of reification: they are not going to people the world with a host of imaginary entities. And the atmosphere of enlightenment results from faithful practice in accord with this animus. The school of empiricists smells clean. It has nothing fishy about it. It lives in clean and noble asceticism of the intellect.

But asceticism is always dangerous, even if occasionally noble. And in their eagerness to avoid any fallacy of reification, members of the school of empiricists have been blind to the full complexity of nature's occurrences. It would be one thing to suppose that "force" is a more than natural or more than empirical entity which makes waves dash against cliffs, makes trees fall on shrubs, and makes winds propel sailboats across a bay. This way of talking proceeds by the fallacy of reification and gives rise to spurious metaphysics. But it is quite another thing to point out that waves dash forcefully against cliffs, that trees fall forcefully upon shrubs, and that winds press forcefully upon sails. *Force* is an abstract noun, and *forcefully* is an adverb. Both are legitimate words to use in making metaphysical analyses, though both, like all words, must be used with discrimination and in justice to the facts discovered. When a metaphysician says that he finds force in nature, he may well be entirely sound. To recoil from that statement because it may be misinterpreted is a bit immature. Every statement may be misinterpreted. We all use abstract nouns: even the most zealous proselyte to the school of empiricists does so. The empiricists assert that they find regularity and sequence in the world around them. But they do not find either regularity or sequence in the same sense in which they find a tree and a wave. The behavior of trees and waves has its specific character. Trees and waves, analyzed in a certain manner, manifest a behavior which can be spoken of as occurring regularly and sequentially. So trees and waves behave forcefully. Or, in other language, there are regularity and sequence and force in the natural order of empirically observable events. Force is no more dangerous a word than sequence or regularity. If the members of the school of empiricists feel that one word is more dangerous than the others, they lack facility in the handling of language. Their linguistic limitations ought not to set bounds to the formulation of metaphysical truths.

As there is force in nature, so there is causality. It may be that the adverb "causally" is the clearest language to use. But the point is the same in either case; and the more adept philosophers ought to be able to employ either abstract nouns or adverbs without slipping into the fallacy of reification. The point is that the forceful behavior of things does not occur in a vacuum: it occurs in a vastly complex set of interactions. And in that set of interactions one thing, in acting forcefully upon other things, brings pressure upon those other things and so makes a difference in the further development of those other things. One thing, that is, acts causally upon those others. It acts causally in the integrity of its own single occurrence; it does not first begin to act causally when it is compared with other similar things and is so found to be typical of a certain class of things. It would seem that the historian might properly sum up the fault of the school of empiricists by saying the following: These empiricists, out of fear of turning the abstract noun causality into an other than natural entity, have abjured causality altogether in any sense in which a metaphysician is interested in it. These empiricists, out of fear of reification, decline to note the adverbially specifiable way in which things behave. Because we empirically find that things behave causally upon one another, we may change our form of speech and say that we have discovered efficient causality in nature. We observe this efficient causality directly in many events, and we infer it, and on good evidence, in other events. And both when observed and when inferred, it is located, not so much in masses of events taken collectively, as in each one of the many events taken singly or distributively.

It is a moot point, in my judgment, whether or not it is wise to go on to speak of necessity in nature. One might be needlessly provocative in introducing the word "necessity" into a metaphysical analysis of nature. For there is no point at which members of the school of empiricists are more adamant than in their resolute denial of natural necessity. Necessity holds between or among propositions, they say, not among things. And the school of empiricism did valiant service back in the seventeenth and eighteenth centuries in pointing out that the relation between premise and conclusion in logic is not the same as that between antecedent and consequent in nature. Against the rationalists of their time, this point was well taken. Necessity, in the sense in which one may speak of a necessary conclusion from a set of premises, is not found anywhere in natural events. The deductive method relies upon noting such necessity, but this method is therefore not suited to unfolding the course of existential things and events. One can construct many logical systems of possible worlds, each with its own internal dialectic and its rigid logical necessity. But the system of nature is quite a different subject matter for investigation, and must come to be known, if, indeed, it is ever known, or in so far as it is known, by observation and experiment; and while deductions from prior knowledge may profitably enable us to formulate hypotheses about further things still unknown, only empirical checks can validate these hypotheses (or give grounds for their correction or abandonment).

If necessity be a term applied solely to the logical bond between premise and conclusion, then necessity is not found in nature, and even the adverb "necessarily" would be a misfit for metaphysical use. But "words are wise men's counters" in the twentieth as much as in the seventeenth century. And there is in common parlance another sense of necessity in which necessity is constantly found in nature. The falling tree crushes the blades of grass. The grass can not resist the tree's impact. The tree *makes* the blades bend and lie prone. There is compulsion here. There is compulsion of that kind throughout nature. One is entitled in philosophical discussions to use terms in accord with an established parlance, and one may therefore say that the blade of grass necessarily bends before a compelling causal force, or that there is necessity in nature. One is entitled to do this. But one need not quarrel about terms. And if members of the school of empiricists are so wedded to their chosen manner of speech that they can not use terms in any other than their set way, then a different language of exposition for metaphysics may be found. But—and this is the vital fact which goes far beyond any linguistic consideration in its importance—no one, no member of the school of empiricists or any other, has the philosophical right to reject the facts indicated by a certain language because they do not themselves choose to use that language. And that is what empiricists have often done. They have denied the facts of coerciveness in nature's operations (that is, what might be called physical necessity) on the ground that natural connections are not like implications among propositions (that is, what might be called logical necessity). This denial is more than an objection to a certain linguistic usage. For, instead of finding a language for the facts which *would* be acceptable to them and to the customary usage of their school of thought, they reject consideration of such facts as are not indicated by the established terms of their own dialectical procedures.[3] And hence it is that the school of empiricism in modern philosophy has become an obstacle to the proper development of an empirical metaphysics.

So much for my two points. I have maintained that we directly observe, and then still further infer on good grounds, the dynamic operations of nature. And I have also maintained that these operations are causal acts of efficacious agents. The two points go together. Both in the thundering crashes of macroscopic forces and in the delicate insistence of microscopic forces, the generating on-goingness of nature in its vast range of productivity is apparent. And instead of recognition of this productivity of natural forces, the school of empiricists is usually occupied with arrangement of selected items of sensuous experience in statistical tables. The statistical tables have great utility; but they do not constitute a metaphysics. The denial, or at least the neglect, of effective operation of natural forces is consequent to description of experience in terms of abstracted items. There is not among the items the causal efficacy which there is in the events from which the items are taken. That causal efficacy can not be recovered by any manipulation of the items, however skillful. As long as experience of the world is supposed to consist initially of separable items, so long the empirical grounds of belief in efficient causality will escape notice.[4]

There is a vast difference between a sensitively empirical view of the world and the impoverished world system of modern empiricists. A sound metaphysics could not be framed on any other basis than empirical attention to facts. There is a sense in which metaphysics ought to be the most empirical of all the sciences. For in the case of other sciences certain selected observations may suffice for at least a considerable course of analysis and interpretation. But metaphysics aims, not so much at the meticulous and prolonged analysis of a chosen area of nature, as at the discovery of generic traits of nature, that is, of traits which are present always and everywhere in the world around us. No limited area of nature, then, gives sufficient grounds for the assertion of any metaphysical proposition. A competent metaphysician will always return to nature, seeking both to make his observations more exact and to take in larger and larger areas of natural events. One of the best "tips" for an ambitious young student of metaphysics would be to make a list of those aspects of nature which are overlooked in the systems of the schools. But even that tip must not turn into a method on which the student relies as a sufficient guide. He ought always to be watchful of the intricacies of nature as well as aware of the limitations of the schools.

STERLING P. LAMPRECHT
Emeritus, Amherst College

On the Nature of Things

1. WHAT PHILOSOPHY IS

In our day, an astute philosopher is supposed to put what he is discussing inside quotation marks, and thereby to realize that he is talking about the use of an expression. Under this strategy my title would have read, "On the Use of the Word 'Thing.'" Well, what I am going to do here is covered by both titles. Moreover, the astuteness that requires a philosopher to exclude all consideration of the nature of things in favor of an account of the terminological jobs of the word "thing" is at present fortunately giving way to a broader wisdom, even in the Oxford camp where it used rigidly to rule. One of their leaders, J. L. Austin, recently declared that the philosopher's business is the phenomenology of language, which includes a look at, and description of, the nonverbal setting in which linguistic expressions are used. Of course it does. Else one would be doing just lexicography or philology or a statistical sort of thing; not the logic of modes of expression.

But a philosopher must straddle this fence between words and things cautiously, or he will get caught in a sort of pseudophysics, like Lucretius. Philosophy fails in its mission when it competes with science—or art or religion. Its mistake then is the supposition that there are esoteric things to be discovered about reality by a penetrating analysis that reaches remote and unfamiliar elements, like physics, though the strange entities may be of a different order. The philosopher must indeed notice things and their natures and draw attention to these, but only in a way that shows what is (at least) implicitly recognized in them right along, as presuppositions of special sophisticated modes of experience and expression. Such aspects of things are so ever-present and close to us that we tend, as nonphilosophers, to overlook them. Philosophy in this sense is analytical and exhibitive. Kant practiced it. Such analysis, however, will not be brought to bear on forms of language alone, but also upon the field of experience and thought, exhibiting the elements that are there for elemental notice, controlling the linguistic performance as a fundamental part of its logic. In this light, philosophy is not so much an instrument of discovery of what was formerly unexperienced or unknown, but rather of exhibiting features of expression and experience that are so ubiquitous or intimate as to pass unnoticed. Philosophy helps us "see" these things. This may raise a question about the importance of philosophy, which presents what is already present. The answer is given by showing the power of such philosophical analysis to dispel obstructions to understanding like sunlight on morning mist, without injury to anything substantial or valuable in the situation. Some indication of this will emerge in what follows.

In Pratt's heyday, the philosophers, great and small, loved epistemological analysis with a sustained and primary passion. Even the New Realists, who wanted to emancipate metaphysics from epistemology, were in effect doing what the Critical were so insistent upon: analysis which revealed ultimate elements in the field of the is-or-could-be-given. They disagreed only on the proposition that the objects of *knowledge* are confined to this field. But that the core job of philosophy is analysis of the above sort, a revelation of what is already present but generally overlooked under pressure of ulterior interests, this they all confidently affirmed. A freer and clearer access to the nature of things was to be had by realizing this, whatever the metaphysics or ontology—this they all believed.

In this light, the present-day conception of the philosopher's task is continuous with the earlier one, though with modifications that make some of the former notions of data appear doubtful. The emphasis now is *not* simply on "sense-data" as a kind of entities universally present, to be distinguished from "physical objects" as always the real things in nature we are trying to know by means of the data; rather, what is now being featured and explored is the more neutral and flexible idea of *things* present as data according to the "way they are looked at." As a kind of *objects*, their "factuality" would then be experienced somewhat as character is seen in a face (Waismann), and such special seeing is not independent of a mode of expression or a "language." Of course, language in this sense is not just a dictionary business but a "form of life" (Wittgenstein). It is this tremendous suggestion that I want to detail here, as applied to the nature of things. In some respects it is an old one, especially in the tradition of idealism and subjectivism, and even currently there are other positions somewhat like it, as for example Whorf's. But the theme has a new ring in its present form among the postpositivistic philosophers of experience and expression, one that subtly redeems it from its earlier limitations or strait metaphysical commitments, without jeopardizing metaphysics wholesale as logical positivism did.

One reason for much of the current misunderstanding of and opposition to the new approach is a bit of poor strategy on the latter's part: calling itself a "grammar" of sorts. To be sure, it does mean by "grammar" something unusual, which it qualifies as "philosophical." But the distinction is not sufficiently made, and the result is, in Gilbert Ryle's words, the difficulty of steering "between the Scylla of a Platonistic and the Charybdis of a lexicographical account of the business of philosophy and logic." I suggest, before I move on to the consideration of the nature of things, that a threefold distinction is necessary: (1) grammar in the dictionary sense, (2) "grammar" as a philosophical examination of the suitability of a language, say, Japanese, to serve, say, a scientific purpose, and, (3) "grammar" in the still more stretched sense of a consideration of the logic of the "language" of science, or art or morals or religion. Notice the quotation marks around even "language," when used thus. The better stratagem would be to use "grammar" only in the first two cases and "logic" in the last. The nucleus or brunt of the philosopher's business is this last thing—disclosing the logic of modes of expression called "scientific," etc. This subjects the concept of logic itself to a wholesome extension beyond the inductive-deductive kind, transforming it into the more neutral and accommodating thing that Ryle calls the "informal logic of the employment of expressions." Or, this would be the phenomenology of language whose own idiom is that of what I have elsewhere called descriptive metaphysics. Anyway, in this essay I shall be moving pretty much in this milieu and making this kind of sense. I like to think of it as a *post*special discipline and subject matter, comparable to the prespecial medium of ordinary experience and its "plain talk" with respect to nonexclusiveness, yet significantly differing from this by a sophisticated or philosophical consciousness of the *special* modes of experience and expression that emerge out of the prespecial matrix, and an explicit transcendence to a position above these categorically determined universes of discourse.

2. THE NATURE OF THINGS: CATEGOREAL ASPECTS

For purposes of a philosophical study, "thing" can be construed too broadly on the one hand, too narrowly on the other. Truistically, "thing" can mean anything. In my preamble, I deliberately used it in very different senses. Anything can be a thing—a function, a mode of expression, a possibility, an impossibility ("round squares are queer things"), a structure, a star, a person. This wonderful latitude is a feature and a virtue of "thing" as used in the very viable thing I am calling plain talk—pejoratively called "ordinary language." (So even a language is a thing; why not?) And such latitude must not be thought of as confusion. So many things ("things"!) are to be done, a kaleidoscopic variety of them, by many words of plain talk; this is their efficacy and meaning—what Wittgenstein calls their life. With "thing" you can do so many things. I remember the traditional philosopher who recently rejected "ordinary language" as containing only crabbed and unimaginative suggestions for a metaphysics of the nature of things. How wrong! Paradoxically, it is the philosopher with a strait-laced or fixed preconception of thinghood who tends nervously to make this accusation against plain talk.

Yet, the dynamics of language in its prespecial uses must be blamed for making the wholesale question—What is the nature of things?—puzzling or even vacuous. Some selection from among the variety of meanings must be made, if the question itself is to make sense. Not only this, but, also, if it is to be a *philosophical* question, there must be another restriction. For example, one might avoid the ambiguity of the question in its initial sprawling form by asking instead what the nature of water or of light is. This is better on the count of specificity, but these questions are not yet philosophical. Failing to make this distinction has tempted philosophers into doing something like physics, by trying to penetrate to an alleged metaphysical *phousis* or substratum underlying all properties discoverable by physics—the "ultimate" reality or nature of things.

But the crucial consideration is that even these questions about the nature of light and water are ambiguous without a presupposition which is philosophical. One man wonders about these things, asks our question, and delivers an answer in the language of natural science. Another wonders about *the same things,* hears our question, and expresses the answer in the language of myth or poetry or painting (the last idiom containing nonverbal terms besides the title). In short, one man sees these things as physical, and formulates them in the appropriate idiom. The other prehends them under a different aspect, and proceeds to the relevant aesthetic articulation.

This accommodation of things to categoreal aspects or "forms" under which they appear as categorically different kinds of objects —physical, aesthetic, etc.—is the setting in which the question, What is the nature of things? takes on philosophical significance. When a *philosopher* inquires into the nature of things, he is in effect asking: What is anything "as physical"? "as aesthetic"? etc. Or, more conventionally, What is an aesthetic object, a physical object? Answers to such questions will plainly *not* involve a closer study of water and light, but will exhibit the over-all controls, the logic which determines the categoreal kind of study in question, and regulates it accordingly.

The philosopher's question, then, is emerging as, What is the nature of things as physical objects? As aesthetic? What is the difference, and how are these categoreal aspects of things related? It is very important to notice that the physicist or natural scientist does *not* ask, What is a physical object? He moves *within* the category of the physical, its outlook ("observation") and its logic of formulation. Of this he is not conscious as a scientist. Rather, this defines what it is to be a scientist. (Remember Wittgenstein's dictum: The limits of the language are the limits of the world.) And so for the aesthetic case. Without the category in operation, things would not even appear as the "data" relevant to, and grounding, the expressions of the special discipline.

But these are already large propositions, calling for elucidation and defense. Let me proceed to this. I begin with an etymological consideration, a bit whimsical to be sure, yet carrying a serious suggestion. It is aimed at dispelling a mistaken notion of "category" as I am using the term. So often a category is identified either as *just* a verbal device over which the user has unlimited option, or *just* a "subjective form" that orders things from the inside out. I am focusing attention on the old question of the subjectivity or objectivity of categories.

The etymology of "thing" has a nice suggestion to begin with. The word has old Saxon and German roots that connote a sort of demand, a bargaining power, that "things" exercise. In that old sense, things were judicial assemblies with power to negotiate and judge. They addressed themselves to you with imperatives having regulative force, though the demand varied with circumstances. In the old sense, "thinging" went on, and things got "thinged" thereby. A thing was a court of appeal, you appealed to it, and it issued declarations. It harangued with you.

Of course, nothing follows logically from this, in view of the way we now use "thing." But it does present a picture of things with wholesome reminders for us who tend toward conventionalism and subjectivism, even vicious relativism, as if *we* make all the demands in our relation to things. It also suggests caution in the opposite direction of technical realism with its notion of things as a special class of mute facts which passively and stolidly appear as, say, physical objects all the time, for anyone who takes a good look at them. This is a common mistake, especially among the physical realists.

I am getting around to the notion that, whatever a category is at most, it is at least a feature of things. It is a way that things have of declaring or presenting themselves, a comprehensive way that defines them as a kind of *objects* for subjects. Even "category" has a Greek root connecting it with the decision of a court, a sort of utterance with the ring of a categorical imperative. Things bespeak themselves in categoreal aspects, aspects which are there for notice when things are looked at in special ways, each relevant to the category in question which is the "form" of the mode of experience or expression.

This raises the problem of the relation of the category to the "way of looking" or the mode of experience. An illustration at this point will throw light on the relation of categories both to the things and to the lookings.

The stock example is by now Jastrow's duck-rabbit picture, thanks to Wittgenstein's featuring of it in his *Philosophical Investigations*, in connection with his theory of aspects. His was *not* a theory of categoreal aspects, but there is something about the noncategoreal aspects he had in view and his treatment of them which suggests the right thoughts about categories such as "physical," "aesthetic," and another which I shall bring into the picture later on. Considering these will provide the answer to the question about the nature of things, in so far as it is a philosophical question.

Well, we are looking at the duck-rabbit picture. Looking at it one way, we see it as a rabbit; in another, as a duck. We call these its "aspects." The description (more mine than Wittgenstein's) of this whole affair goes as follows: (*a*) we cannot see both aspects at once; (*b*) the *picture* does not undergo any substantial change during a change of aspects: to the picture "in itself" nothing happens while it presents different aspects; what it is in itself is simply a picture, namely, lines in a field of contrasting color, and this is certainly as noticeable as the aspects, though in a different way; it is not a Kantian *Ding-an-sich*; (*c*) without some sort of experience or knowledge of ducks and rabbits, we would not see the picture as either one or the other—we would be "blind" to these aspects; (*d*) yet, what we see, when the aspects dawn, are features *of the picture*; such that, if the looking involves a kind of imagination and the aspects are "images," something is present nevertheless, for *perception*, for anyone who is not aspect-blind; the aspects are the picture as perceived in a certain way; (*e*) we may say either that the *picture* presents itself, appears, as a duck, or that *we* see it as a duck; in other words, that the duck aspect dawns on the picture, or on us; or both of these alternatives; the aspect, then, is as connected with the picture as with the way of looking necessary to seeing the aspect; it is neither just objective nor just subjective; so this distinction does not significantly apply to aspects; (*f*) when we say we are aware of this or that aspect, the truth of what we say is decided by our say-so, not by any further "empirical" considerations; in this respect, the logic of aspect expressions is like the logic of reports of, say, afterimages or pains; this justifies thinking of aspects as a kind of images, provided we are careful about the subjective-objective distinction in this use of the term; (*g*) though the picture is properly said to be seen "as a rabbit," etc., the picture itself is not seen "as a picture"; this would be an improper locution; but we certainly may come to see "that it is a picture"; seeing "that this is a picture" is different from seeing the *picture* as something; the truth of the expression, "I see that this is a picture," is certainly *not* decided just by the say-so as in the case of the aspect expression—e.g., seeing the picture as a rabbit; moreover, we could see that this is a picture—a drawing on paper—without seeing it "as" anything, though this is difficult after we have discovered that it is a picture of something; the aspect then makes demands on us, it takes over; (h) to see the picture as, say, a duck is to see it in a space, or with space properties, that it does not have "in itself."

With this final factor (h) of the description of noncategoreal aspects in view, let me pass abruptly to the account of categoreal aspects. There is a common assumption among theorists in our Western scientific ethos that the picture "in itself" is a physical object in physical space, and is to be seen that way or as such, while not being seen as a duck or a rabbit. The latter condition, they will admit, does make the picture appear in a quasi-imaginative setting, in a problematic relation to any physical location; and this, they say, is why there is something subjective about the aspect. But you had better see the drawing itself as a physical object if you want to see it as it is "in itself." There is nothing aspectual about this, the physical realists would say. It is rock bottom, the very limit of objectivity.

The critical realists of Pratt's camp make a subtle distinction at this point. They say that "the picture" is a complex notion. It involves a presentationally immediate or direct element called the datum which "means" or signifies something else, namely, a factor never simply present in the field of consciousness, and it is this transcendent X which, strictly speaking, is the picture as physical object. The other elements of the presentation are closer to subjectivity, in relations of greater dependence on the subject's station and general condition for their mode of appearance or even being. Aspects, they say, are connected with the latter, while the picture *as physical* is not.

This gets me to the nerve of my matter. I anxiously turn now to a persuasive account of things—anything, not just our picture—which will show that their being physical is a fundamental, a *categoreal*, way of appearing (aspect) which has categoreal alternatives ontologically on a par with it, neither more nor less "subjective" than the thing's presentation as a physical object.

The categories are the pervasive and sustained demands that things make, and the capacity to understand and satisfy such a demand involves an educated or "objective" way of looking, an achieved mode of experience. This is the difference between seeing the cloud as a camel and seeing it as, say, a physical object. The latter involves a certain sophistication, a technical achievement; this is not true of the former. The cloud is not simply present as a physical object—the physical realists were right about this, but misconstrued it—nor does it require this view of it. "In itself" it is just a cloud, a thing *simpliciter* in the field; white, convoluted, glowing, slow-moving in a blue field; yes, all this, but all these terms have a precategoreal sense gravid with the categories but not yet under the explicit, special control of any one of them. This is the sense of plain talk, and is phenomenologically prior to the senses they acquire *under a category* such as "physical" or "aesthetic." The thing and its field may make, however, a special categoreal demand (appearance) "as physical," and with this goes a mode of expression, a "logic," that defines the language of science; and this puts a special construction on the above descriptive terms. Under this category, perception becomes "observation" for what this means to science, and this view is elaborated in the hypothetico-deductive-inductive language of scientific formulation. Notice, it is the *view* that is conceptually formulated, without ceasing to be an outlook. N. R. Hanson exhibits this nicely in his book *Patterns of Discovery*.

The field in which the cloud is "simply" present is not as such a space. It becomes a kind of space with the dawning of a categoreal aspect. Suppose this is the category of the physical. Then the space is physical space. It is a complete mistake to suppose, as physical realists have, that "perceptual space" is one thing, and "physical space" something "outside" it. Perception is a large term covering various modes of experience. If you are *observing*, then things are already appearing in physical space as the data evidencing (positively or negatively) the scientific description and explanation; things *as physical objects*. (That statement is a part of the "grammar" of science, not an empirical report.)

To see things this way, then, is to see them in a kind of space; and this is of the essence. The adequate philosophy of space, or, better, spaces, has yet to be composed. (This would involve some considerations of times as well.) The classical philosophers were wisely aware of how fundamental the question about space is. Some of them were so impressed that they overstated the case, like

Descartes. They said that physical space is the essence of physical objects. This locution, in its material mode, invites an impossible reductionism of physical objects to just space, and misses the truth that such space is the categoreal condition under which things appear as physical objects and are then accounted for accordingly, with a view to whatever properties—such as energy and color—they may be *observed* to have. Notice also that though scientists now explore spaces in the plural, as post-Newtonians, they *assume* physical space as a category, and then show how different spaces can be determined, all of them "physical" for any interpretation made of the metrical system whatsoever. So their question is not a philosophical one. Philosophers get behind this categoreal assumption, looking for other *such* alternatives with which it is related. Such phenomenological inspection answers the *philosophical* question about the nature of things. The philosopher, paraphrasing Plato, is the spectator of all spaces as categoreal forms and of all existence in them in relation to the forms.

Well, how does anything look when observed as physical? Perhaps I should have raised this question sooner, before the above grand preliminaries. But these may now be illuminated in retrospect, as I answer. In the first place, caution should be exercised against trying to see through something given to a physical source of stimuli behind it. The physical factuality of a thing is seen "in" it somewhat as the duck is seen in the picture, or merriment in a laugh. These "aspects" are not behind or beyond the laugh or the picture; neither is the categoreal aspect of the thing-as-physical behind the thing.

We have seen the duck and rabbit aspects dawn on, and disappear from, Jastrow's picture—or on us in relation to the picture. Let us now notice the dawning and disappearance of the categoreal aspect which presents something as physical, or as a physical object. Suppose this is an apple in a bowl on the table. That it is an apple, and round and red, may be simply noticed without any dominant criterion "fixing" the shape and the color, though several such criteria are present as potentials in the situation. But now look at the rotund apple in a specially controlled way, one which shows that only a very small part of its surface would touch a rigid foot rule held up against it. Such factors may be *seen* as properties of the apple, but only if the looking is educated into observing. These to-

gether tend to define—or, if you like, determine—the rotundity of
the apple-as-a-physical-object. Even the color *under observation*
gets caught in a scheme of physical-space relations which, to subsequent scientific thought, structure it as wave frequencies. To see
the apple the observational way is to *experience* it in physical space,
as a physical subject. And such seeing, while it is an experience of
the thing, is also a first-order formulation or expression of it, a
categoreal ordering that legislates over the thing's mode of appearing, which is at once a demand that the thing makes on the way it
is to be looked at (experienced) and that the latter, as observation,
makes on the way the thing is to appear (as physical object). As
this category becomes operative, it dawns on the situation, including the thing and the looking. The categoreal aspect of the physical
becomes a sort of prescriptive logic, a kind of synthetic *a priori*. The
statement that the apple is appearing or present as a physical object
is certainly not just empirical like the subsequent description given
of it *under* the category. The logic of this statement is rather like
that of an image—or sensation-report—the say-so decides it, together
with the consideration that the language of observation is known
and in use. Thus, that "there are physical objects" will be intelligible
and maintained except in cases of aspect-blindness, where the aspect
is the category of the physical. In this sense, the category is to be
noticed much as, say, the duck aspect of Jastrow's picture, though
in this categoreal case what is noticed is a pervasive architectonic
which can finally, in the space of educated observation and scientific
construction, structure the whole world. Even the observer, vis-à-vis
things in this view of them, is then seen as a psychophysical organism whose description is properly "physicalistic"—Kant's "empirical
self." The basic appeal here is not simply to "thing-language" (Carnap) but to the language of things-as-physical.

The categoreal aspect of things as physical objects, though it is
the condition under which *things* are observed or observable, is
itself certainly not an object of observation. (Perhaps this is clear
from the foregoing remarks.) Yet it is present for a nonobservational
sort of notice, as are the aspects of the duck-rabbit picture, with the
reservations already made about the difference between such aspects
and the categoreal.

One more point about the logic of this mode of perception and
expression. When observing fails, or is not feasible in the circum-

stances, it collapses into "sensing." Then things appear as "sensations," which is a way of saying they fail to appear as physical objects; they fall short of the objectivity of location in physical space. And since to be at all in this "world" is to be objective under the category, a sensation has no being; it is nothing. In this respect, things are nothinged, where the demand for physical being is made but not satisfied. However, some failures of observation result from the thing in question being too far, or too small, or too big, etc., to permit observation in the basic sense, in the stereoscopic zone. It is then that scientific *conception* is challenged and gets to work, discovering what may even "in principle" be unobservable, such as subatomic events and structures, the distance of galaxies, etc. But the connection with observables will not be broken, since this provides the evidence for the theory. So much for the logic of the terms "sensing" and "sensation." They are indeed parts of the vocabulary of science, but not working parts.

Now, let us return to the apple in the bowl and look at it as the artist does, say, a painter. We now see the thing as an aesthetic object—the *same* thing. It lends itself as readily to this mode of perception as to the physical, and then is certainly not still "there" as a physical object, though the apple, the thing *is* still there. Only very ineptly would one say of things that they are physical objects which occasionally appear as aesthetic objects as if what is primordially there were physical objects. This would be a category mistake, analogous in some respects to the mistake of taking Jastrow's picture as a duck picture which occasionally appears as a rabbit picture, as if one of the aspects were fundamental. (Of course, *another* picture of which this is true could be drawn.) One can understand, however, that where the physical categoreal aspect has "taken over," or become the sustained and dominant demand in a situation prevailed upon by the scientific ethos, it seems as if things are "fundamentally there" as physical objects; the aesthetic aspect then being naturally mistaken as a kind of accretion upon, or derivative from, the physical. It is the job of descriptive metaphysics—phenomenology of things-in-relation-to-forms-of-expression—to show that categoreal outlooks are special and disclose the various alternatives.

Probably what sometimes induces the notion that, say, the apple is a physical object *ab initio* is another meaning of "physical object," different from the one I have been featuring. By "physical object" I have been meaning things as objects of physics, or, more generally, in the view of them that finally emerges as scientific. But frequently when people think of the apple as a physical object, they are distinguishing it from *ideas* of the apple, which are "mental" and "subjective." Then whatever is not mental about the thing is thought of as physical. This is the old mind-matter distinction which tends to coalesce with the subject-object distinction as a fixed stereotype. "Physical" here is a general term for anything that appears as a *bona fide* object. And the term in this metaphysical-dualistic use does not serve to distinguish things as aesthetic objects from things as scientific objects. It is this latter distinction that I am exploring here, suggesting that the "subjective" is itself categorically modified vis-à-vis the kind of objectivity that things take on, under the category in question.

The path is now clear for continuing the description of things under another categoreal aspect, that of the aesthetic. This too can dawn on the situation and become quite pervasive and, as in the physical case, this involves some sophistication in so far as it is special or exclusive, approximating the condition of the "purely" aesthetic case. As the aesthetic aspect dawns, things again appear in a characteristic space; but here the stereoscopic properties—depths, volumes, distances, shapes, textures—are determined by felt light-and-color-and-sound relationships. How far, how big, how flat, how solid the thing appears as aesthetic object depends on brilliance, hue, and in part on linear arrangements outlining the color areas. In such a space, the thing has properties which it does not have either in itself (*simpliciter*) or as a physical object. Moreover, this kind of space, not being physical, is a natural habitat for feeling. This is why it is called aesthetic. In it, the autumn sunset is sad and its color warm. If Berkeley had been more intelligently concerned to provide in his theory for such facts, he would not have been satisfied with a blanket attack on space as a metaphysical ultimate. His mistake—a common one—was the supposition that space is either physical or nothing. And since "spirit" is not at home or prevalent in physical space, he felt he had to get rid of that medium, leaving no real extension at all for apparently voluminous experiences resonant with various "tonalities" (color and sound).

It is worth noticing that, in the aesthetic situation, things are tinctured even with kinaesthetic qualities. This enters into the dynamics of aesthetic space. In view of all this, the tendency of some aestheticians to characterize it as "purely visual" is a sorry mistake. Even in the case of a so-called visual work of art such as a (great) painting, the space of the picture is vibrant with properties beyond the purely visual, though they are "realized" by light-and-color relationships. A sorrier mistake is the supposition that these aesthetic qualities are projected out of the subject into the object. This error is prompted by a supposed analogy with hallucination for what this means under the category of the physical—the empirical self mistaking sensations for physical object. This overlooks the fact that when perception becomes aesthetic, it ceases to be observation. I shall call this categoreally controlled way of looking "prehension." When the categoreal aspect that demands this outlook dawns or prevails, things are structured as aesthetic objects, and the *empirical* subject-object distinction breaks down, together with the stimulus-response concept of empirical psychology. (I am using "empirical" this way; these remarks are grammatical ones, connected with the logic of the modes of perception and expression.)

Prehension, as a mode of perceptual experience, is nevertheless a first-order formulation or *expression* of the nature of things. And as "observing" occasionally fails, then going under the head of "sensing," so there are abortive or unformed prehensions, and these are called fancies. Fanciful experiences and expressions fall short of the objectivity of the mature aesthetic grasp called prehension. And as scientific theoretical constructions formulate and educate the seeing called observing, so works of art express and cultivate the seeing called prehending. Thus is perception assisted by appropriate "languages" into more special, exclusive ways of looking, while presenting things as data more and more relevant as evidence to the kind of interpretation in question. Thus does the categoreal aspect dawn and elucidate the field of things; or, thus is the demand (category) of things satisfied that they be presented in a certain way, and of a way of looking that things conform to it.

Having prehended things in aesthetic space, the artist turns to his medium to portray them in it, doing this in a way that exhibits their aesthetic potential or status more clearly than they themselves do in the state of nature. Finally, the work of art which depicts the thing is "seen as" the thing, but not at all by simple representation.

To see that something is *like* something is different from seeing it *as* something. In the work of art the "essence" of the thing is exhibited, meaning nothing more esoteric than that it has become articulate in aesthetic space, with considerable attention being drawn to the latter for its own sake. Notice again the option as to how this may be put: either the thing becomes articulate in the work of art, or, the artist does. Both artist and thing have "had their say" in the work of art. The categorical demand has been satisfied on both counts—two sides of the same coin. And the work of art "expresses"—formulates, articulates—both the thing and the aesthetic experience at once. Indeed, the "prehension" of the thing *is* its presentation as the sort of datum that makes it specially relevant as evidence for the subsequent elucidation in the work of art. The latter is neither supported nor rejected by things unless they are perceived this way. And the logic of this aesthetic formulation in the art work is like that governing the report of seeing an aspect of the duck-rabbit picture. The say-so decides it, together with the exhibition of the aspect in the medium. Failures in this respect may result either from (categoreal) aspect-blindness, or from an inept or inexpressive use of the medium.

There is one (and only one) more categoreal aspect the account of which will complete this *philosophical* sketch of the nature of things. (Spinoza was wrong about reality having an infinity of attributes only two of which are manifest; what could this mean?) Until this third category is brought into the *Weltanschauung*, one of the latter's fundamental features cannot be accounted for. Neither observation nor prehension of things, nor a combination of them, will provide a foundation for the view and expression of the nature of things relevant to morality and religion and, at base, to the outlook of a will-full (purposive) "making" of something into something and the actions subservient to this. To look at things with a general view to a making, or a having been made, or a what-could-be-made, is to see things as material or means in relation to a design, a purpose, an end. And the development of this view yields morality and religion as its theoretical elucidation.

Now, of course, even the artist and the scientist have occasion to view things this way, as when the former views something as material for a bit of experimental apparatus—he must make it—and as when the artist looks at his medium with a view to making a

work of art out of it. But, still, this is different from observing something (as evidence for a descriptive report or an explanation), or
prehending it as an aesthetic object. Moreover, the telic view can
become prevalent over the prehensive and observational ones. As
this category dawns in a sustained and comprehensive way, the
physical and the aesthetic wane, and thus does the field of things
become a theater of action (vital *action,* not just movement, however
dynamic). Again, a kind of space becomes the form under which
things are presented as data now functioning as evidence of some
action to be taken, or being taken, or that has been taken. This vital
space of purposive action I call *Lebensraum.* In it, things appear
neither as physical nor as aesthetic objects. The categoreal aspect
of *Lebensraum* has dawned on the situation; and accordingly, things
present themselves—are given as guides to action or signs of action
already taken. They *look* that way, and this sort of seeing is neither
observation nor prehension. Without this sort of perception, things
do not serve as evidence corroborating judgments of right or wrong
actions, good or evil things.

Just how, then, do things look in *Lebensraum?* They are seen as
indications of the right (or wrong) things to do or of what has been
done. The significant feature here is that, in *Lebensraum,* things are
not seen as just happening, nor are they *observed* as effects of causes
or causes of effects. Rather, they present themselves as reasons for
beliefs of the form "x does (did, will do) y," where this is a report
of responsible action and so carries with it the notion of "ought"
and of value. This is built into the descriptive predicates of the
language relevant to this categoreal aspect. For example, if I am
looking at a pencil this way and say that it is sharp, I commend
it as good for something, namely, writing. And the crucial point here
is that the pencil appearing sharp in this view of it addresses itself
to a will-to-do; it is a challenge and a guide to action-to-be-taken.
Thus a value-judgment is implicit in the simplest descriptive report
in this idiom. The property will be *seen* differently—under a different aspect—from the way in which, say, an *observer* notices the
sharpness and the softness of the pencil point, with no relevance to
action. The space in which the thing appears modifies the properties
it presents.

When this categoreal aspect dominates the field, the tendency is to
see *everything* not only as a reason for further action but also as a

sign of action already taken. Not only is the pencil seen as having been purposely sharpened; so also is the constellation of the heavens perceived as the embodiment of design. Thus, where the human will is not discernible in the pattern of things, another will is; since all things in *Lebensraum* are relevant in some way or other to the will-to-do. So the not-my-will-but-Thine consciousness supervenes and intervenes; and things take on a religious aspect. The theoretical development of things appearing in this space of action is formulated as religious beliefs, educating and expressing the will-to-believe which, under this aspect, is certainly different from the will to make-believe; though the grounds or reasons for religion are just as certainly *not* things as "observed." But neither are they imperceptible things. Perception has categoreal modes, two of which we have called observation and prehension. Let us call our third mode "proception." Then, things as *proceived* are the grounds of religion.

There are many fine distinctions in this area—between the ethical and the valuable, the technical and the moral, the moral and the religious—which in this short essay must be neglected. But that they all are relevant to the experience of things as appearing in *Lebensraum* has a prima facie plausibility, which can be shown to have a deeper connection with the nature of things under the categoreal aspect exhibited in proception.

Here ends the account of the phenomenon of categoreal aspection —the dawning and the disappearance of spaces which determine the kinds of data things are presented as, and the relevant languages or modes of expression. The noting and stating of the categoreal aspect is nonempirical, though descriptive in a phenomenological sense, and *this* account is a bit of "descriptive metaphysics."

Interaspect questions naturally arise and, as Waismann has remarked about the relations between "language strata," these are the delicate and difficult questions, involving the transition from one logic (or mode of appearance and expression) to another. Suffice it here to remember the features listed in connection with the duck-rabbit picture, and to notice that the account I have given stresses the categoreal aspects each in a highly special separation from the others, as it becomes systematically prevalent. Of course, in the more usual cases, the aspects dawn and disappear more intermittently, alternating in a less special or exclusive presentation of the nature of things. But any one of them can blossom into an exclusive full-blown *Weltanschauung*, the "sense" of which will not be readily grasped without specially educated insight. Again, however, a much more detailed breakdown is called for, after the brief suggestions in this essay. Things, and the perception and expression of them, are not so systematic as this account of them suggests. It was Wittgenstein's genius to realize this, without any loss to philosophical intelligence. What has recently been said of the British novelist Anthony Powell applies exactly to Wittgenstein, and to the quality of mind of those under his influence: "It is as if we had come suddenly on an enormously intelligent but completely untheoretical mind with a vision of experience that is deeply penetrating yet wholly familiar, beautifully subtle in ordination and yet unostentatious in technique, and, above all, undistorted by doctrine" (Arthur Mizener's review of Powell's *The Music of Time*, in *The Kenyon Review*, Winter, 1960). The description also fits Shakespeare. In philosophy, the phenomenologists of language are *showing* us our languages—assisting us to *see* them—as Shakespeare made us see the human predicament.

VIRGIL C. ALDRICH
Kenyon College

American Realism: Perspective and Framework

In this paper I am going to emphasize two interconnected things which I regard as important for philosophy as a systematic enterprise, namely, perspective and framework. Perspective concerns itself with point of view, the gate of entry. Framework, on the other hand, is an affair of conclusions drawn, the outlook justified. The disciplines associated with theory of knowledge cluster around perspective and have been prominent in modern philosophy. But the background motivation is a concern for light shed on the nature of things, on what is technically called ontology or metaphysics. What for instance, is the place of mind in nature?

Philosophy is of the nature of a debate which shifts from one topic to another. Yet, in the long run, there is advance. Now it will be my thesis that the American realistic movement was a healthy one which raised basic issues. As a survivor (along with Lovejoy) of that movement, and since I have had considerable time to meditate on American realism in the light of developments both in science and philosophy, I feel a certain responsibility to indicate structural lines which might serve to give the movement new vitality. Because both groups (new and critical realists) concentrated on perception, it may well be that a more adequate analysis of *perceiving* will carry us over the hump. In perceiving, we make cognitive contact with the world. But just how?

I intend to be quite personal in expounding and defending the conclusions I have myself reached. They have been a matter of growth in the cultural setting of the first half of the twentieth century. On the whole, American philosophy in this period was international in its intentions and contacts. And the impact of science and secularism was marked. Such concern with science was outstanding in the work of Peirce, James, and Dewey; and I took it quite for granted. This is not the place for a study of the cultural spectrums of English, French, and German philosophies. In my early days I found French philosophy interplaying with science, as in the work of Poincaré. Under the influence of Husserl, German philosophy tended to bracket objective existence and engage itself in eidetic intuition. This activity was, unfortunately, associated with a dislike of scientific naturalism, and the terminus was a revival of subjectivism and idealism. Postwar tensions linked this technical development with Kierkegaardian *fideiam* to give various types of existentialism.

It was unfortunate that a popular version of pragmatism was only too often adopted as symbolic of American thought. Dewey's stress on experimentation and scientific method was ignored and the American realistic movement was set aside. One reason for this was, undoubtedly, the fact that young American philosophers regarded it as ending in an impasse. And attention had swung to the stipulations of logical positivism and the linguistic techniques of English thought. These had to work themselves out. That they have enriched philosophy there can be no doubt. But it would seem that the time is again ripe to get down to fundamentals. Perhaps American realism can serve as a framework. Language is not enough, for we must concern ourselves with the extralinguistic. I would argue that the compromise of philosophical behaviorism with its rejection of consciousness and what we can directly note is failing. As I see it, the situation is *analogous* to that which confronted the American realists. I am quite ready to admit that technical resources have increased, but these may easily mislead if they are not properly directed.

But let us return to pragmatism, instrumentalism, experimentalism. Its popular formulation was given by William James in terms of a modification of the British empirical tradition. I shall leave out the consideration of the more balanced statement by C. S. Peirce. I have recently analyzed this as tied in with the outlook of "immediate perception" directed against Locke and against Kant's things-in-themselves. Dewey developed his instrumentalism as he moved down from Hegelianism to experiential behaviorism under the influence of James, Darwin and, in some measure, Mead. I shall argue that, upon coming East to Columbia, he was confronted by an outburst of interest in epistemology which rather perplexed him. Studying it, he found weaknesses in the searchlight theory of knowing of the new realists and in the *essence* notion of Santayana. So far as I know, he never explored my own leads, which I shall develop in this paper. Dewey's longevity and continued intellectual vigor made his influence persistent. And he was, *in his own way*, naturalistic and realistic. But, in my opinion, his outlook was epistemologically vague and his ontology was unable to absorb the new concepts of science with their enrichment of our thought of nature. "Experience" was too blanket a term.

It so happened that I entered the field of philosophy at the time of the great debate among idealists, pragmatists, and realists as to the status of truth and the nature of human knowing. In giving my perspective, I shall try to be as fair and as objective as I can be. Unfortunately, I cannot go into much detail. Professor Pratt belonged to the critical realist group. In outlining my own position I shall have his in mind.

Along with the debate on truth went the question of the merits of the shift from transcendentalism and theism to naturalism and humanism. It was in the direction of evolutionary levels and emergence that I myself moved. I shall try to *triangulate* here and connect up perceiving with *true* as an endorsement of a cognitive claim and *free will* as a term for the human level of causality involving choice after deliberation and the use of criteria. In all this, I hold that epistemology interplays with ontology.

The emphasis upon epistemology had been inaugurated in the seventeenth century with the breakdown of Aristotelian cosmology and the advance of astronomy and physics along mathematical, mechanistic, and experimental lines. The result was that mind was extruded from nature. The topic, the place of mind in nature, is still a recurrent one. In terms of Cartesian and Lockean schematism, mind and the subjective were somehow confronted by "matter"— conceived more after the manner of Democritus than of Aristotle— and the objective. It was a wholesale contrast, and both domains were thought of in substantival terms. But how could "mind" get knowledge of the material world? It was the urgency of this question which forced epistemology to the forefront. And it was, quite naturally, looked upon as philosophy's business. Descartes, Locke, Berkeley, Hume, and Kant made their moves.

On the whole, the result was skeptical in import. Percepts, ideas, and thoughts tended to become terminal for mind and its primary objects. How could mind transcend itself and reach the material world being explored by the sciences? Concepts like mass, acceleration, gases, chemical elements were enriching man's thought of the physical world. And there seemed no place in nature for mind and the self. It was only in our own day that the evolutionary approach began to offer clues for the naturalization of mind.

In the English-speaking world toward the close of the nineteenth century, what is usually called Anglo-American idealism dominated the scene. And then came the challenge, first of pragmatism and then of realism. The idealists had worked out a coherence theory of truth in which the meaning and the tests were largely identified. At present, Professor Brand Blanshard of Yale is the most persuasive defender of this view. It is opposed to correspondence implications and to pragmatic emphasis upon working and the future. The traditional correspondence theory was set aside because it involved an impossible type of verifying confrontation. If ideas are our sole terminal objects, how can we get beyond them? Until a different epistemology was worked out, the argument was strong. But what of the material things we denotatively perceive in the framework set by response? I shall argue that the adjective "true" expresses a favorable verdict on a cognitive claim, having referential import; and that it contextually implies that the statement involved is an achievement able to give facts about its object because it has been reached by using data and methods under external control. If perceiving is a guided operation using information communicated by our sense organs, we can understand how it is connected with adjustment and decipherment. Sensory patterns are employed in perceiving. That is, we perceive *through them* at the object. And we go on to explore, developing and testing concepts as we do. The start may be humble, but it can be taken up and expanded in terms of scientific methods.

The essential thing is to get the right framework; and I doubt that could have been grasped before biology and psychology had become intertwined. Modern neurology is adding its bit. One important thing to do is to realize how artificial is Cartesian and Lockean dualism. Mind would seem to be an affair of functional activities evolving from lower to higher levels. The unit in human perceiving is an interplay of stimulus patterns and response, with response the dominant pole. That is where safety beckons. From quick reaction to the delayed responses of visual observation we are oriented to the world. We decipher things through sensations, and apply our concepts denotatively to the things around us. Ideas are not terminal; they are functional.

As I look back at the historic debate accompanying the rise of pragmatism, I am still surprised by its fervor. It is clear that it stood for a cultural reorientation. But this was not so marked in James. It was Dewey, following the lead given by Peirce, who tied in philosophy with scientific method.

But the realists felt there was something amiss. Because there were weaknesses in the new realism and in Santayana's essence gambit, Dewey turned his back on the directness of cognitive claims and stressed the *reconstruction of experience*. Thus his work became tangential to the problem set in the seventeenth century.

The uprush of interest in epistemology was connected with a strong feeling that both the idealists and the pragmatists had ignored the possibility of novel approaches in this field. On the whole, the "new realists" searched for a direct realism of a presentational type which, however, made it hard to distinguish between being and seeming. Lockean representationalism, which made ideas primary, was to be avoided at all costs. One could not get from ideas to things. It would be a more fruitful strategy to rechristen presentations and move in the direction of a pan-objectivism and a behaviorism. The subjective and consciousness, it was held, constituted an unnecessary domain which should be got rid of. William James and G. E. Moore had already moved in that direction. Accordingly, the new realists used all their ingenuity to construct a direct realism of a presentational kind in terms of external relations and a "searchlight" givenness. As a hypothesis, it was deserving of careful consideration, much as logical positivism was to be later. But it was confronted by obvious difficulties; and these were soon pointed out.

Now the critical realists were men of about the same age and maturity in philosophy who were trying to avoid the Lockean gambit in another fashion. J. B. Pratt, A. K. Rogers, and A. O. Lovejoy, particularly, had much in common. They were ontological dualists, and laid much stress on the *mind*. It was the job of the mind, in cognition, to transcend its own states in some intentional way and get to objects. This was a *sui generis* achievement. Because they were dualists, they did not explore the possibility of a natural mechanism for this development. It seemed to them ultimate, something inborn, so to speak. I, on the other hand, was seeking just such a natural mechanism to explain the referential moment in perceiving. I usually put it, now, by saying that stimulus-and-response is the natural biological unit and that sensations guide perceiving. This approach leads me to emphasize reference rather than transcendence. I shall later examine statements made by Pratt, Rogers, and Lovejoy on this issue. We were all agreed as to the unsatisfactoriness of the new realism's move with its ever-present, cognitive searchlight. John Dewey's subsequent critique of it only confirmed us. That was not the way out. But we were equally agreed that Lockean representationalism which made ideas *terminal in perceiving* was not the way out. Hence we rather resented Montague's and C. I. Lewis's attempt to insist on such an identification for us. Lewis was defending phenomenalism and Montague, the new realism. I was certainly seeking a new analysis of perceiving. It would need to be direct and referential and regard sensations as not terminal but guiding.

There was a third try for a direct realism in the cooperative book of the critical realists, the *essence* doctrine. This doctrine was supported by Durant Drake, C. A. Strong, and George Santayana. Later, Strong rejected it. It was an identification of what is before the *psyche*, or entertained, with what is in the object. This development had a long history involving the distinction between sentiency and "consciousness." Drake was here influenced by Strong. The subject is a complex one into which I cannot here go. On the whole, I am inclined to think that Santayana was more literary in his approach than either Drake or Strong. Neither of these would, I think, have fallen back so easily on "animal faith."

To sum up, there were three strands in critical realism: (1) the notion of mind as having the power of self-transcendence; (2) the essence-doctrine; and (3) the re-analysis of perceiving as a referential operation guided by sensations and founded on a biological mechanism of the sensorimotor type. In all three there was the search for a direct realism as against Lockeanism. All three held that presentationalism was not the answer.

Now I think it should at least be clear that epistemology is not an easy subject. Yet a clarification, using the proper clues which modern biology and psychology offer, might well put philosophy on its feet and enable it to integrate itself with science. The seventeenth century extrusion of mind and the self from nature might then be healed in an evolutionary way. This, of course, has been my thesis and project. It has often seemed to me that philosophers were determined to ignore it and to employ their great analytic gifts along as many blind alleys as they could locate. But the maze analogy is a false one. What we have are enrichments which will find their place in the pattern.

Looking back at this complex development, my feeling is that it deserved more continued examination than it received. It became the fashion to say that the new realism and critical realism canceled each other out. Dewey turned his back on epistemology and pursued thinking and the logic of inquiry. I shall put in the proper qualifications later. The gambit of Locke and Kant of unperceived things and "things-in-themselves" was eschewed by common consent. But, since there was no clear idea of guided perceiving terminating on physical things, the physical world *enriched by scientific exploration* had a dubious status. Atoms, elements, molecules were often classified as *fictions* by both scientists and philosophers. The epistemological logic of this was clear. If one begins with "immediate perception" as an affair of *experience,* then radical empiricism, neutral monism, sense-data are the ultimates. The only alternative to some kind of *givenness* was something reached by an unbased inference to what is not given. But who could guarantee an "inference license" of this sort? Russell drew the conclusion of logical construction, and Carnap followed in his wake.

Now the only answer to this development which could never do justice to either common sense or science was a more adequate analysis of perceiving. Some kind of "breakthrough" was here needed. I have argued that neither the American new realists nor the British neorealists had the proper cue. G. E. Moore, I take it, was handicapped by his lack of firsthand knowledge of biology and psychology. He at least tended to take his problems from books and conversation; and persistent analysis without theory will not do. I have much the same feeling about Wittgenstein, while recognizing his contributions in logic and in the handling of language.

The approach of the critical realists was more fluid. There were, as we have already indicated, three strands. The more conservative one was the appeal to the power of the "mind" to transcend its own states. This is exemplified in Pratt, Rogers, and Lovejoy. Drake, Strong, and Santayana rested their case on an identity of "essence" as entertained and as in the object. The difficulty here was in giving empirical status to these essences. I was exploring a referential view of perceiving as a guided operation connected with stimulus-and-response as the unit. And I was led to locate sensations in the brain. The objective import of perceiving had, then, to be correlated with the response pole, with looking at, manipulation, the formation of attitudes, expectations, and concepts. Many critics recognized my integration of the analysis of perceiving with the mind-body problem but, unfortunately, drew the conclusion that it only complicated matters. My reply must be that I think that perceiving is a quite complicated achievement. It begins with guided response and is lifted, at the human level, to the "here" and "there" of demonstratives and the application of descriptive terms. The human perceptual situation has risen to a field of applied pronouns connected with percipient bodies.

I shall say little about the "essence" doctrine and its connection with skepticism and animal faith. The translation of sensory experiences into entities of the nature of particular universals seemed to me arbitrary and, in a way irrelevant to knowing, since I thought of knowing as essentially conceptual. And I saw no good reason to lapse into subjectivism of the Cartesian type, to be rescued only by the *salto mortale* of animal faith. All in all, this schematism struck me as artificial and as reflecting the application of inherited forms of thought. It did not seem to me to bring out the diverse roles of sensations and concepts. I admired Santayana's literary gifts and enjoyed his needling of Dewey's *experientialistic naturalism*. I must confess that I was of the opinion that Dewey had not integrated his philosophy at the high level of an interlocked epistemology and ontology, though he got along remarkably well without it.

Let us turn briefly to the first gambit, that of *mind* transcending its own states in some intentional way. Pratt, Rogers, and Lovejoy are very clear about this move, though I think their dualism of process shut out any adequate theory of the mechanism involved. Thus to say with Brentano that the mind has intentions is not

enough. We must have a clear idea of the semantics of the term
"mind," and connect it up with the brain which is, clearly, the organ
of the mind.

It is, as we have already said, clear that there was no attempt to
return to Locke, as Montague and Lewis insisted. Pratt is very
definite about this. In volume two of *Contemporary American
Philosophy,* he writes as follows: "The assertion of Locke that 'the
mind hath no other immediate object save its own ideas' not only
is false, it is the root of many hopeless vagaries in both epistemology
and ethics." [1] And then he goes on to appeal to the power of transcendence on the part of mind. Somehow it goes beyond its states.
Lovejoy also invokes intentional transcendence without any existential self-transcendence. "If the notion of 'intentionality' seems to
some a paradox and a mystery, I reply that, on the contrary, it is a
notion obviously entertained by the plain man and by most philosophers in their normal moments." I take it that Lovejoy regarded this
intentional transcendence as a sort of descriptive fact tied in with
the distinctions human beings make between the present and the
past, the physical and the mental. But, if so, it is of the nature of a
challenge. It is in this respect like "free will." The problem is to find
a satisfactory theory of its mechanism. That is, precisely, what I
undertook. The naïve realism of common sense is, surely, a resultant
of complex operations. And I take it to be a framework upon which
other distinctions developed. I prefer "reference" to transcendence
since it indicates an operation. Knowing, I think, is of the nature of
a directed and testable claim.

Looking back, as I do, after the lapse of some decades, I can quite
understand why many thinkers were attracted to critical realism
and yet were puzzled. The essence wing was easily attacked, as by
Dewey. But I do not think justice was done to the other two strands.
The quip of the time was to the effect that the new realists could not
account for error and the critical realists could not account for
truth. The result was a sort of stalemate and vacuum into which
logical positivism rushed, making something of an alliance with
pragmatism. It is for this reason that I have taken the pains to
revise the correspondence theory of truth, putting a tested knowl-
edge-claim in the forefront. I developed this thesis in my *Philosophy
of Physical Realism* (1932). Let me put it this way: Correspondence
is an *achievement* essential to knowledge and rests on the role of the

sense organs and the controlled development of concepts. It is thus an implication of knowledge and not a special confrontation test of the Lockean type. I suppose this view fits in more with the Aristotelian tradition. But I do not see that that tradition has a clear idea of the mechanism of perceiving and of testing. It is well to note that, in perceiving, we are always testing our perceptual judgments for their adequacy and using sensations and the way things *appear* in so doing. We are not at all surprised that things look smaller at a distance; or that they look different from different angles. While we regard things as public and perceivable, we recognize that the mode of perceiving is affected by conditions and relations. Language has handled all this pretty effectively, but philosophy has been puzzled, just because it had no clear idea of the framework of perceiving. Only too often entities called sense-data and appearances were set up and reified. Suppose I put it this way: Perceiving is referentially direct, but our cognitive thinking of objects rests upon a functional interplay of sensory factors and concepts.

What I have suggested, thus far, is that I had sympathy with the "transcendence motif" of Pratt, Rogers, and Lovejoy, but was persuaded that they leaned too heavily on "mind" taken in an introspective and dualistic way. That is, I was working along the lines of a psychophysical monism in an evolutionary setting, and was on the lookout for mechanisms and operations. I wanted to correlate genetic growths and analytic requirements. Was there not something in common between response, reference, and transcendence? Of the three, transcendence seemed the most mystical and opaque. Reference, on the other hand, could be given linguistic development —as has been done recently—and also connected with response. I would break down "intentionality" in much the same fashion. After all, what we have to do with is a gifted organism functionally concerned with its environment. I was doubtful of an abrupt "dualism of process." What seemed to me more likely was an evolutionary "levels of causality." I even envisaged a level of rational causality directed by rules and tests. Naturally, I was led to reject the *predetermination* scheme of classical physics, and to put stress on causality as a going concern involving time as a dimension. What we experience as free will could thus be theoretically interpreted as *open* causality. One must not impute wonders to it, but it has its possibilities, personal and social.

I think I can justly claim to have been something of a pioneer in this perspective. At least, Lloyd Morgan devoted an appendix to my outlook in his book *Emergent Evolution*. It was S. Alexander who called his attention to my *Evolutionary Naturalism*. Emergence was an expressive term, and soon gained vogue. And it had something in common with *Gestalt* theory, as Köhler remarked to me when he visited Ann Arbor at the end of the First World War. It is curious how these things work out. American biologists like Ritter, Jennings, and Wheeler recognized my work. But a gap in bibliography soon followed. Novikov's excellent article on integrative levels attracted attention long afterward.

Now the importance of this stress on levels of causality was that it played into my analysis of perceiving. I began to think of stimulus-and-response as a causal unit. But it was a unit which could be enriched by cortical insertions. Broadly speaking, it would thus become S-C-R. With concepts would go inhibitions and facilitations and redirections with methods of checking and verifying. What we may broadly call judging would thus operate, even at the level of perceiving.

This perspective led me to coordinate what I may call three "parameters": (1) the biological mechanism of perceiving, (2) the consciousness-brain complex, and (3) the reflective level of *comment* expressed in such nondescriptive terms as true, good, and beautiful. A few words on each of these parameters are in order.

I have recently noted that both Blanshard and Chisholm regard my location of sensations in the brain as a complication which at once distinguished my theory of perceiving from that of others and made it more difficult to carry through. On page 429 of Volume I of his systematic treatise *The Nature of Thought*, Blanshard writes as follows: "Because writing with the mind-body relation more explicitly before him, he seems to me to reveal most candidly the difficulties which it entails for the theory of knowledge." But, as I see it, the difficulties are, rightly taken, the opportunities. They led me to regard sensations as not terminal in perceiving but as guiding. What we are concerned with, in perceiving, is the object to which we are responding. Thus we look at things *through* our visual sensations. The correlative of the thing perceived is the percipient; and language quite clearly so expresses it. Of course, this does open the door to ontological questions which I met in terms of levels and double-knowledge. One problem does lead to another; but this is the way it should be. For instance, it points squarely to a revision of the correspondence theory of truth, making correspondence an achievement resting on the *interplay* of the sensations, controlled in us by our sense organs, and the concepts developed in the attempt to decipher the objects we are perceiving. While *true* means the endorsement of a cognitive claim (statement) as a case of knowledge, it contextually implies this kind of achievement. Had Blanshard studied these mechanisms more carefully, I doubt that he would have been satisfied with the coherence theory of truth. Thought and object are, for him, too easily identified. As I see it, human knowledge is in terms of deciphered facts about the world. It is an achievement resting on reproductive communications and logical operations, a really wonderful accomplishment. Knowing can be clarified, but it is not reducible to something else.

Terms like "true," "good," and "beautiful" are of the nature of comments, and reflect man's status as knower and agent. All involve the use of criteria and, in the idiom of today, are of the nature of *meta* appraisals. They are connected with man's status and dignity in the world.

The flaw in traditional materialism was that it tended to identify itself with a too reductive and dead-level picture of the world. Since it began ontologically with the material world, it was hard put to it to find a place for mind and consciousness. And it was never strong in theory of knowledge. Here Kantianism and idealism had an advantage. It remained for evolutionary thought to give new leads. It has remained a step-by-step affair. On the scientific side, the assumption of deductive, mechanical predetermination had to be qualified and more room left to time and novelty. On the philosophical side a new kind of realism had to be worked out. All this would take time. Meanwhile, there would be semantic confusion with condemnation of ethical materialism and much appeal to the spiritual. In the long run, the whole situation had to be cleared up. It was this strategy I had in mind when I correlated what I have called the three "parameters." I think that logical positivism did a disservice when it sought a short cut. Much, of course, depended on the full import of empirical statements. Are they about material things or about actual and possible sensations?

Quite obviously, the job to do is to put mind back into nature in an evolutionary way. Perceiving must be seen as a natural two-way operation. If the human mind is put "under-the-hat," it must be understood as a functional affair, one of sense-organ communication and of directed response, able to use in this activity the high service of symbols. And justice must be done to human appraising, its standards and rules. No form of materialism can be adequate which does not give full recognition to the status and stature of man. After that, it will be a matter of semantic adjustment. Naturalism may well be a mediating term. But I think it is the task of science and philosophy, working together, to clarify the whole situation.

So much in the way of general perspective. In the remainder of my paper I shall go into more detail and also make comments on contemporary movements. I shall, in point of fact, weave in and out. First, I shall offer some historical notes indicating the impact of the new science upon philosophy. I shall then go in more detail into the climate of thought represented by the American realistic movement, new and critical. And I shall conclude by indicating unfinished business. Where I allow myself to pass judgment, it will always be tied in with perspective and emphases. After all, philosophy has a broad front and there are many workers in it.

My historical notes must be brief. I wish again to call attention to the reasons why modern philosophy lapsed into subjectivism and into concern for the status of mind. The medieval outlook was teleological and hierarchical. But the "new sciences"—to use Galileo's phrase—were mechanical and mathematical. The inorganic world was described in terms of the mass and movements of *bodies*. The culmination of this was in the celestial mechanics of Newton. As new sciences developed, man's thought of nature was enriched by the development and application of new concepts. Philosophy became specialized by way of contrast. It could not do the job the sciences were doing. But it was concerned with its import. Epistemology and the mind-body problem were pushed to the front.

I cannot go into the complexities of the interaction between rationalism and empiricism. Rationalism tended to be too intuitionistic and deductive, while empiricism linked itself with sensations and images and the causal approach to perception. This was what I call a one-way approach, stressing stimulation and ignoring response. Kant tried to initiate a counterrevolution *without really solving the problem of perceiving*. Like Locke, he could not get back to the physical world. Fichte, Schelling, and Hegel gave objective idealism its romantic proportions. I do not deny their contributions but regard their work as topheavy. It required Darwinism and the general advance of science to give perspective.

In the meantime, philosophy had entrenched itself behind epistemological dicta, such as no object without a subject and the physical world is phenomenal. Science made its counterthrust in terms of behaviorism. It was in this general climate that American pragmatism and realism were born. I am persuaded that the impacts involved were more direct and vital because less academically cushioned than in England or the European Continent.

But before I return to the American scene I want to make a few remarks on Neo-Aristotelianism, dialectical materialism, and existentialism. These will illustrate what I called, above, weaving in and out.

I have always had a certain sympathy for the Neo-Aristotelians. After all, Aristotle had tried to unify the *psyche* and the body except for the "active reason." And there was some substance to Aristotelian empiricism. But its corporeal theory did not express an interrogation of nature in a methodical way. It lacked the conception of mass, and was opposed to atomism. Its cosmology could offer no alternative to Newtonianism.

But it had certain leads in psychology, ethics and logic. To some extent, these were more an affair of "experience," and were not so likely to be completely mistaken. But logic has been revised and ethics enlarged and more carefully analyzed. A vital point to note is that Aristotelianism always protested the "subjectivism" and "dualism" into which modern philosophy fell as mind was extruded from nature. It held to the objective "intentionality" of mental acts, though it had no clear idea of the "mechanism" on which it was founded. It was Brentano who exploited this schematism. We shall see that Lovejoy appealed to some such intentionality as an empirical fact. Roderick Chisholm would seem to be exploring the same lead. I, on the other hand, have been exploring *reference* as developed on response and taken up into language. Professor Wilfrid Sellars has been analyzing language and its idioms in this setting.

I suppose my feeling is that modern philosophy took the hard road and is only now working its way back to objective import and psychophysical monism. Science in its full range is now the complement of philosophy. The so-called *philosophia perennis* cannot escape the implications of this situation. As is well known, Aristotle had worked back from Plato's fervid mind-body dualism toward monism but he knew nothing about the causal economy of the brain. The philosophy of mind must now be worked out in this setting. My own hunch is that the Neo-Aristotelians would have little objection to my location of sensations in the brain: less than pragmatists and idealists probably. The rub would come in the handling of thinking. The neurology of linguistics, with all it means for concept-formation and integrative, causal novelty, is the key point.

From the technical point of view, dialectical materialism is hard to deal with. It is critical of mechanical materialism, and stresses time and history. In the period of Marx, it was opposed to Hegelianism of the right and had a strong element of eighteenth century Enlightenment. Thus it was to the left of Anglo-American idealism. On the other hand, it was more close-knit than academic philosophy, which soon underwent the dissolving influences of developments in logic and in theory of knowledge. On the other hand, Lenin's protests against Machian positivism had justification. However, too many points on theory of knowledge, the mind-body problem, and general ontology were left blurred. But one could also say that the neat phenomenalism of much of English thought was just as unsatisfactory. Where among Wittgenstein's followers, for example, does one find discussions of the neurology of linguistics? And how about the mechanism of perceiving? Yet, in saying this, I recognize that philosophy has a broad, working front.

Existentialism seems to have been, primarily, a cultural phenomenon in a Franco-German after-the-war setting. It is hard to say how much is living and how much is dead about it. It had no clear theory of knowledge, for it mingled a subjective view of truth as trust and loyalty with Kantianism and with phenomenological description and idealism. And it was even divided in its loyalties. I was recently somewhat surprised by a reference in Professor F. H. Heineman's able book *Existentialism and the Modern Predicament* to American *materialistic humanism*. Of course, I come under that caption; but so, in a way, does Sartre. Let me make certain contrasts.

American thought combines rationalism with empiricism and does not put essence before existence. Sartre seems to me a Car-

tesian behaviorist with phenomenological trimmings and a penchant
for the "absurdity" of existence, all very effectively used in a dra-
matic way. I can find no clear theory of perceiving or of valuation.
Jaspers is essentially a Kantian with the transcendent overhang of
the unbounded. Heidegger is an etymological ontologist able to
use that remarkable instrument, the German language, in striking
ways. Of course, we are all seeking authentic modes of living, and
dislike anxiety. One should read, now and then, the *Thoughts* of
the Emperor Marcus Aurelius. He had a tough-enough time. Marcel,
I would class with Hocking, both depending much on the weakness
of the traditional, causal theory of perception. The emphasis shifts
to participation in a rather mystical fashion. Now, in all this there
is a strong sense of the human situation and a stress on *being* rather
than having. All in all, it is a rather heterogeneous assemblage.
One must remember that the note struck is that of human existence,
philosophical anthropology, the human situation, the human predicament. While I do not think that existentialism has accomplished
much technically, it is of the nature of a challenge to a too optimistic
humanism.

These brief surveys, I hope, drive home my point that Neo-Aristotelianism, dialectical materialism, and the evolutionary realism I
favor are moving in much the same direction, in the field set for
them by the vast development of science. Our knowledge about the
universe has been conceptually enriched. There is more to this
than the adoration of scientific method. Objective knowledge of
the texture and mode of working of nature is involved. And man's
status and standing must be understood and commented on. It is
not impossible that all this will come to a focus in our day. The
United States will make a mistake if it allows its tradition of anti-
intellectualism to blind it to the import of such a development in
which technology may find itself subordinated to theory in the
Greek sense, that is, to intellectual vision.

After these analyses I come again to comments on the positions
taken by J. B. Pratt, A. K. Rogers, and A. O. Lovejoy. My purpose
is to bring out the difference between mental transcendence and
reference. In any larger treatment of critical realism, I should have
to explore Durant Drake's position. He was one of the keenest of
the group. Probably time has helped me to bring together response,
concepts, and language.

Pratt took his stand on a dualism of process, and stressed the capacity of the mind to transcend itself. Just *how* it could do this was, I fear, not brought out very clearly. The point for him was that it was an accomplished feat. I think it was much the same for Rogers and Lovejoy. They were all dualists, whereas I was not, and therefore I sought a biological base for reference.

While Pratt was not a personalist, he emphasized the power of the "self" to know what was other than its own states, to will, and to interact with the body in such a fashion as to change the outcome of the mechanistic laws of nature. Teleology was set over mechanism as a dualism of process. In all this, I take it, he reflected the outlook of his beloved teacher William James, though he was not a pragmatist. I have the feeling that he had begun to recognize the pull of naturalism in his later years. Note this sentence: "The world we live in is the kind of world that produces selves." [2] And there is the use of the term in a title of a book. His ethics is explicitly naturalistic.

In his stress upon a dualism of process, Pratt had advanced beyond the tradition of a dualism of substances, mind and matter. As I saw it, what he really did was to issue a challenge to the rising evolutionary approach. The alternative was emergent levels of process and modes of causality. It was this line of exploration which I undertook, and I know that Pratt studied my efforts with care. A crucial point would be the handling of perceiving. If sensations and images operate in the stimulus-response unit, then reference might be a natural development made explicit in gestures and language. The biopsychology of language is making immense strides these days. This is something the Neo-Aristotelians will also need to reckon with.

People were too accustomed to speaking of the body as a brute, physical thing. But we are realizing today what a marvelous sort of thing it is with its complex, internal adjustments, its wisdom or homeostasis. And the brain with its pattern-forming cortex is being studied with the aid of new, electrical methods. There are indications that every activity modifies its working. It has a job to do. May it not be that the self is intrinsic to that agency and participates in its high type of causality, which involves the use of criteria for decision? I am persuaded that thinking, with its use of language, is a historical achievement which man has added to nature with nature's support. In this fashion, symbols and their meanings have attained directive, causal import. I might call this level that of "open" or self-governing causality. There is always the possibility of significant origination. Up to the level of psychology, science has tended to stress external knowledge built around perceiving. The semantic integration of behaviorism with introspection is one of the tasks of the present. This will be the apex of that enrichment of our thought of nature for which pure science has stood. In this evolutionary way, the breach between *res extensa* and *res cogitans* may be healed. That, I may remark, was one of the tasks I set myself in my first book, *Critical Realism* (1916).

A. K. Rogers is a neglected thinker, partly, I think, because of the complexity of his style. He emphasized precision of statement. Like Pratt he was an empiricist but not of the Humian school. That is, he did not think that our firsthand experience was reducible to the components emphasized by traditional British empiricism. What he had in mind is the context of beliefs and attitudes. There is a touch of common-sensism as in C. S. Peirce. One can call it a rational empiricism. I think that Lovejoy had much the same outlook. Thus he emphasizes the rationalistic element in Locke. I suppose that it was intuitionism which Hume was attacking. *The controlled rise of concepts which apply* was the unmastered problem. I shall point out later that I do not think that C. I. Lewis has quite got it in hand.

Rogers's dualism comes from his emphatic recognition of the physical world. He is impatient with those idealists of his time who tried to explain it away. But this leaves him in a situation quite like Pratt's; and, like him, he resorts to theism. It is interesting to note that neither of them found themselves able to take the path of pragmatism. Like myself, they found it tangential and of the nature of a compromise with idealism. It seemed to them to blunt the point of epistemological inquiry. As I would put it, cognitive claims were subordinated to the method of inquiry and the reconstruction of "experience." The language became that of transactions, plans of action, and warranted statements. This linguistic shift expressed Dewey's perspective very accurately. To this, Rogers—and I think quite rightly—was opposed. He puzzled away at the correspondence theory of truth.

Lovejoy sums up very well his own movement away from the *idealism* of his teachers with its absolutism and its neglect of time. He became a temporalist and a pluralist.[3] In epistemology, he was led to regard knowledge as "somehow the apprehending of one bit

of experience by means of another which is not identical with it."
Knowing, our most characteristic human function, seemed to him
to involve a potential reference to, an evocation and apprehension
of, a beyond. Particulars must do duty for other particulars. Cognition would then be indirect and substitutional.

I am inclined to think that Lovejoy's concentration on memory
and the past had much to do with this formula. He had been debating Dewey's and James's emphasis on the future. Now memory has
its peculiarities so far as it is recollection. A factor of retention
enters in. It is *as though* I were living an experience over again;
and yet aware that I am not. But I am inclined to hold that the
framework of perceiving and doing must be taken as a background.
It was upon this that I concentrated my attention. As I increasingly
saw it, perceiving is a guided operation of a response, and denota-
tive, type. And what we look at we can ordinarily handle. Language
and thought lift this framework to the level of reference and characterization. We are concerned, in perceiving, with things and
events and their relations. Language patterns itself on this categorial
syntax. I am quite aware of the proposals of the linguistic, cultural
relativists; but would hold an intermediate position between cultural
relativism and any simple reading off of categorical traits. Perceptual knowledge is of the nature of an exploration under guidance
and practical needs, just as scientific knowledge reflects an exploration with sophisticated methods.

I have the impression, accordingly, that Lovejoy, an acute critic,
was so engrossed in the consideration of the weaknesses of the
presentationalism of the new realism and the allied objective relativism of Whitehead and Murphy that he did not explore the possibilities of a reanalysis of perceiving. I take it that the introspective
tradition was still dominant, whereas my approach expresses the
stage of an integration of behaviorism and introspection. We look
at things *through* our visual fields. And we rightly and inevitably
take the visual field to give information about the things around us.
That is our biological make-up. Such a position lies between the
kind of epistemological monism of Perry and any epistemological
dualism which tends to make knowing terminate on ideas. Let us
call it direct, referential perceiving. Now I think that all the critical
realists had some such goal in mind, since they all wanted to move
between the Scylla and Charybdis of Berkeley and Locke. I have

argued that the essence gambit was not successful and that the transcendence move depended too much upon supposed, innate powers of "mind." What I explored was the sensorimotor mechanism which connected stimulation with response-adjustments to the environment, adjustments which could be furthered cortically and conceptually.

It was not surprising that C. I. Lewis and other phenomenalists (Berkeleians) did not appreciate what we were trying to do. In their eyes we were seeking an *invisible path* between truth and error, in much the same way as Honor Tracy's priest exhorted his congregation to keep to the straight and narrow path between right and wrong. If sensations are terminal in perceiving, Lewis was quite right. The logical thing to do was to add the a priori Kantian touch in a predictive, pragmatic way. I have always regarded him as more analytic than Dewey.

Because Lovejoy was concerned with objective knowing, he did not take kindly to Russell's location of "percepts" in the brain. He called this the "under-the-hat" theory of mind. Now the flaw in Russell's position was that it confused "percepts" and their sensory components with perceiving. He got to the extracerebral world by postulation. If, however, we take the brain to be the organ of behavior, we can connect it up with perceiving as a guided activity. The whole rich content of consciousness can be given functional status. It involves, as Hebb points out, continually changing, selective responses. While, therefore, I have sympathy with Lovejoy's feeling that both the English neorealists—G. E. Moore, for example —and the American new realists were sterilizing consciousness, I do not agree with his alternative, which was dualism. The alternative I pursued was that of a more adequate psychophysical monism. This can be noted in my first book, *Critical Realism*, in which I seek to enlarge the notion of the physical along evolutionary lines. Here I anticipated Russell; but, in connecting perceiving with response, I had a less purely introspective conception of mind. Even if the brain-mind is "under-the-hat," it is concerned with linking stimulus patterns with guided response. It has a job to do.

Now both Bergson and Perry had ejected consciousness from the brain; and early behaviorism did not like consciousness at all. But I am persuaded that the tide has turned. Neurology is enlarging its conceptions.

But one must have not only "a patterned-stimulus and guided response" view of perceiving but also some idea of the way in which language is inserted to give human beings more control of thought. Fortunately, psychology is beginning to conduct controlled experiments in this field. It is becoming clear that sensations act as cues for the assignments of attributes and class concepts. Words are tied in with public references and characterizations: and their meaning arises in this context. The application of a word, like "table" to a thing is, at one and the same time, the application of a concept to the thing. Thus language in use is as objective in import as is perceiving.

What a wonderful creature language has made of man! He can give his signs objective reference and talk about himself and the Other One, developing pronouns for discourse in the human situation. And he can hand down cultural achievements, explore nature, acquire methods of investigation, achieve new concepts applicable, in a tested way, to nature. I take it that this perspective undercuts subjectivism and phenomenalistic positivism and puts the human mind back into nature on its own functional terms.

Let me illustrate by taking some of the thought-models against which it has struggled. Man, the speaking creature, had made for himself tales and rituals involving gods, fate, and divine decrees. He did not, as yet, have much control over events and over his destiny. And he could hardly think in impersonal terms. Then, when science developed, he found regularities he called laws. And he came to think in terms of machines and predeterminations. He could use these routines technologically. But did they not reach up to bind himself? In what sense, if any, was he a law to himself, and self-governing?

Here is where an adequate philosophy of mind is needed. I am inclined to suggest that the notion of free will, of self-determination, has a close connection with the high level of causality displayed in language. Thinking, as Plato already saw, is largely discourse with oneself. There is an openness about it. But there is also a logic to it. I cannot, here, go into the intricacies of the topic. Somehow we must combine the notions of responsibility and opportunity, of relevance and creativeness. Here is where my third "parameter" of appraisal and comment comes in. I would define man as the criteria-using animal. Responsible conduct signifies criteria-using conduct in the temporal mode of deliberation. Here an individual's culturally educated cortex in actual, or possible, communication with other persons, so endowed, is the organ of reason and commitment. The semantics of "materialism" must adjust itself to this perspective.

In this abbreviated survey of perspectives, I have largely concerned myself with the new realists and the critical realists. It is true that I have made some comments on the behavioristic experientialism of John Dewey to the effect that he tended to by-pass cognitive claims and their epistemology, and concentrate on the logic of inquiry. The only valid reply to this move is to work out an epistemology which avoids his charges of passive spectatorship. Surely, human knowledge is an achievement. Dewey seems to have had Plato and Locke almost equally in mind. I have never been a Platonist; and I think I have shown how Locke's gambit can be circumvented by a more adequate view of perceiving. I have decided, therefore, to examine briefly the position of C. I. Lewis. I shall try to be just to him while indicating contrasts. There are signs that he is trying to escape from phenomenalism to realism. Now I am persuaded that the only defensible avenue of escape is some such analysis of the mechanism of perceiving as that which I have outlined. Let us bear this in mind.

We can, I think, best examine Lewis's framework under three headings: (1) the status of concepts, (2) the mind-brain complex, and (3) the nature of physical things. As I see it, there is a strong element of Platonism in his theory of concepts. As regards the mind-brain complex he is a dualist with, at most, a correlational program. With respect to the nature of physical things, he makes sensory findings terminal.

Now, as to the first heading, I would regard concepts as developments under criterial control. The framework is that of directed response and the use of informational cues. The setting is, at first, concrete and only gradually does the manipulation of signs secure some independence in what we call thinking. This genetic approach in terms of what he calls psychologics has been carefully explored by Piaget. His thesis is that the higher psychological processes grow out of biological mechanisms. Recently, other psychologists—notably Bruner and Osgood—have studied cognitive activities, such as the strategies used in the attainment of concepts and the mediations upon which denotation and connotation rest. All this leads up to the view that the meanings of terms are selective, referential, and largely public.

Coming now to Lewis as an accomplished logician, it would be only natural for him to stress analysis rather than genesis. Concepts are there to be "entertained." Empirical knowledge involves the application of concepts to what is perceptually findable. The epistemological query then is: Just what is perceptually findable? Is this the sensory given as terminal? Such would seem to be the Berkeleian and phenomenalistic element in Lewis. Conceptual "If . . . then" implications are of the nature of predictions. Now, in contrast, I would hold that perceiving terminates referentially upon bodies, that the framework at the level of human perceiving is that of percipient organism and thing perceived. I would regard sensory data as informational cues and evidence whose distinctness from the body observed is blurred in naïve realism. It will be recalled that my assignment of sensations to the brain was regarded by my critics as introducing unnecessary difficulties. I do not think so. They play a role in guiding perceiving, connected, as they are, with patterned stimuli, and become, at a reflective level, of evidential value. As we all know, linguistic signs are conventional patterns which secure meaning in use. Speaking technically, phonemes become morphemes.

As I see it, then, Lewis is operating within the tradition of "immediate perception" of James and Peirce. Immediate perception meant the rejection of Lockeanism and Kantian things-in-themselves. I, on the other hand, am working within the referential view of perceiving.

"Immediate perception" gravitates in the direction of phenomenalism and idealism and neutralism. Referential perceiving supports physical realism. Now Lewis is quite aware that cognition involves objective reference, some kind of representation, the application of concepts, the possibility of error. He speaks of cognitive apprehension through representation. Believing is inferential in significance. Thus empirical knowledge has two conditions: conceptual and perceptual. And there must be correspondence of character between knowledge and the "perceptually findable." With these principles I am in essential agreement. The divergence lies in foundations. This brings us to the brain-consciousness complex.

I am particularly interested in this question since Professor Kuiper appealed to Lewis's handling of it in terms of correlation to reject my monistic, double-knowledge approach.[4] According to Lewis, the answer takes the form of a correlation of the inspected psychical with descriptions of brain-states. To correlate sound waves with sound sensations, light frequencies with color sensations is one thing. To assert a functional unity of sensations with brain-states is something else again. But, surely, if the analysis of perceiving, itself, upon which science rests, indicates that sensations intervene between the stimulus pattern and the response, the connection must be causally intimate. And, really, is there any reason to deny this functional unity but a false notion of the reach of descriptive knowledge founded on perceiving and, perhaps, the ghost of the tradition of Cartesian dualism?

Let me now try to bring my exploratory analysis to a conclusion. I shall put my results under headings.

1. All the critical realists were seeking some path between Berkeley and Locke. The problem was to understand the objective import of perceiving. Drake, Strong, and Santayana set up "essences" as at once before the mind and in the object. Pratt, Rogers, and Lovejoy regarded mental states as terminal entities which pointed beyond themselves in an intentional and transcending way. I, on the other hand, was exploring the possibility that the mechanism of perceiving was such that sensations had the role of guiding response to things, that they were "informational" in import. So taken, they would not be terminal, as in traditional British empiricism, but factors in an activity of deciphering the terminal concern, which would be the thing to which the organism was responding. In a quite literal sense, one would be looking at the thing *through* the visual field. Here would be the birthplace of that transcendence which has so bothered introspective thought. Concepts would develop in this framework as the higher cortical centers were called into play in connection with manipulations and explorations, all objective in import. The added techniques and strategies of language would permit the use of conventional signs and their combinations to make more abstract explorations.

2. From this development, resting in the final analysis on the informational role of sensations as linked with stimulus complexes playing upon sense organs, a thickened empiricism would arise, directed at the world. Analytically, it would manifest itself as the tested application of concepts to denotables. The denotables would

be *observables* disclosed by the informational use of sensations. The relevant sensations would be employed criterially in strategic ways with which both psychology and scientific method are familiar. I take it that Dewey, Lewis, Pratt, Rogers, and Lovejoy had such a conceptually thickened empiricism in mind but hardly knew how it was achieved. I repeat that my location of sensations in the brain, which seemed to so many a courting of disaster, enabled me to put them in the service of perceiving and to avoid that impasse of mental states somehow transcending themselves. As I see it, the "logical atomism" of Russell and Wittgenstein had no such framework in mind.

3. Now there has been a great advance in the appreciation of the logic of language. Having a criterial and combinatorial job to do under perceptual and social control, it could not have escaped a logical matrix. But I am persuaded that a good epistemology will enable formal logic to avoid misinterpretation of its existential signs and variables. A clear understanding of the idioms of natural language should be of help here. The prime purpose of formal logic is consistency and inference. "Truth tables" concern this context. In thinking about the world we are working out its categorial texture. We found our "inference licenses" on such texture as taken up into language. If language has its logic, thought must have a corresponding one. It has its structures, tests, and strategies, as psychology is beginning to note. It strikes me that Piaget and Bruner are on the right track.

In developing and defending this perspective, I have inevitably sketched the framework of my own philosophical position. Call it either evolutionary naturalism or nonreductive materialism. The point is that it breaks sharply with any mysterious transcendence of the sort Jaspers still clings to. We are quite naturally *in* the world, not thrown into it, erupted from some Absolute or *Urgrund,* of the Schelling-Tillich type. As I see it, that is a rationalization of what is essentially mythology. The ultimate cure is a naturalization of mind which will do it justice.

Both Husserl and Russell boggled at an inference from consciousness to that which was beyond consciousness. Dewey and the philosophical behaviorists, like Ryle, gave it up. But is not the problem badly set? Is not cognitive reference an activity within a natural framework developed around response? Do we not look at things through our visual field and concern ourselves with them in a deciphering, exploratory way? More complex cognitive activities carry on. We look at things from different angles, manipulate them, break them to pieces. Science takes over from the broad conquests of common sense. But I cannot see any mystery in it. Yet, until cognizing as a human activity is naturalized and clarified, all the stops will be pulled on *homo viator,* man the pilgrim.

In cognition and deliberative appraisal, man becomes a rational creature lifting his head above the world which he knows and appraises, and commenting upon it. He is the thinking reed of Pascal. As I see it, this is the only kind of transcendence he can achieve, the transcendence of objective knowledge, slowly achieved by activities resting, in the last analysis, upon the communicative capacities of the sense organs enhanced by logic and experimentation. This enhancement has a cultural history. And there have been many false starts and twists and turns. Within limits, knowledge gives man power. Since science and philosophy are complementary, it would seem their duty to talk the situation over. Something of the nature of *wisdom* might ensue.

I am going to summarize in an abrupt fashion. The weakness of Greek thought lay in the fact that it had, as yet, no idea of the intricate mechanisms involved in nature. The modern world has traced them upward from the inorganic realm to living things and, thence, to minded organisms. "Forms" have been transmogrified into action patterns. And new action patterns are built on old ones. How will the Aristotelian deal with this situation? Traditional empiricism made sensations and images terminal, and could never escape from subjectivism. Its value lay in its attack on a priorism. Dialectical materialism got the material world reflected into the brain but had not arrived at the realization of the importance of the clue of the guided response. There has been too much yammering and *fideism* in existentialism, and too little technical analysis. The Continent has forgotten the need for cultural cross-fertilization. For all its concreteness and stress on scientific method, pragmatism made the mistake of too easily getting discouraged about the objective import of cognitive claims and the objective status of the entities—electrons, neutrons, atoms, molecules, coded protein templates, etc.—which scientific exploration had found in nature.

The American realists, I believe, raised and faced the whole gamut of problems. How near to a "breakthrough" they came the reader must judge.

Professor Pratt invited me once to become a colleague of his at Williams. I could not see my way clear to an acceptance. But I was grateful to him; and I have often thought of the delightful times we would have had seeking to "follow the argument" in Socratic fashion.

ROY WOOD SELLARS
Emeritus, University of Michigan

Three Bases of Objectivity

Ever since Protagoras propounded the paradox that "that which appears to each man is to him," the possibility and the extent of objectivity in human judgment have been much disputed. Of late the controversy has been chiefly about the "normative" as opposed to the "descriptive" variety of judgments. But apart from the difficulty of drawing this very distinction—since the ideal of a true description looks very like a norm—Protagoras's pronouncement remains a paradox in the ancient sense of being contrary to received opinion, which on this point makes no distinction according to the subjects about which we judge.

Although this essay will be concerned with some of the alternative grounds to which reflection may appeal in support of this common opinion, it may be appropriate to remind ourselves briefly of its stability, and of how much our daily practice depends upon it.

We are in fact congenital and incorrigible propounders of judgments, forever ready with pronouncements about anything and everything. In this we are as often as not pretty light-minded, "talking through our hats" in the forms and usages of considered judgment without being prepared to establish either what we say or our right to be taken seriously in saying it. But still, since vanity and irony are possible only because some things are serious, and blasphemy makes no sense in a company where reverence is unknown, the declaration of every judgment, making no matter how casual a claim, presumes that it is capable of being true in some sense. Otherwise the indicative mood that we use to make judgments would be as ill adapted for all our foolery, irony, and hyperbole as it would be unsuited to carry the burdens of sober truth.

There are, of course, considerable differences among the judgments that we make or go through the motions of making, and in just what ways they all claim to be true it is not easy to say. It is, indeed, my purpose to clarify some of these differences, and the corresponding

differences in the ways in which it is appropriate to support or
question our claims. And since our time is one in which we are most
uncertain about the better and the worse, and about what, in view
of what we know about ourselves and our circumstances, we ought
to do, it is "value judgments" of various sorts that will concern me
most, while the descriptive variety will be introduced principally
for purposes of comparison and contrast.

But let the differences among our judgments be as they may, my
initial point concerns all of them, simply as judgments: it is, to
repeat, that Protagoras has propounded a veritable paradox, for
nobody believes him. Nobody believes him, that is, if we go by the
testimony of our constant involvement in the practice of claim-
staking and its use of the language of objectivity. What some theorist
may say or think about Protagoras's doctrine is quite another matter,
and so is the question whether he may actually have been right—
whatever that could mean. But what men say as thinkers they do
not necessarily believe as agents, even if they believe that they do.

At any rate, the presumptive claim of every judgment is a con-
comitant of the indicative mood by which we make them. It has
little to do with their varying "substance"—with whether any particular one has merit or is even put forward for serious consideration
—but much to do with their common form. It is by having this asser-
tive form, for example, that falsehoods sometimes pass as truths,
and it is by using it that fiction and drama imitate our experience
in all its action and passion. In many uses of the indicative, to be
sure, the likelihood of justifying what we say with it is not only
remote but irrelevant: it would spoil the game to press the question.
But despite all this, both the claim that is characteristic of the indicative (which is a condition of its use for play and pretense as well
as for instruction and guidance), and the existence of such a form
of expression at all, require that it should always make sense to ask
whether what we say in that form is true or publicly warrantable.
And this in turn depends upon our presumption that such claims
are for the most part decidable *de jure*. For if they were not generally
thought to be, it would be futile to make them.

This general condition of using the forms of assertion has a specific
application to each principal species of claim: if it were thought that
no claims of a particular sort could possibly be made good, it would
become impossible to make any of that kind. We should have only

an ironic use for the usages of judgment about such matters. It is conceivable, of course, that some judgments owe all their plausibility to their looking like the more respectable members of the family. But such impostors would have to be occasional individuals rather than whole companies of them. A wandering wolf may occasionally profit by wearing sheep's clothing, but only in a territory where sheep are the usual thing. And so again, the phenomena of the uses of judgment are unequivocal: were no claims of a certain sort generally thought (whether rightly or wrongly) to be sound, it would become fruitless to try, or even to pretend, to make one.

If we now shift our attention from the practice of claim-staking and the objectivity which it presupposes, and turn instead to the possible grounds of this presumed objectivity, Protagoras's position appears very much stronger, and particularly when the varieties of value judgment are in question.

According to Protagoras, there is no sense of "true" over and above what appears or seems to this person or that. And if so, discourse can be effective only in the way he set out to make his own efficacious, that is, by affecting how things seem or appear—or by influencing our attitudes toward things. So he cultivated the art of bringing about changes in men by means of words, as the art of medicine produces them by drugs or exercise. Now, of course, either travel or instruction may equally improve a man's opinions as well as his health; and there is no reason to doubt that beliefs and other dispositions may be induced and altered in many ways. But the philosophically interesting and important question concerns not only whether but when discourse can have a measure of success other than its effects upon our attitudes—that is, when it can be objectively justifiable as well as effective.

On this point it is interesting to note that, while no one goes the whole way with Protagoras any more, he is not without his modern-day followers. Professor Stevenson, who is perhaps a representative example, conceives the business of normative discourse as being "to direct and redirect attitudes," quite as Protagoras did; but about issues of "belief" he is as objectivist as the next man, as it would be hard not to be in this scientific age.[1] Beliefs, he says, are true or false as conforming to what they are about, and they may be affected by other beliefs and statements of belief which are related to them "logically," as evidence, and not only "factually," as causes.

But "attitudes" of approval and esteem, and dispositions to pursue or avoid, not being intended to conform to any object, are neither true nor false, correct nor incorrect. They may, indeed, be altered by alterations in belief as well as by other causes; and although he calls the modification of attitudes by way of our beliefs a "rational" method of affecting them, there is a more important sense in which he thinks no method in influencing attitudes can possibly be rational. For a belief, however true and rationally grounded, can be related to an attitude only "factually" and causally, never "logically" and cogently; and in this respect it is no different from any other source of influence.

Hence arises a perplexity as old as human reflection. It is practically impossible not to affirm the validity of each general kind of judgment many times over every day, although we recognize that any particular claim may be unfounded. But at the same time, the validity of some types, and with it the capacity of their instances to be significantly wrong rather than vain and senseless, often seems impossible to account for. Strange, so many centuries after the injunction "Know thyself," if we are still self-deceived in making whole classes of fatuous claims and seem condemned to continue doing so as if by some kind of original sin. Yet it is no less strange, if they are not groundless, that we should be so much at a loss in identifying their grounds.

2.

In everyday usage the man of "objective" judgment is no doubt often so called because he has regard for the facts of the case: his judgment is determined by its object, rather than by anything "subjective." At the same time, as one might expect, he is the man who judges impartially, taking the disinterested view as opposed to the "subjectively" biased. Here reference is made not only to the traits of an antecedent object of judgment, but to similarly (or perhaps alternatively) essential traits of the judge who estimates a disputable value. And finally, since one's "object" need not always be a "thing" or state of affairs which is there to be known or evaluated, but rather, as in "the object of his ambition," what one seeks to bring about or achieve, to be "objective" is to resist distraction by the practically irrelevant. And so in yet a third sense, the objective

judgment may be measured by the requirements of effectively purposive action.

These distinctions of perspective, which we find sometimes
coalescing and sometimes occurring alone in the usages of common
speech, have been developed with considerable sophistication in
the works of philosophers; and each has been regarded as the primary basis for valid judgment. I shall examine some philosophical
experiments with the capacities of each alleged basis, to see how
far the nature of an antecedent object, the disinterestedness of a
judge, or the imperatives of action may be a sufficient ground for
objective judgment, and to see whether or not one of these is always
primary and indispensable while the others are derivative and dis-
pensable.

The predilections of common sense suggest that objectivity in
judgment requires conformity to an object independent of the judge,
and that our questions therefore converge upon an "ontological"
doctrine about the character and status of the objects of knowledge,
of action, and of evaluation.

Let me therefore [says Mr. Vivas] call myself an axiological realist. . . .
I believe that the moral man *discovers* the values he espouses, in the same
way in which the scientist or the logician discovers the laws of his science.
. . . Values are real and antecedent to our discovery of them; this is what
I mean when I say that they have "ontic status." [2]

This affirmation undoubtedly expresses something significant in
moral and aesthetic experience. So does the following:

To the extent to which it is operative, this capacity to discover values
is the pivotal point in the moral process, since it enables men to correct
what they incline to consider right and good by comparison with what
they discover to be right and good.[3]

There is, in other words, something about deliberation or evaluation which is like the passage from opinion to knowledge, and we
should often like to say that that is exactly what it is. In any case
this view has characteristic answers to our questions. The kinds of
objectivity are at least generically the same and are realized in
propositions that are true of their respective objects, though some
of them may be more difficult to establish than others. Therefore
the vindication of objectivity in morals and criticism requires a

common recognition of objects concerning which their assertions may be appropriately and peculiarly true.

Congenial as it is to the way we are inclined to think, this view is grievously embarrassed. No specifically "axiological" objects or qualities seem to be identifiable, or tractable with any objectivity in discourse, as the tedious debates of naturalists and nonnaturalists in value theory amply witness. The former point to many things but not to the specific objects which would differentiate ethics and aesthetics from psychology, sociology, and history.

> A primrose by a river's brim
> A yellow primrose was to him,
> And it was nothing more.

On the other hand the unanalyzable and supervenient qualities of nonnatural value, though they might, if palpable, provide our sought-for subject matters, are yet like the light that never was on sea or land.

3.

Taking note of this common failure of the axiological realists to communicate insights about the "ontic objectivity of value," yet aware that our estimates are often communicable none the less, and that community of sentiment is sometimes achievable, a second plausible view comes forward to justify a kind of objectivity of value which is different from the objectivity of knowledge.

> In expressing a moral attitude, [says Winston Barnes] . . . I should be implicitly claiming, though I should not be asserting, that . . . it will commend itself to anyone who considers the facts and allows them to register on his moral sensibility.[4]

Both the "facts" and whatever principles may be required for knowing them are relevant and essential, but they are not the specific determinants of this sort of judgment—if "judgment" is still the name for what "claims" without "asserting." Rather, certain attitudes are supposed to be sufficiently stable and widespread to determine community of response to the same persons, acts, or objects; and in judgment the determinant of the response would be attributed by a figure of speech to the object which was only its occasion.

Sentiments as a class are congenitally capricious and relative to the individuals whose affections they are, but perhaps some feelings and attitudes reflect uniformities which are not only circumstantial and variable but generically human. The question of fact is not in principle unanswerable. The realist's dour view of the waywardness of passions not determined by an object may be too sweeping.

To take this standpoint, I suggest, is to adopt one version of the aesthetic judgment as one's model, at least in the sense of Kant's remark that "we might even define taste as the faculty of estimating what makes our feeling in a given representation universally communicable without the mediation of a concept." [5] It should not be surprising that much recent thinking about art and morals, from crude emotivism to the more sophisticated attitude theories, is easier to understand when looked at in this way, for these accounts of normative discourse emphasize Kant's two marks of the judgment of taste: the presence of communicable feeling and the absence of a determining concept.

Stories of the sentimental dispositions vary, but their generality and power as principles were best worked out by Hume. He, we may remember, projected a complete system of the sciences based on the experimental investigation of human nature, a "foundation almost entirely new" and certainly radical in its reliance upon feeling, or the "secondary impressions," according to which "reason is and ought only to be the slave of the passions." But this project makes no sense unless there are certain common "principles of the human make," for, as he observes, "the faculties of the mind are supposed to be naturally alike in every individual; otherwise nothing could be more fruitless than to reason or dispute together." [6]

As for the realist, so for Hume, the kinds and grounds of objectivity are generically the same; but this time they all depend on the "internal fabric" of the human mind, which determines our characteristic responses and is detected by observation of its effects.

Thus even the idea of necessary connection, essential to every judgment of fact and existence, is traced to a secondary impression determined neither by the given data of sense nor by the understanding's arbitrary comparisons of ideas which we call "reason," but by custom, a universal tendency of sentiment. Since this principle of all "factual" knowledge is itself noncognitive, there is no reason why similarly "emotive" but specifically different dispositions should permit less reliability in other judgments. And so we can understand why Hume's "reformation in all moral disquisitions" enabled him to treat the problems of criticism and morals with confidence.

Moral and aesthetic judgments are unlike those of mathematics and experimental science in being noncognitive; that is, they are not concerned either with necessary relations of ideas or with the expected course of experience. Like judgments of fact and existence, however, they are determined by appropriate principles of the internal fabric; and although they are not true or false except by courtesy of metaphor they may nevertheless be more or less well founded and subject to correction by standards presumably objective. Beauty, for example, is not to be discovered among the qualities of the circle which Euclid noted and so thoroughly explained; yet these same qualities move us by touching "a string to which all mankind have an accord and symphony." [7] And moral judgments report no special qualities, or relations between agents or their acts, but express dispositions toward them which "are not only the same in all human creatures and produce the same approbation or censure; but . . . also comprehend all human creatures." [8]

Error, or rather caprice and subjectivity, in these matters springs from two sources: fugitive and irrelevant passions and inadequacy of knowledge. In moral judgments we easily misinterpret the motives and tendencies of action in its concrete setting. Justice, founded upon our estimates of social utility, is variable according to conditions of life which are hard to diagnose. In the second place our approvals are so alloyed with personal interest and the "violent passions" that the disinterested and universal feelings may be ineffective or go unnoticed. But as enlightenment moderates the former failings, so the latter are corrected by steadiness of moral character or "strength of mind." As other wise men have agreed, the man of good character is the good judge. And similar considerations apply to aesthetic judgments, explaining why the art of every time and place is accessible to informed and disciplined taste as well as why the strange seems barbarous and why the preferences of the vulgar are chaotic.

The accommodation of men's appraisals is imperfect and difficult even when successful; but the difficulty is not about the objectivity or universality of their principles so long as Hume's main principle is granted—if the faculties of the mind are not supposed to be naturally the same in every individual, nothing could be more fruitless than to reason or dispute together. He was no stranger to cultural and psychological relativism, but they bothered him not a bit. He even found them a source of wisdom, teaching us how to allow for the circumstances which alter cases and to appreciate, without looseness of principle, the flexibility and variety which life requires and culture fosters.

I have not lingered over Hume in this way because I regard his account of objectivity as all-sufficient or above criticism. He should remind us, however, that there is more than one way to skin a cat. Philosophy, above all disciplines, demands that our principles survive in dialectical battle with their ablest opponents rather than with the tired sparring partners of our polemics or with mere understudies. The capacities of Hume's doctrine to illuminate the successes as well as the failures of moral and critical objectivity are much greater than we may be at first inclined to think. Moreover it can handle phenomena of the moral consciousness which at first sight presuppose an "ontic objectivity" of value. The moral man's discovery of standards which correct his prejudices and inclinations is still accounted a discovery of laying bare of the primary sentiments of humanity beneath the overlay of temporary and strident feeling. Even as Mr. Vivas so accurately reports,

the man confronted with a radical moral perplexity must undertake a descent into the depths, a painful inquiry into his actual as opposed to his ostensible, motivations and values.[9]

Or, as we might restate it in the mode of Hume, he must be apprized of the facts; then, rather than explore the realms of being with ontological manual in hand, it befits him to search his soul. The man who has found himself and his place in the moral world—the *integer vitae*—responds immediately, as if by intuition. But so, of course, does the prisoner of convention. Custom may counterfeit nature, and intuition is no guide save for the man already disciplined.

A second lesson to be drawn from these reflections is that we philosophers too readily underestimate the place of emotive factors among the objectives as well as the obstacles of the good life. If philosophy can be the guide of life, as the Phi Beta Kappa motto promises, it will not rule by the enunciation of propositions and syllogisms alone or even principally. Community of values requires

both sound knowledge of a common world and harmony of sentiment based no doubt on nature but cultivated by habit and culture.
What we choose or enjoy has no exclusive dependence upon the
nature of the immediate object, but reflects our own characters;
and we should find no fault with Mr. Stevenson's truism that disagreements about value are often in part, and sometimes entirely,
reducible to disagreements in attitudes. But we should object to
his presumption that, such oppositions being noted, no significant
questions remain except about Protagorean devices for molding
other people's attitudes in the image of our own.

Finally we should question some distinctions fashionable among
the followers of Hume's empirical tradition. Most take the hard-
boiled stand that empirical science at least is objective by conforming to the "facts," leaving agreement about the noncognitive to such
consilience as may occur in attitude and taste. We have seen both
how this invidious distinction is ignored in common practice and
how it is denied at both ends by Hume. What do our contemporaries
say to this?

While this is not one of the untenable dualisms recently attacked
in Cambridge, it might well have been. If with Mr. Quine one
thinks that

the totality of our so-called knowledge or beliefs, from the most casual
matters of geography and history to the profoundest laws of atomic
physics or even of pure mathematics and logic, is a man-made fabric
which impinges on experience only along the edges,[10]

one notices that the changing design of this fabric is controlled by
"our vaguely pragmatic inclination" or "natural tendency" toward
"conservatism" and "simplicity." Are these still further "universal
principles of the human make?"

Let us grant the unsuspected possibilities of this kind of objectivity: something seems to be missing. You will remember that we
had asked what could be accomplished if we gave an architectonic
role to the judgment of taste, defined as one which claims com-
municability of feeling without the mediation of a concept. We
found that much could be done on this basis—more indeed than
we often achieve when trying to make sense of objectivity in action
and appreciation. But we also began this inquiry by asking about
the place of intelligence and judgment in the life of action, taken

broadly. As it has turned out, we have heard much of judgment but little of intelligence save as it is—as Hume said it ought to be—the slave of the passions. Has it no further role?

4.

Let us get a new perspective on this question from a third possible generic view of the problem of objectivity—and one, incidentally, in which intelligence is more prominent. Instead of the true theoretic proposition or the communicable estimate of taste, it takes the maxim of action as primary. Its name, of course, is pragmatism, and I shall illustrate it by brief references to Dewey.

Here again objectivity is tested by, and achieved in, communication; but attempts to base it upon disinterested feeling or references to an antecedent reality are alike rejected as "spectator theories," signs of the pathology of intelligence. "Experience" does not mean something passively undergone, nor is it a name for the turbulence of data impinging upon the edges of the fabric of knowledge. It is the interaction of an agent with his world, an activity guided by thought and in its characteristic forms always social, shared, involving communication. That is why Dewey said he ought to have avoided misapprehension by speaking of "culture" instead of "experience." To analyze the process of social experience, or communication, therefore, is to exhibit the grounds of objectivity.

This interactive process is most intense when habitual activities are blocked, as they constantly are, by circumstances. The outcome of such a problematic situation must be made determinate in one way or another; we make over ourselves and our worlds as we go along. Fortunately, problematic situations are not isolated, for we are what our biological and cultural pasts have made us, giving us more or less serviceable instruments of all sorts, from organs literal to organs metaphorical—that is, tools and their uses and the generalized habits of thought and action called sciences and arts. This equipment, shared to an increasing degree as we deal with people in situations like or overlapping our own, is one of the conditions of objectivity.

In the second place, as I said, the situation is going to turn out some way. What we do or don't do will in any case be a determinant of it and of the endless consequences that follow. Responsibility is

not to be evaded; in this world there are no spectators; our "engage-
ment" is complete. (My slipping into the language of moral responsibility was also, I think, not to be avoided, as I shall explain.) Action
then is required to solve a problem; and action in this generic sense
may be differentiated into the more special activities which make up
experience on the human scale. Still, it is fair to say that, as the
maxim or rule of action is the principle which structures experience, so the focus of the problem of objectivity will be upon the
objectivity of these rules of action.

We are, then, faced with a problematic situation. The first order
of business is to determine what its elements are; and these are
both in us and external to us. That is, as we were saying when Hume
was under examination, we must be apprized of the "facts" and we
must search our souls, discovering further facts about our motivations and commitments. This much is a search for knowledge, if
you like, and no doubt sentiment too may respond with a communicable feeling of approbation or disgust. But these are here only
the elements, not the solution, of the problem. The question is,
What to do? Well, first we *think*. (That is a word, by the way, which
I have not needed to use so far in this paper except as a sign of
opinion—"I think." Its appearance now is significant.)

Sometimes thinking requires little more than an act of subsump-
tion, a recognition of the situation as being of a kind resolvable by
familiar concepts; and it should be noted that a concept here—as
for Kant but with a difference—is a rule which unifies a manifold:
in this case a rule embodied in some available habit or institution.
But on other occasions the situation is more radically problematic,
in which case thinking must be correspondingly more reflective.
That is to say, again borrowing from Kant, in a reflective judgment
we need to find a rule that will tie antecedents and consequents
together in a realizable whole.

From here inquiry may take on either of two emphases. If the
tendencies of the external situation are uncertain, inquiry becomes
predominantly theoretic or scientific, devising and testing alternative
hypotheses and often developing a derivative interest in laying up
treasures for future exploitation. But if the fault is in ourselves, a
disorientation of drives and habits, calling for a redirection of character and attitude, then thinking is primarily deliberative and the
problem is proportionately moral. And the moral, like the theoretic

interest, is capable of indefinite expansion. For our ends in view—
the movable targets at which we aim the maxims that regulate current activity—may comprehend the purposes of others according
to the idea of a moral community.

Finally, though all these strands of reflective experience are
intertwined, concepts or hypotheses or rules of procedure (they
are here all one) need to be tested in operation. Should they fail
there is in that respect no warranted cognitive judgment, no moral
expansion of the self, no achievement of value. We try again. If
we succeed, the confused and capricious situation will have been
put in order with the guidance of articulate thought. Thought and
its object having been brought into conformity with each other,
assertions will be truly warranted. The agent, having new understanding and command of himself and his activities in accordance
with a rational principle, will have increased in virtue; and survey-
ing the "consummatory" phase of his activities in the reorganized
situation, he will realize its aesthetic values, even as the Lord rested
after his labors and saw that they were good.

Objectivity in this analysis is not determined by antecedent realities or by the fabric of the human make; for antecedent realities are
never objects of thought in the present sense of "object" and
"thought," and the "human make" is always remaking itself in the
respects immediately relevant to action and appraisal. Objectivity
is a function of communication, and we communicate in virtue of
our common history, giving us a common equipment for facing the
present. We communicate further by engaging in common action
according to common procedures for resolving common problems.
And we communicate, finally, by sharing meanings and values realized in the experience of the community.

Toward the end of *The Public and Its Problems,* Dewey tells of
a remark by an old Yankee neighbor:

"Someday these things will be found out, and not only found out, but
they will be known." The schools may suppose that a thing is known
when it is found out. My old friend was aware that a thing is fully
known only when it is published, shared, socially accessible. . . . Knowledge cooped up in a private consciousness is a myth.

Interpreted, this fable comes to this: There are no objective problems, therefore no objective judgments, until people already asso-

ciated by nature and history become aware of their common involvement in conditions which call for control. Although several projected
measures may have been "found out" or "thought up" which, their
authors opine, will solve a problem, none have any objective status
until they are known—that is, until they are communicated and
tested in action by the relevant public. Similar considerations apply,
adjusted to the appropriate circumstances, in the worlds of science
and the arts as well as in society at large. In each case the relevant
communicants may, as problems vary, make up a larger or a more
exclusive circle. Moreover art, as the special activity or aspect of
activity that embodies meanings and values in forms available to
their publics, is the prime instrument of social experience or communication. Art in this sense includes, of course, "the incomparable
Mr. Newton's" demonstrations as well as the King James Bible,
"The Midnight Ride of Paul Revere," and the World's Series. But
in the end all the sciences and arts are subject to architectonic
principles of moral choice and practice; and the chief problem about
the moral community, Dewey insists, is intellectual.

So Dewey, even as Hume before him, was untroubled by any
special difficulties about the objectivity of value judgments. Infinitely
more dubious—in fact mythical—were the merely theoretic truths of
the spectator theory. But his critics, persisting in the assumption
that he meant what they did by "empirical science," kept wondering
how he could answer such questions as whether *Oedipus Rex* is a
greater tragedy than the *Death of a Salesman* by the "scientific
method," and if so, how he could avoid the naturalistic fallacy. The
answer is simple. There is no kind of question about which he could
care less, unless it might be some casuistical puzzle invented by a
moral intuitionist. These questions are not fit for a sensible man's
attention. They are strictly meaningless, having no foundation in
a problem but only in the debating topics of the schools. However,
if you wondered which of these plays you should advise your children to read, why then, having a determinate problem, you might
find a reasonable answer also.

5.

By this time we have watched something loosely called "the
problem" of objectivity transform itself, like Proteus, through three

forms. According to the first, all serious claims turn upon the establishment of a cognitive relation to an object—assuming that the requisite objects can be found. If there are values—as of course there are—how "are" they? It is hard to say. In the second place, we can look at every issue as if it were to be settled by being referred to the responses of an impartial judge: and it seems that Hume's philosopher is a connoisseur, meeting whatever experience presents to his view with appropriate dispositions and sentiments. But are the "calm passions" which he sought at the base of all judgments in fact "common to all mankind"? And are they perhaps in turn subject to some intellectual regulation? Dewey, finally, moralizes everything. Science and the arts acquire objective significance as ingredients of the active life, that is, of experience conceived as active thought determining us to thoughtful action. Some speculations, he keeps insisting, it is frivolous if not wicked to entertain. But while we may concede potential practical relevance to all issues, does it follow that this is their sole source of objective significance?

Considering separately the standpoints of verifiable knowledge, intelligent action, and critical appraisal, I think that each does bear at some point upon every occasion that calls for judgment. And taking them together, we see that, rather than marking off three exclusive classes of subject matter, they each have something to contribute to every subject matter. Thus scientific inquiry, as we are constantly being reminded, requires of every inquirer not only a stock of information but also the spirit and habit of impartial or "objective" judgment, together with a good deal of practical "know-how" about the means of discovery and the controlled validation of hypotheses. Similarly, the qualities of the good man must include more than obedience to a code; he must know and understand his world, as well as having a critical appreciation of the values it makes available to him. And the good life, whether for men individually or in civil society, would be mutilated without both achievement in and appreciation of the sciences and arts.

But all this overlapping, which we recognize, should not confuse us about differences in the specific questions that may range over the same materials. It is, therefore, at this point that I must differ with each of the theories which we have been considering—not differing with them because of the various bases of objectivity which they recognize and exploit, but because they push each beyond the limits of its capacity. There are, I should think, at least three interrelated problems of objectivity, not just one, and if it is the business of philosophy to distinguish questions and to direct inquiries along negotiable paths, why then each of these theories, despite its truths and virtues, is philosophically deficient to the extent that it treats what is different as the same.

That there is a place for good taste in all things, in science and human intercourse as well as in appreciating the beauties of nature and art; that good taste usually goes with good morals; and that judgments of taste are communicable among the cultivated and the informed, I entirely agree with Hume. And I should agree that the principles of taste, though identifiable and sharable, are not themselves cognitions, whether they be natural tendencies of sentiment or whether, as for Kant, they rest upon the noncognitive interplay of all the cognitive powers. But to treat questions of scientific truth as being like those of taste is to fail to exploit one's available resources. Knowledge is relative to its object as well as depending upon the impartial objectivity of the inquirer. And when one's problem is practical the objectivity of the agent is again insufficient, but so too is an appeal to any existing states of affairs; for now one's "object" is something to be realized, either as an activity or as what is to be brought about by means of activity, so that now the conception is independent of and prior to its realization and, together with what one knows of the circumstances, determines the rules that guide action.

Since what used to be called practical reason has recently been under suspicion, I think we owe much to Dewey for showing how intellectually formulable rules may have an objective role in determining what choice is morally or technically right without thereby reducing practical problems to questions of simple knowledge. But I should think that, while all problems have more or less practical and even moral relevance, as he has reminded us, they need not all be practical problems in any literal sense. Dewey does, also, illuminate the place of art and the "consummatory phase" of experience among the other forms of cultural activity; but may not more be said about what is peculiar to it as art? But nevertheless conformity to an antecedently given object does seem to make sense when we are engaged in a theoretic investigation of nature, in spite of Dewey's strictures about the "spectator theory."

It should be evident, then, that I think objectivity and an ontological reference go together when we ask, What can I know? But what I should do is only metaphorically among the things that I may discover, and to deliberate is in no proper sense to inquire about what there is, even though it may incidentally require that I do so, lest my deliberations suffer from the shortcomings characteristic of the superstitious and the ignorant. Knowledge is something of which none of us ever has too much, but it does not of itself settle questions of right or of value—which are not literally cognitive questions.

The precise formulation of the needed distinctions is not now my main concern. I can think of several versions which might serve as a beginning. Aristotle, for example, speaks of the *logos,* or intelligible structure, that we discover in natural things; of the *logos,* or rational rule, which guides choice and is embodied in institutions and in the dispositions which are the virtues of thought and character; and of the *logos,* or form, which we construct and enjoy in a work of art. And Kant, in slightly different fashion, explains that to know is to determine the concept of an object given in experience; to act, whether morally or technically, is to bring one's performance or its product into conformity with a concept; while in the reflective judgment concepts do not determine anything, but have a regulative or suggestive role.

Such schematic distinctions, as I have said, might serve as points of departure for further reflection, and indeed I have so employed them in this essay. But quite apart from that, I have principally tried to expand understanding and discussion of the possible grounds of our presumptively objective claims by developing the possibilities of two alternatives which do not regard objectivity as coextensive with cognition.

WARNER A. WICK
University of Chicago

James Bissett Pratt:
A Biographical Sketch*

James Bissett Pratt was born in Elmira, New York, on June 22, 1875. His father, Daniel R. Pratt, though also born and raised in New York State, was descended from a long line of New England ancestors. For many years the father was a very successful banker and investor, an important public figure in Elmira, then a town of 30,000 people. Dan Pratt, as he was known, was president of the bank, director of various companies, builder of a large business block which housed both the bank and the opera house, trustee of Elmira Female College, and a trustee of the Presbyterian Church. In the late 1880's an unfortunate series of investments resulted in a financial calamity, and Dan Pratt was obliged to give up his bank and sell the palatial brick house in which young James had been born. But he was able, with the help of friends, to start a building-loan association from which enough was earned to support the family, send James to college, and contribute regularly to the church.

James's mother, born Katherine Murdoch, was the daughter of a Presbyterian minister who had left his native Scotland to help evangelize Canada. After five years in Canada, he took his family to New York State, eventually settling, in 1850, in Elmira where, after a number of controversies with certain elders of the church, he founded the "Second Presbyterian Church" (still known today as "Dr. Murdoch's Church"). Katherine Murdoch was the second wife of Daniel Pratt, the first having been Katherine's younger sister, Isabella, who died a year after the birth of her fourth child. By his own testimony, the most important single influence upon young James Pratt was that of his mother. They were extremely

* All quotations attributed to Professor Pratt in this sketch are taken from an un-published "letter" written to his two children not long before his death.

close to each other in temperament and interests, and from the mother the son inherited his intense love of literature and concern for religion. James's mother enjoyed, indeed insisted upon, discussing religious topics and reading aloud her favorite authors with her professorial son until the very last days of her life.

Another boyhood influence was James's favorite uncle and his mother's favorite brother, the man for whom James was named. He was James Bissett Murdoch, a distinguished physician, Dean of the Medical School of the University of Pittsburgh, and one-time president of the American Medical Association. His frequent visits were always jolly ones, and the companionship and understanding he provided his youthful nephew were always gratefully remembered. Many years later James Pratt observed that his uncle James Murdoch and his teacher and friend William James reminded him of each other; no one else he encountered quite possessed the same charm and vigor of personality that distinguished those two men.

In 1893 James graduated, as valedictorian, at the age of eighteen, from the Elmira Free Academy. He and his mother had planned for him to attend Princeton. "So far as I can recall, the chief reason for choosing Princeton was that my mother was thoroughly averse to my going to Yale." But a close friend of the family, Dr. Isaac Jennings, a Presbyterian minister in Elmira and an alumnus of Williams College, persuaded Dan Pratt to send his son to Williams. "So in September, 1893, Mother and I started out on my new adventure: the Erie to Binghamton, the D and H to Albany (where we had time to visit the new capital), and then, on the Fitchburg Railroad, an invasion of New England. The thought that I was actually going to be in New England had produced in my mind a kind of awful thrill. New England, where Emerson and Longfellow, Hawthorne, Lowell and Webster lived; where the Pilgrims had first landed and where American Liberty had been born; and where also (though this produced only a minor part of the thrill) my father's family had lived since 1631. And for once, the realization was better than the anticipation. To my young eyes . . . the 'mountains' around Williamstown, three times as high as our Elmira hills, opened up a vision of beauty—a vision which even now, as I approach threescore years and ten, had never lost its wonder. The college campus, too, made at once a deep impression on me; and the occasional glimpses (as Mother and I walked about) of the reverend and learned professors who taught the wonderful courses described in the catalogue whetted my eagerness to drink at this famous font of scholarship." But James suddenly became ill with a fever, believed then to be typhoid, and was so long in recovering that he was prevented from entering Williams until the following year.

Two of Pratt's main interests—philosophy and hiking—were developed during his undergraduate days. He came to know the Berkshire hills perhaps as thoroughly as one could, and when he returned to Williams as a faculty member he continued to tramp up and down the surrounding mountains until 1938. In that year a blood clot tragically necessitated the amputation of a leg, thus ending one of his favorite hobbies. His being drawn to philosophy was the work of Professor John E. Russell, teacher of philosophy and religion. Russell was a distinguished scholar who, besides publishing several books, engaged in a remembered controversy with the Oxford pragmatist F. S. C. Schiller, in the *Journal of Philosophy*. Pratt was to be Russell's colleague for twelve years until the older man's death in 1917. Besides Russell, the teachers whose influence Pratt especially felt were President Carter and Professors Bascom, Rice, Wild, Goodrich, Peck, and Mather (names familiar to older alumni of Williams College as well as to younger ones who recognize here the source of the names of some of the college houses).

The yearbook of the Class of '98, dedicated to Professor Russell, shows that Pratt received numerous academic and college honors and was held in high regard by the entire college community. In his sophomore year, for example, he took first prizes in Latin, Greek, and Mathematics. He held a major scholarship in his sophomore and junior years, was elected to Phi Beta Kappa and to Gargoyle (select senior society), and was president of the Philosophical Society. The same yearbook also records that in answer to the questions, Why did you come to Williams, What is your favorite novel, and What is your favorite girls' college, Pratt's answers were, respectively, My father knew a good thing, *Les Misérables*, and Elmira College. In 1898 Pratt graduated, as valedictorian, in a class of fifty-nine. The class included sixteen who were twenty-four or older, four who were twenty-seven, and one who was twenty-eight. There were three who were the youngest at twenty; Pratt was twenty-three, approximately the average age of the class. As of this moment, there are fourteen surviving members of the class of '98.

Pratt then entered the Harvard Graduate School to study philosophy under James, Royce, Palmer, Münsterberg, and Santayana. While naturally impressed by this galaxy of thinkers and teachers, he was also confused and somewhat discouraged by the constant arguments and disagreements among his mentors. "To hear James and Royce contradict each other in successive hours, and to be further confused by what the other powerful thinkers had to offer, was too much for me." Consequently, Pratt decided to abandon philosophy, and the following year, in accordance with his father's long-standing desire, entered the Columbia Law School. But he found the study of law intolerably dull, and after his year at Columbia he returned to Elmira to teach Latin for two years at the Elmira Free Academy. He had now decided to return to philosophy, and the Elmira assignment was taken on in order to acquire funds for an anticipated year's study in Berlin.

The year 1902–1903 was spent in Berlin where one of his fellow students was William Ernest Hocking. In general, Pratt was disappointed by his German professors, with the exception of Otto Pfleiderer and his course in the philosophy of religion. He later ranked Pfleiderer with James and Royce as a major influence upon his own development. In the spring of 1903 Pratt traveled extensively for several months—Constantinople, Beirut, Damascus, Jerusalem, Egypt, Greece, Italy, Spain, Austria, Hungary, Germany, and Belgium. This was the first of many journeys to all parts of the world. Finally, after four years away, he returned to Harvard, and in June, 1905, received his doctor's degree in philosophy.

Despite his published differences (notably, *What is Pragmatism?* in 1907) with William James's pragmatism, Pratt never wavered in his affection for his former teacher. He had written his doctoral thesis, in the psychology of religion, under James's guidance, and was therefore often invited to his professor's home for consultation and "the evening meal." Pratt once wrote, "A memory picture which I hope will never be erased, is of James, sitting in his great study, all four walls covered with books to the ceiling, and his adoring setter and adoring me, sitting at his feet, as he talked and we listened." James's interest in the subject of religious consciousness was of considerable inspiration and help to Pratt, and is reflected in his first book, *The Psychology of Religious Belief,* in 1907, as well as in his later, more famous work *The Religious Consciousness* (to which, said Pratt, he gave more time and thought than to any of his other books).

Possibly, however, the most important result of Pratt's association with James was his eventual inability to subscribe to the monistic idealism of Royce and Palmer. The "earthiness" of James's own approach to philosophy finally made it impossible for Pratt to keep trying to validate in his own mind the idealistic philosophy that seemed more friendly than pragmatism, for example, to his deeply rooted religious concerns. Unable to accept the position of Dewey and James, but equally unable, largely because of the impact made upon him by James's opposition to it, to accept idealism either, Pratt was compelled to search on his own for an epistemology compatible with his metaphysical and religious convictions. The 1916 meetings of the American Philosophical Association marked a significant turning point in this search, for it was here that a small group of philosophers, including Pratt, initiated a movement that culminated in 1920 with the publication of *Essays in Critical Realism*—a famous moment in American philosophy. There was, however, not much agreement among the Critical Realists upon what Pratt considered to be the most important, the "ultimate" issues, so he continued on his own, publishing in 1922 *Matter and Spirit.* Here he attempted to establish the ontological status of the mental, and thus refute any form of naturalism. It laid the groundwork for the position he finally arrived at and detailed in his *Personal Realism,* which appeared in 1937. This was thirty-two years after his return to Williams as an instructor in philosophy.

Until 1911 Pratt lived a bachelor's existence, residing with the other single members of the faculty at the Faculty Club, or "Monastery" as it was generally called. During those years "Jim" Pratt, as he was known to his colleagues, did much of his thinking and conversing while tramping the hills covering portions of Massachusetts, Vermont, and New York State. It was to resume his favorite hobby of undergraduate days, and he seemed to feel an almost mystical identification with the mountains. When he and his wife later built their home in 1917 on the college campus, it was deliberately placed looking toward the north where their favorite eminence,

"The Dome," was ever in view. These were the quiet years of preparing classes and pondering possible lines of philosophical commitment. "Except for the publication of two books, and a hurried trip to Italy in the summer of 1909, nothing of importance happened to me until my Father's death in the Spring of 1910, and my meeting with Zia in the following August."

In recounting the major influences shaping his life and thought, Alfred North Whitehead made special mention of his wife, remarking that her contributions to his manner of conceiving things were so fundamental that it was necessary to list her as a primary factor in his philosophical output. In the unpublished "letter" previously referred to, James Pratt makes a similar moving testimony to the indispensable role that his wife played in all aspects of his life. Theirs was a remarkable storybook relationship of mutual love and dedication, and it seems genuinely impossible to exaggerate the amount of carry-over of the thought and character of Mrs. Pratt to that of her husband during their thirty-three years of marriage.

They met in the summer of 1910 in Chicago. Pratt was visiting a former Williams classmate who had married an Italian girl. She had a younger sister, Catherine Mariotti (to be known later by her husband and friends affectionately as "Zia," the Italian for "aunt"), who was making her second transatlantic visit with American relatives. Her intent was to return to Italy and to fulfill her ambition of becoming a nun (a plan which her family hoped always to discourage). Catherine Mariotti's mother was an American girl, born Melanie Durfee, who had gone to Germany to study piano. She became ill, and was advised to rest in Italy, and it was in Florence that she fell in love and decided to live the remainder of her life in her husband's native land. Coincidentally, since her brother, Charles Durfee, had been a student at Williams College, Melanie had visited and remembered the campus which her daughter was to make a permanent home as the wife of a professor of philosophy. Catherine Mariotti's father was an important official in the royal household of King Humbert. He was later to be appointed Director of the Royal Houses in Milan and Monza, and after that in Genoa and Palermo.

Catherine Mariotti and James Pratt saw each other every day for ten days in Chicago. Plans were made for Catherine and her aunt to visit Williamstown in the autumn, and Pratt left Chicago with that prospect uppermost in his mind. Shortly thereafter, Catherine, upon receiving word that her mother was seriously ill, was forced to cancel her American visit at once. Pratt was notified, and he made a special point of being at the New York dock to say a short farewell to Catherine before she sailed for Italy. A month later, in October, 1910, he mailed a proposal of marriage. He did not have to wait long for the letter of acceptance. The following summer he went to Milan, and on the 5th of August, 1911, in the chapel of the royal palace Catherine Mariotti and James Pratt were married.

From the outset they reciprocated each other's religious convictions and sentiments. That one had been raised a Roman Catholic and the other a Presbyterian was of small moment. Though Professor Pratt originally offered to raise their children as Catholics, the eventual parental decision was to send their two children, Edith and David, to the Episcopal Church. Mrs. Pratt has always remained a devout Catholic, attending early Mass every Sunday at the French Church in Williamstown. At the same time she cherished their trips, during sabbaticals, to India and the Orient, and the opportunity to learn with her husband, at firsthand, the different ways of Buddhism. From these trips came his widely consulted *India and Its Faiths* (1915) and *The Pilgrimage of Buddhism* (1928), as did much of the material for his course in the history of religions given over the years at Williams. (His interest in the history of religions, especially the religions of India, had been awakened in his freshman year at Harvard by Charles Carroll Everett—a man for whom he retained an abiding affection.) Mrs. Pratt was ever disposed to be impressed more by the parallels than by the dissimilarities between different religions, and she now laughingly recalls that, whenever the attempt was made to ascertain Professor Pratt's denominational allegiance, he would reply, "I belong to the church of Jesus Christ at Williams College." This was in reference to the fact that he regularly attended Sunday services at the college chapel, as well as suggesting that he wished his own devoutness to be taken as transcending usual methods of classification.

When the Pratts were not traveling about the world during sabbaticals and college vacations, they were—when writing and teaching duties permitted—"at home" to virtually the whole of Williams College and surrounding Williamstown besides. They stayed at home every Sunday afternoon from four to six, for thirty years, having spread the word that any Williams student could drop in during those hours for tea, tobacco, and talk. The Pratts were renowned for the generosity and elegant simplicity of their hospitality and entertainment, and even today one fortunate enough to be Mrs. Pratt's dinner guest has no trouble in picturing the cordial, merry occasions once typical of the Pratt household. Though her English was generally excellent, Mrs. Pratt was somewhat prone to confound the order of words in certain phrases, and very often caused her husband and guests great amusement by speaking of "a button-shoe," "a wild chase-goose," or "a blue-sky ribbon." People she found dull were apt to be called "drum-drum," and she was always pleased when a notorious bluffer was compelled "to pass the bucket."

Meanwhile, Professor Pratt's writings, professional accomplishments, and honors steadily accumulated. In 1923–1924 he taught at the Chinese Christian University in Peking and in 1931–1932 was visiting lecturer in Rabindranath Tagore's School at Santiniketan, India. As a glance at his bibliography will reveal, he was constantly busy with articles and books. These brought him offers from other institutions, including one from Harvard in 1928. When he decided to remain at Williams, a few of his faculty colleagues and hiking companions gave a small dinner in celebration of his choice, one which he had to remake several times subsequently. In 1934–1935 he was elected president of the American Theological Society and also received honorary degrees from Amherst and Wesleyan. The next year he was elected president of the Eastern Division of the American Philosophical Association. In 1940 he was awarded the Rogerson medal by Williams College for service, loyalty, and achievement by an alumnus of outstanding merit. Upon his retirement in 1943 his alma mater again expressed its appreciation by conferring on him the honorary degree of Doctor of Letters. On this occasion he was cited by President James P. Baxter, III, as "the ideal Williams professor—who by his incomparable teaching and by his example made philosophy a living force in the lives of countless students and faith stronger in the hearts of all who knew him well." Thus concluded an official relationship with the institution which had welcomed him as a freshman a half-century minus one year earlier.

When James Bissett Pratt, Mark Hopkins Professor of Intellectual and Moral Philosophy, died on January 15, 1944, and was buried in the college cemetery near the graves of former hiking companions and that of his teacher, John Russell, the Williams College community lost one of its most distinguished members in its long history. The final years had been difficult ones, but cheerfully accepted nevertheless. After the operation at Albany Hospital in March of 1938, resulting in the amputation of his leg above the knee, Professor Pratt, aided and nursed by his wife, resumed his classes within the space of a single month! He met classes in his living room, seated at a card table with a purple robe draped over his knees. His remaining days were subject to intense physical suffering, but he refrained at all times from mentioning the operation or its effects. There were occasional moments when, should a student or guest depart leaving them alone, Professor Pratt said to his wife, "When people are around, there's no pain, but when they leave, it returns." He learned to wear and use an artificial limb and got about with the aid of a cane. When he resumed his classes in Hopkins Hall, he was always accompanied by Mrs. Pratt, who carried his books and wheeled him to the left or right on his cane if an especially difficult turn in the route should be needed. In such manner he was able, until the moment of his retirement, to bring to his students the benefits of experience and learning consonant with his reputation here and abroad as a genuine lover of wisdom.

Gerald E. Myers

Notes

Some Glimpses of James Bissett Pratt (pages 1–8)

[1] R. B. Perry, *Thought and Character of William James*, II, 202.

The Self: Existence or Substance? (pages 11–25)

[1] James Bissett Pratt, *Personal Realism*, New York, 1937, p. 277.
[2] *Ibid.*, p. 279.
[3] James Bissett Pratt, *Matter and Spirit*, New York, 1922, p. 217.
[4] *Personal Realism*, p. 274
[5] *Ibid.*, p. 275.
[6] *De Civ. Dei*, 9:26, quoted by Cochrane, *Christianity and Classical Culture*, New York, 1944, p. 404.
[7] Martin Heidegger, *The Way Back into the Ground of Metaphysics*, in *Existentialism from Dostoevsky to Sartre*, selected and introduced by Walter Kaufmann, New York, 1956, p. 214.
[8] Karl Jaspers, *The Perennial Scope of Philosophy*, New York, 1949, p. 60.
[9] Martin Heidegger, *An Introduction to Metaphysics*, New Haven, 1959, p. 14.
[10] See *Personal Realism*, p. 9, pp. 353 ff.
[11] Erich Frank, *Philosophical Understanding and Religious Truth*, Oxford University Press, New York, 1945, p. 43.
[12] *Thus Spake Zarathustra*, Chap. 24.
[13] St. Augustine, *Confessions*, 1:i.

An Imputation Theory of Free Will (pages 26–44)

[1] The remainder of the paragraph makes use of information appearing in "Letter from Washington" by Richard H. Rovere in the *New Yorker* magazine of April 19, 1958, pp. 75–82.

Existence—Self—Transcendence (pages 45–65)

[1] Cf. My *Philosophie der Endlichkeit*, pp. 193 ff., 1951, 1960; English edition, *Beyond Existentialism*, Allen and Unwin, London, 1960.
[2] Translator's note: The "one"—*das Man*—is the indefinite subject that acts, not as an individual self, but does what "one" is supposed to do, avoids what "one" does not do, believes what everyone believes, etc.
[3] *Sein und Zeit*, pp. 43, 117, 175, 259, 318. *Platons Lehre von der Wahrheit: Mit einem Brief über den Humanismus*, pp. 67, 70 ff. (1947). *Was ist Metaphysik?* Introduction, p. 14, 1949.

229

[4] Kierkegaard, *Die Krankheit zum Tode,* p. 19; *Philosophische Brocken,* 249 ff.; *Entweder-Oder* 11, 139 ff., ed.: H. Gottsched und Chr. Schrempf, 1921–25.

[5] *Die Beziehungen zwischen dem Ich und dem Unbewussten,* 91, Reicher Verlag, 1928.

[6] For further elaboration cf. my *Der Wertgedanke in der Europäischen Geistesentwicklung* I, on Eckehart, 272 ff., 1932.

[7] I tried to explain this matter further in an article on *Philosophia cordes* (*Der Europäische Mensch,* 37 ff., 1957).

[8] Cf. C. G. Jung: *Seelenprobleme der Gegenwart, Psychologische Abhandlungen,* III, 122 ff., 1931.

[9] Cf. Charlotte Bühler, "Basic Tendencies of Human Life: Self-Realization, 476 ff., 484 ff., in R. Wisser, *Sinn und Sein: Ein philosophisches Symposium,* 1960.

[10] On this problem in general, cf. Heidegger, *Identität und Differenz,* 1957. The self may be preserved meanwhile; indeed it may thereby become "great in essence" (Albertus Magnus, *magnanimitas*).

[11] In the religious sphere, cf. Kierkegaard, *Krankheit zum Tode,* page 10; *Der Begriff der Angst,* pages 36, 93, 100.

Self and Introspection (pages 66–80)

[1] *Personal Realism,* New York, The Macmillan Company, 1937, p. 305.

[2] *Ibid.,* p. 309.

[3] *Ibid.,* pp. 311–312.

[4] Gilbert Ryle, *The Concept of Mind,* London, Hutchinson's University Library, 1949, pp. 195–198.

[5] *Ibid.,* pp. 312–313.

[6] *Ibid.,* pp. 313–314.

[7] *Ibid.,* p. 314 (italics mine).

[8] *Ibid.,* p. 315 (italics mine).

[9] *Ibid.,* p. 275 (italics mine).

[10] Erik H. Erikson, "Ego Development and Historical Change," *Psychological Issues,* New York, International Universities Press, Inc., 1959, Vol. 1, No. 1, p. 23.

[11] E. G. Boring, "Mind and Mechanism," *American Journal of Psychology,* 1946, 59, p. 176 (quoted by C. E. Osgood, *Method and Theory in Experimental Psychology,* Oxford University Press, 1953, p. 647).

[12] G. E. M. Anscombe, *An Introduction to Wittgenstein's Tractatus,* London, Hutchinson University Library, 1959, p. 168.

[13] C. E. Osgood, *Method and Theory in Experimental Psychology,* Oxford University Press, 1953, pp. 647–648.

Comprehending Zen Buddhism (pages 122–126)

[1] The "Ten Ox-Herding Pictures" are allegorical paintings originally done by a Zen master, Kaku-an Shi-en, of the Sung Dynasty. A Zen priest, Shubun, of the fifteenth century, copied Kaku-an's paintings, and these, which are the ones referred to here, may be found reproduced in half-tone plates in Dr. Suzuki's *Manual of Zen Buddhism,* Grove Press, Inc., New York, 1960. Each of the pictures is titled, and as a series they show a boy looking for an ox, finding it, taming and herding it, separated from it, and finally entering "the Market Place" on foot and without the ox. They are delicate, charming creations of considerable aesthetic interest in addition to their symbolic significance for Zen. Notes by the editor are only

intended to give the reader some conception of the appearance of the pictures, without regard to their allegorical meanings.—Editor's note.

[2] *Meister Eckhart,* translation by C. de B. Evans, London, John M. Watkins, 1947, p. 162.

[3] Picture VII is titled "The Ox Forgotten, Leaving the Man Alone." It shows the boy, now without the ox, on his knees with hands together in an attitude of prayer, looking toward the distant mountains with the moon overhead.—Editor's note.

[4] Picture VIII of the series is titled "The Ox and the Man Both Gone out of Sight." For the Western viewer, it is especially arresting and indeed amusing, since it depicts nothing more than an empty circle with a shaded perimeter.—Editor's note.

[5] Picture IX is titled "Returning to the Origin, Back to the Source." This is a partial landscape, showing a craggy tree with exposed, unusual roots dominating the foreground and left portion of the circular painting. The tree is not yet in full bloom, and the boy is still absent.—Editor's note.

[6] Picture X is titled "Entering the Market Place with Bliss-Bestowing Hands." This is a particularly engaging picture. It shows the boy again, with a staff and attached small sack over his shoulder, meeting a fat, bare-bellied jovial man who also carries a staff, with a huge sack attached, over his shoulder. They stand under the craggy tree which is now in bloom and with its roots apparently firm in the soil. The reader is referred to Dr. Suzuki's *Manual of Zen Buddhism* for further comments on this picture as well as the whole series.—Editor's note.

[7] R. B. Blakney's translation, New York, Harper & Brothers, 1941, p. 167.

What Metaphysics Is Good For (pages 127–141)

[1] *The Principles of Science,* Macmillan and Company, Ltd., 1905, pp. 581, 583.

[2] "Discursive entities" are utterables, recognizable each as the same in the various utterances of it. A more detailed account of them may be found in the writer's *Nature, Mind, and Death,* Open Court Publishing Company, 1951, pp. 371–373.

[3] "Freud's Legacy to Human Freedom," p. 115 of Vol. 1, No. 1, Autumn, 1957, of *Perspectives in Biology and Medicine.*

[4] *Introduction to Philosophy,* New York, Henry Holt & Co., 1906, p. 83.

Metaphysics and Empiricism (pages 145–155)

[1] Sometimes these selected items which we may call ideas or sense-data are already present in the world out of which they are chosen. Sometimes they are first brought into existence by acts of transformation of that world. An illustration of the former would be the shape of a track in the snow which means "deer" or "squirrel." An illustration of the latter would be the color of a precipitate which a chemist produces by pouring an acid into his unknown liquid, which color might then mean sulphur. John Dewey made a great deal of the way in which experimenters produce ideas with deliberate intent to solve problems. For logic, the distinction between "natural" and "artificial" ideas or sense-data may be important. But for metaphysics, at least for the metaphysical discussion of this essay, the distinction has, so far as I can see, no importance. And to take constant account of it in the text of this essay would be to complicate every statement needlessly.

[2] For example, take a statement by Bertrand Russell in his essay "Physics and Metaphysics," published in *The Saturday Review of Literature* for May 26, 1928, p. 910: "Causation, like every other traditional notion, appears to be concerned with what happens to things in the mass, not with what happens to them individually."

(One wonders what other "traditional" notions Russell means to dispose of so glibly!) Russell has repeated this position concerning causality often since 1928. And many other members of the school of empiricists have done likewise. Cf. Moritz Schlick in an essay reprinted in Feigl and Sellars, *Readings in Philosophical Analysis* (1949), p. 516. Members of the school of empiricists usually suppose that they are following out the teaching of Hume in regard to causality. But their supposition is, I think, a misunderstanding of Hume. I cannot here deal with historical questions or give an analysis of Hume's thought. But I have reviewed Hume's theory of causality and his relation to subsequent developments of the school of empiricists in *Nature and History* (1950), Lecture II, especially pp. 30–48, and in *Our Philosophical Traditions* (1955), especially pp. 328–344.

3 Dewey made the same point against traditional empiricism which I an seeking to make. For example, "things," he wrote, are connected "with one another, in efficiency, productivity, furthering, hindering, generating, destroying" (*Experience and Nature*, p. 84). Or, as he wrote in the same paragraph, "coercive necessity" is a "self-evident" aspect of experience. And self-evidence is not a matter of deduction by necessary implication from prior premises; it is, rather, "obviousness of presence" in our dealings with the world around us, a world we are intimately involved in before philosophical analysis begins. Dewey was himself conspicuously an empirically-minded thinker. And it was because of his empirical-mindedness that he became as caustic a critic of traditional empiricism as of rationalistic systems of philosophy. He objected to empiricists' conception of experience for several reasons, among which are both of the points I have made above in this essay. Against the narrow views of traditional empiricism, he sought by genuinely empirical observations to direct men's attention once more to the full and rich and complex world which it is the business of philosophers to keep in mind throughout even their most refined analyses.

4 My criticism of the antimetaphysical position of the school of empiricism in modern philosophy can be expressed simply in Aristotelian language. Empiricists, when they say that causality is found only when a particular case of something is viewed as an instance of a general formula, are noting "the formal cause." That aspect of causality is a genuine one. For some logical purposes, and in connection with some types of experimental research, it is the most important aspect. Empiricists usually err, however, in claiming that all other phases of causality are nonsense. They neglect or deny both "the material cause" and, even more emphatically, "the efficient cause." And among the semanticists of the last decade or two (who are a type of empiricists), "the final cause" is overtly and deliberately denied to be more than an idle fancy. The school of empiricism will not recapture any metaphysical wisdom unless and until empiricists can take the larger view of the world we encounter in ancient philosophy instead of remaining in the dialectical confines of a modern tradition.

American Realism: Perspective and Framework (pages 174–200)

1 P. 216.

2 *Contemporary American Philosophy*, Vol. 2, p. 217.

3 "A Temporalistic Realism," *Contemporary American Philosophy*, Vol. 2.

4 *Journal of Philosophy and Phenomenological Research*, 1954, pp. 48–64.

Three Bases of Objectivity (pages 201–217)

1 Charles L. Stevenson, *Ethics and Language*, New Haven: Yale University Press, 1944. The distinction between beliefs and attitudes is fundamental in his attempt to "obtain a general understanding of what constitutes a normative *problem*" (p. 2).

[2] Eliseo Vivas, *The Moral Life and the Ethical Life*, Chicago, The University of Chicago Press, 1950, p. viii.

[3] *Ibid.*, p. 186.

[4] W. H. F. Barnes, "Ethics Without Propositions," Aristotelian Society, Supplementary Vol. XXII, 1948, pp. 26 ff.

[5] *Critique of Judgment*, Sec. 40.

[6] *Enquiry Concerning Human Understanding*, Sec. VIII, Part I, par. 62.

[7] *Enquiry Concerning the Principles of Morals*, Sec. IX, Part I, par. 222.

[8] *Ibid.*, par. 223.

[9] *Op. cit.*, p. 230.

[10] W. V. Quine, "Two Dogmas of Empiricism," *Philosophical Review*, LX (1951), pp. 39 ff. Cf. Morton G. White, "The Analytic and the Synthetic: An Untenable Dualism," in *John Dewey: Philosopher of Science and Freedom* (New York, 1950).

Bibliography of the Works of James B. Pratt

In Chronological Arrangement

"The Ethics of St. Augustine," *International Journal of Ethics*, Vol. XIII, (Jan., 1903), pp. 222–235.

"The Place and Value of the Marginal Region in Psychic Life," *Psychological Review*, Vol. XIII (Jan., 1906), pp. 50–59.

"Types of Religious Belief," *American Journal of Religious Psychology and Education*, Vol. II, No. 1 (March, 1906), pp. 76–94.

The Psychology of Religious Belief, New York, The Macmillan Company; London, The Macmillan Company, Ltd., 1907.

"Truth and Its Verification," *Journal of Philosophy, Psychology, and Scientific Methods*, Vol. IV, No. 12 (June, 1907), pp. 320–324.

"Concerning the Origin of Religion," *American Journal of Religious Psychology and Education*, Vol. II, No. 3 (June, 1907), pp. 257–271.

"On the Philosophy of Socrates," *Open Court*, Vol. XXI, No. 9 (Sept., 1907), pp. 513–522.

"Truth and Ideas," *Journal of Philosophy, Psychology and Scientific Methods*, Vol. V, No. 5 (Feb., 1908), pp. 122–131.

"The Psychology of Religion," *Harvard Theological Review*, Vol. I, No. 4 (Oct., 1908), pp. 435–454.

What Is Pragmatism?, New York, The Macmillan Company, 1909.

"Die Religionspsychologie in den Vereinigten Staaten," *Zeitschrift für Religionspsychologie*, Band. III, Heft 3 (June, 1909), pp. 89–98.

"An Empirical Study of Prayer," *American Journal of Religious Psychology and Education*, Vol. IV, No. 1 (March, 1910), pp. 48–67.

"The Philosophy of the Enlightenment, by J. G. Hibben" (book review), *The Nation*, Vol. 90 (May 19, 1910), pp. 513–514.

"Mysticism in Heathendom and Christendom, by E. Lehman" (book review), *The Nation*, Vol. 91 (Sept. 22, 1910), p. 267.

"A Mistake in Strategy," *American Journal of Theology*, Vol. XIV, No. 4 (Oct., 1910), pp. 572–588.

"The Psychology of Religious Experience, by E. S. Ames" (book review), *The Nation*, Vol. 91 (Dec. 1, 1910), pp. 524–525.

"Studies in Spiritualism, by Amy E. Tanner" (book review), *The Nation,* Vol. 91 (Dec. 8, 1910), p. 554.

"Pragmatism and Its Critics, by Addison Webster Moore" (book review), *The Nation,* Vol. 92 (Jan. 5, 1911), pp. 13–14.

"The History of Ethics Within Organized Christianity, by Thomas Cuming Hall" (book review), *The Nation,* Vol. 92 (Feb. 2, 1911), pp. 118–119.

"Reason and Belief, by Sir Oliver Lodge" (book review), *The Nation,* Vol. 92 (March 2, 1911), pp. 217–218.

"The Alchemy of Thought, by L. P. Jacks" (book review), *The Nation,* Vol. 92 (April 13, 1911), pp. 374–376.

A Japanese translation of *The Psychology of Religious Belief,* 1911.

"Peter's Toothache Once More," *Journal of Philosophy, Psychology and Scientific Methods,* Vol. VIII, No. 15 (July, 1911), pp. 400–403.

"The Newer Spiritualism, by Frank Podmore" (book review), *The Nation* Vol. 93 (Aug. 10, 1911), p. 127.

"The Application of Logic, by Alfred Sidgwick" (book review), *The Nation,* Vol. 93 (Oct. 12, 1911), pp. 341–342.

"Science and Religion in Contemporary Philosophy, by Emile Boutroux, transl. by Jonathan Vield" (book review), *The Nation,* Vol. 94 (Feb. 8, 1912), pp. 141–142.

"The Psychology of the Religious Life, by Georgy Malcolm Stratton" (book review), *The Nation,* Vol. 94 (May 16, 1912), pp. 495–496.

"The Sources of Religious Insight, by Josiah Royce (The Bross Lectures for 1911)" (book review), *The Nation,* Vol. 94 (May 23, 1912), pp. 516–517.

"The Religious Philosophy of William James," *The Hibbert Journal,* Vol. X, No. 1 (Oct., 1912), pp. 225–234.

"Professor Perry's Proofs of Realism," *Journal of Philosophy, Psychology and Scientific Methods,* Vol. IX, No. 21 (Oct., 1912), pp. 573–580.

"The Psychology of Religion," *Journal of Religious Psychology,* Vol. V, No. 4 (Oct., 1912), pp. 383–393.

"Present Philosophical Tendencies, by R. B. Perry" (book review), *The Nation,* Vol. 95 (Sept. 26, 1912), pp. 283–285.

"The Realistic Movement" (reviews of *The World We Live In,* by E. S. Fullerton, and *The New Realism,* by E. B. Holt, W. T. Marvin, W. P. Montague, R. B. Perry, W. B. Pitkin, and E. G. Spaulding), *The Nation,* Vol. 95 (Oct. 17, 1912), pp. 357–358.

"Thy Rod and Thy Staff, by A. C. Benson" (book review), *The Nation,* Vol. 95 (Dec. 5, 1912), p. 539.

"The Meaning of God in Human Experience, by William Ernest Hocking" (book review), *The Nation,* Vol. 95 (Dec. 26, 1912), pp. 613–614.

"The Twelfth Annual Meeting of the American Philosophical Association," *Journal of Philosophy, Psychology and Scientific Methods,* Vol. X, No. 4 (Feb. 13, 1913), pp. 91–95.

"The Subconscious and Religion," *Harvard Theological Review*, Vol. IV, No. 2 (April, 1913), pp. 109–228.

"A Psychological Study of Religion, by J. H. Leuba" (book review), *The Nation*, Vol. 96 (April 3, 1913), pp. 341–342.

"The Interpretation of Religious Experience, by John Watson" (book review), *The Nation*, Vol. 96 (April 10, 1913), p. 364.

"The Autobiography and Life of George Tyrrell" (book review) *The Nation*, Vol. 96 (April 10, 1913), pp. 388–389.

"Winds of Doctrine, by George Santayana" (book review), *The Nation*, Vol. 96 (June 5, 1913), pp. 574–575.

"The Positive Evolution of Religion, by Frederic Harrison" (book review), *The Nation*, Vol. 97 (Aug. 28, 1913), pp. 188–189.

"The Awakening of India," *The Nation*, Vol. 98 (June 11, 1914), pp. 690–691.

"Social Christianity in the Orient, by John E. Clough" (book review), *The Nation*, Vol. 100 (Feb. 18, 1915), pp. 199–200.

"Society and Its Problems" (reviews of *The Gospel Jesus and the Problems of Democracy*, by Henry C. Vedder, *Interpretations and Forecasts*, by Victor Brandford, and *Social Heredity and Social Evolution*, by Herbert William Conn), *The Nation*, Vol. 100 (March 18, 1915), pp. 305–306.

"The Sentimental Teuton" (letter to the editor), *The Nation*, Vol. 100 (April 29, 1915), pp. 467–468.

"Modern Religious Movements in India, by J. N. Farquhar" (book review), *The Nation*, Vol. 100 (June 24, 1915), pp. 713–714.

"The Idealism of War," *Forum*, Vol. 54, No. 4 (Oct., 1915), pp. 392–405.

India and Its Faiths: A Traveler's Record, Boston and New York, Houghton Mifflin Co., 1915.

"Safety First" (letter to the editor), *The Nation*, Vol. 102 (March 16, 1916), pp. 310–311.

"Professor Ladd's Philosophy" (review of *What Can I Know? What Ought I To Do? What Should I Believe? What May I Hope?*, by George Trumbull Ladd), *The Nation*, Vol. 102 (March 16, 1916), pp. 312–313.

"The Elementary Forms of Religious Life, by Emile Durkheim" (book review), *The Nation*, Vol. 103 (July 13, 1916), pp. 39–40.

"New Wars for Old John Haynes Holmes," *The Nation*, Vol. 103 (July 27, 1916), pp. 85–86.

"India Begins To Uplift Herself," *The World-Outlook*, Vol. II (May, 1916), pp. 11–13.

"Mysticism," *The Psychological Bulletin*, Vol. XIII, No. 12 (Dec. 5, 1916), pp. 471–475.

"The Confessions of an Old Realist," *Journal of Philosophy, Psychology and Scientific Methods*, Vol. XIII, No. 25 (Dec., 1916), pp. 687–693.

Democracy and Peace, Boston, R. G. Badger Co., 1916.

"War and the World's Hope" (reviews of *The Free Man and the Soldier*, by R. B. Perry; *Towards an Enduring Peace: A Symposium of Peace Proposals and Programs; The War and the Soul*, by R. J. Campbell; *War, Peace, and The Future*, by Ellen Key; *Questions of War and Peace*, by L. T. Hobhouse), *The Nation*, Vol. 104 (Jan. 11, 1917), pp. 47–48.

"John E. Russell" (letter to the editor), *The Nation*, Vol. 104 (March 15, 1917), p. 312.

"The Psychology of Religion, by George Albert Coe" (book review), *The Nation*, Vol. 104 (March 15, 1917), pp. 315–316.

"Why Men Fight, by Bertrand Russell" (book review), *The Nation*, Vol. 104 (March 29, 1917), pp. 367–368.

"A Defense of Dualistic Realism," *Journal of Philosophy, Psychology and Scientific Methods*, Vol. XIV, No. 10 (May, 1917), pp. 253–261.

"The Nature of Peace, by Thorstein Veblen" (book review), *The Nation*, Vol. 105 (July 5, 1917), pp. 14–15.

"What the Reformers Are About," *The World-Outlook*, Vol. III (August, 1917), pp. 14–17.

"The Idea of God in the Light of Recent Philosophy, by H. Seth Pringle-Pattison, Gifford Lectures for 1912–13" (review), *The Nation*, Vol. 105 (Oct. 25, 1917), pp. 457–458.

"Professor Spaulding's Non-Existent Illusions," *Journal of Philosophy, Psychology and Scientific Methods*, Vol. XV, No. 25 (Dec., 1918), pp. 688–695.

"Again What Is Christianity?", *The Hibbert Journal*, Vol. XVII, No. 2 (Jan., 1919), pp. 242–247.

"The Problems of Eastern Europe," *North American Review*, Vol. CCIX (April, 1919), pp. 482–489.

"Some Psychological Aspects of the Belief in Immortality," *Harvard Theological Review*, Vol. XII, No. 3 (July, 1919), pp. 294–314.

"Realism and Perception," *Journal of Philosophy, Psychology and Scientific Methods*, Vol. XVI, No. 22 (Oct., 1919), pp. 596–603.

"Can Theology Become an Empirical Science?", *American Journal of Theology*, Vol. XXIV, No. 2 (April, 1920), pp. 180–190.

The Religious Consciousness: A Psychological Study, New York, The Macmillan Company, 1920.

"Critical Realism and the Possibility of Knowledge," in *Essays in Critical Realism*, London, The Macmillan Company, Ltd., 1920.

"Why Do Religions Die?", *Journal of Religion*, Vol. 1, No. 1 (Jan., 1921), pp. 76–78.

"The Historical Study of Religions," in *Theological Studies Today* (address delivered at the 75th anniversary of the Meadville Theological School, June 1–3, 1920); Chicago, Illinois, University of Chicago Press, 1921, pp. 1–24.

"Fear in Religion"; "Psychical Research"; "The Psychology of Religion"; "Suggestion," *The Dictionary of Religion and Ethics*, edited by Shailer

Mathews and Gerald B. Smith, New York, The Macmillan Company, 1921, pp. 165, 357, 358, 429.

"The New Materialism," *Journal of Philosophy*, Vol. XIX, No. 13 (June 22, 1922), pp. 337–351.

Matter and Spirit, New York, The Macmillan Company, 1922.

"Behaviorism and Consciousness," *Journal of Philosophy*, Vol. XIX, No. 22 (Oct. 26, 1922), pp. 596–604.

"Mahaban and Sri Krishna," *Asia*, Vol. XXII, No. 12 (Dec. 1922), pp. 990–993.

"Religion and the Younger Generation," *The Yale Review*, Vol. XII, No. 3 (April, 1923), pp. 594–619.

"Mr. Moore's Realism," *Journal of Philosophy*, Vol. XX, No. 14 (July 5, 1923), pp. 378–384.

"Natural Religion; Consciousness and Its Implications," *Harvard Theological Review*, Vol. XIV, No. 4 (Oct., 1923), pp. 287–304. (Reprinted with revisions in *Religious Realism*, edited by D. C. Macintosh, New York, The Macmillan Company, 1931.)

The Nature of Christianity (pamphlet-address), Peking, The Peking Union Medical College, 1924.

"A Report on the Present Conditions of Buddhism," *Chinese Social and Political Science Review* (Peking), Vol. VIII (July, 1924).

"Essential Values for Religious Liberals," *The Christian Register*, Vol. 105 (May 6, 1926), p. 417.

"Objective and Subjective Worship," *Religionspsychologie* (Veroffentlichungen des Religionspsychologischen Forschung-Institute, Wien, 1926), Vol. I.

"Remarks at the Ephraim Williams Smoker," *Williams Alumni Review*, April, 1927, pp. 269–272.

"The Unity of Buddhism," *The Eastern Buddhist*, Vol. IV (Sept., 1927), pp. 122–144.

"Difficulties for Religion in an Age of Science," *Religious Education*, Vol. XXIII (April, 1928), pp. 284–288.

The Pilgrimage of Buddhism and a Buddhist Pilgrimage, New York, The Macmillan Company, 1928.

"The Place of the Four Noble Truths in Indian Buddhism," *The Maha-Bodi*, Vol. XXXVIII, No. 2 (Jan., 1929), pp. 3–5.

"Personal Realism," *Contemporary American Philosophy*, edited by George P. Adams and William Pepperell Montague, London, George Allen and Unwin, Ltd.; New York, The Macmillan Company, 1930, Vol. II, pp. 213–222.

Adventures in Philosophy and Religion, New York, The Macmillan Company, 1931.

"Buddhism and Christianity," *The Visva-Bharati*, Bulletin No. 16, Vol. 16 (March, 1932), pp. 1–20.

"Is Idealism Realism?", *Journal of Philosophy*, Vol. XXX, No. 7 (March 30, 1933), pp. 169–178.

"Recent Developments in Indian Thought," *Journal of Philosophy,* Vol. XXX, No. 19 (Sept. 14, 1933), pp. 505–517.

"What Is Speculative Idealism?", *Journal of Philosophy,* Vol. XXX, No. 25 (Dec. 7, 1933), pp. 673–683.

"Buddhism and Scientific Thinking," *Journal of Religion,* Vol. XIV, No. 1 (Jan., 1934), pp. 13–24.

"Once More Unto the Breach!", *Journal of Philosophy,* Vol. XXXI, No. 8 (April 12, 1934), pp. 199–215.

"Logical Positivism and Professor Lewis," *Journal of Philosophy,* Vol. XXXI, No. 26 (Dec. 20, 1934), pp. 701–710.

"Buddhism and Inter-Cultural Contacts," *Modern Trends in World Religion,* edited by Eustace Haydon, Chicago, Ill., University of Chicago Press, 1934, pp. 34–45.

"Ramakrishna's Attitude Toward the Absolute and Finite God," *The Prabuddha Bharata,* Feb., 1936, pp. 118–120.

"What Was Ramakrishna's Power?", *The Vedanta Kesari,* Vol. XXII, No. 10 (Feb., 1936), pp. 392–394.

"The Present Status of the Mind-Body Problem," *Philosophical Review,* Vol. XLV, No. 2 (March, 1936), pp. 144–166.

"The Function of Religion in Modern Life," *The Hibbert Journal,* Vol. XXXIV, No. 3 (April, 1936), pp. 418–429.

"Liberal Religion and the Function of Unitarianism," *Unitarians Face a New Age,* Boston, American Unitarian Association, 1936, pp. 53–60.

"Sincerity and Symbolism," *Christendom,* Vol. I, No. 3 (Spring, 1936), pp. 488–497.

"The Thought and Character of William James, by R. B. Perry" (book review), *The New England Quarterly,* Vol. IX, No. 2 (June, 1936), pp. 317–324.

"God and the Moral Law," *Harvard Theological Review,* Vol. XXIX, No. 3 (July, 1936), pp. 153–170.

Personal Realism, New York, The Macmillan Company, 1937.

"What Can Christians Learn from Buddhism?", *Visva Bharati Quarterly,* Feb., 1937, pp. 49–68.

"Books on Buddhism" (reviews), *Review of Religion,* Vol. I, No. 30 (March, 1937), pp. 279–286.

"The Transiency of Humanism," *The University Review* (University of Kansas City), Vol. III, No. 4 (Summer, 1937), pp. 245–246.

"Descartes and the Psychological Problem," *Travaux du IXᵉ Congress International de Philosophie,* Paris, 1937, Vol. I, pp. 167–172.

"The Twenty-five Hundredth Anniversary of Buddha," *Christendom,* Vol. III, No. 3 (Summer, 1938), pp. 392–401.

"Universalism in Religion," *The Prabuddha Bharata,* Jan., 1939.

Naturalism, New Haven, Yale University Press; London, Oxford University Press, 1939.

"Concerning Empirical Philosophy," *Journal of Philosophy,* Vol. XXXVI, No. 10 (May 11, 1939), pp. 269–271.

"Why Religion Lives," *The Personalist,* Vol. XXI, No. 4 (Autumn, 1940), pp. 352–373.

"Why Religions Die," *University of California Publications in Philosophy,* Berkeley and Los Angeles, Calif., University of California Press, Vol. XVI, No. 5 (1940), pp. 95–124.

"Notes on the Use of Christian Words," *Journal of Religion,* Vol. XXI, No. 1 (Jan., 1941), pp. 48–50.

"Reply to Professor Moore," *Journal of Philosophy,* Vol. XXXVIII, No. 3 (Jan., 1941), pp. 78–80.

Can We Keep the Faith? New Haven, Yale University Press; London, Oxford University Press, 1941.

"Therefore Fight, Arjun," *Vedanta Kesari,* Vol. XXVII, No. 12 (April, 1941), pp. 442–443.

"The Implications of Self-Hood" (Ingersoll Lecture for 1939–1940), *Harvard Divinity School Bulletin, 1040–41,* Cambridge, Harvard University Press, 1941, pp. 5–18.

"The Nature of Value," *Science, Philosophy and Religion, Third Symposium,* New York, Conference on Science, Philosophy and Religion in their Relation to the Democratic Life, Inc., 1942, pp. 85–95. (Also, Pratt's comments on other articles by E. S. Brightman, pp. 9–10; Richard Kroner, pp. 55–58; H. N. Russell, pp. 114–116.)

"Three Trends in the Philosophy of Religion" (address at the 75th anniversary of the Episcopal Theological School, May 13, 1942), published in *The Anglican Theological Review,* Vol. 24, No. 4 (Oct., 1942), pp. 289–306.

"The New Supernaturalism: Peril to 20th Century Christianity" (selected from *Can We Keep the Faith?*), *Religious Liberals Reply,* Boston, Beacon Press, 1947, pp. 96–147.

Reason in the Art of Living, a Textbook of Ethics, New York, The Macmillan Company, 1949.

Eternal Values in Religion, New York, The Macmillan Company, 1950.

DATE DUE

NOV 30 '65			
MAY 6 '71			
GAYLORD			PRINTED IN U.S.A.